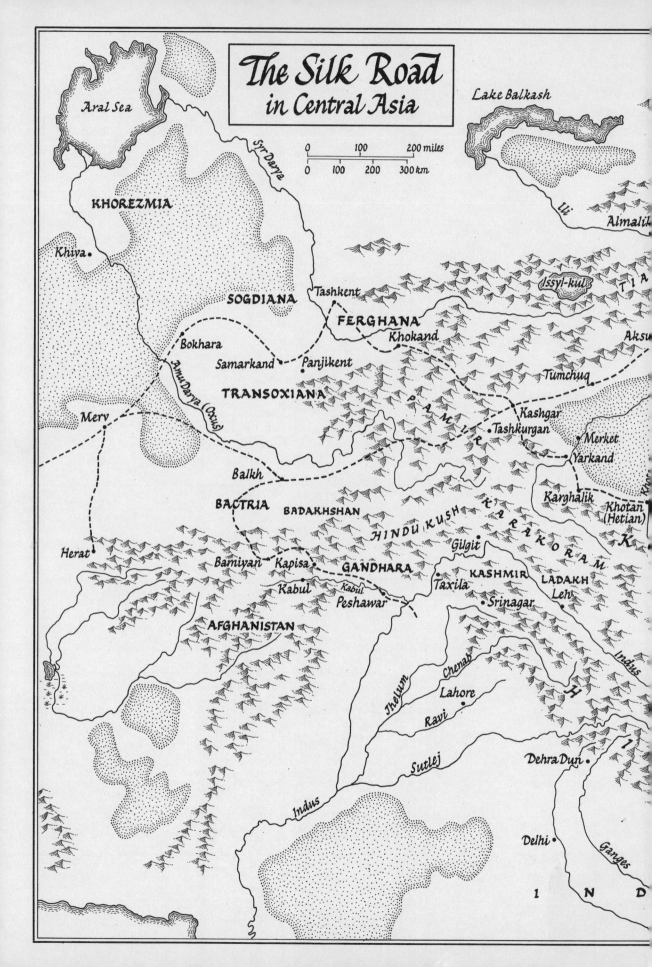

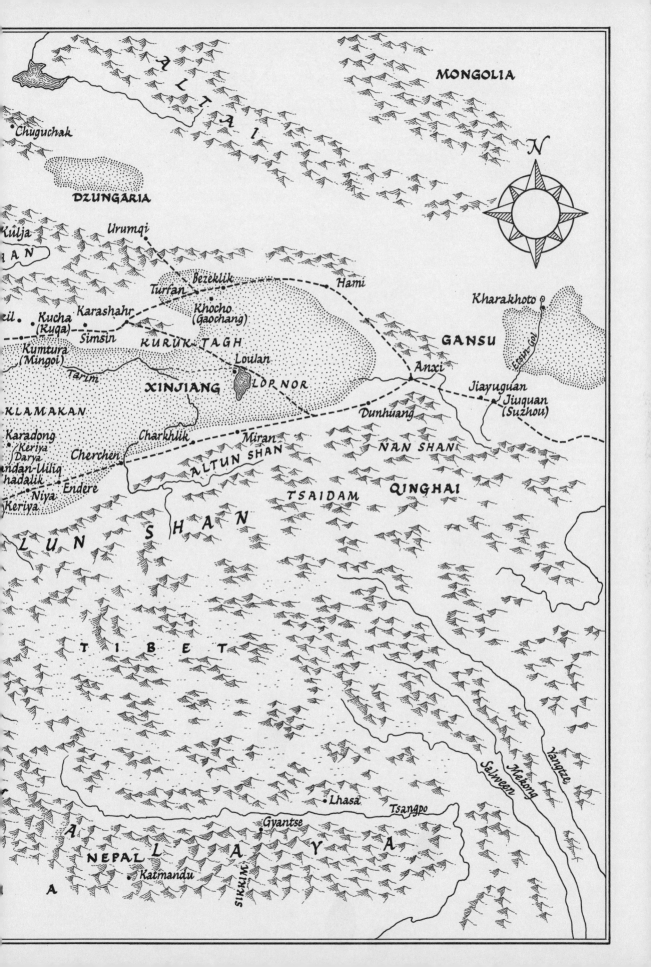

The Silk Road

The Silk Road

FRANCES WOOD

UNIVERSITY OF CALIFORNIA PRESS

BERKELEY   LOS ANGELES

University of California Press
Berkeley and Los Angeles, California

First published by The Folio Society Ltd 2002

Endpaper maps drawn by Reginald Piggott

Published by arrangement with the British Library

Cataloguing-in-publication data is on file with the Library of Congress

ISBN 978-0-520-24340-8

10   9   8   7   6   5   4

Typeset at The Folio Society in Sabon with Ondine for display

Printed and bound in Germany by Firmengruppe Appl, Wemding

Contents

Note on spellings

I think this is the most complicated book I have ever written when it comes to spelling place names. The combination of huge geographical spread and thousands of years of history, complicated by the rise and fall of very distinct civilisations with their own languages and scripts, some of which are still only half-deciphered, and the confident idiosyncrasy of many of those who recorded their travels in the area, makes it incredibly difficult to choose a rendition for a place.

It is important to remember that the transcription of foreign names has always provoked problems. Transliterations imposed on parts of the British Empire – 'Bombay' and 'Burma', for example – seem to have been the result of somewhat cloth-eared research. When Bombay announced recently that it wanted to be known as Mumbai, some Westerners assumed that this was a change of name. In fact, Mumbai has always been Mumbai to its inhabitants: it was only some half-deaf British administrator of the eighteenth century who wrote the name down as Bombay. The same is true of Burma. It did not change its name to Myanmar, but simply asserted the use of the real name of the place rather than that misheard by a British official.

Transliteration systems were invented by foreigners in an attempt to fit local names to their own phonetic range. Where there were rules, these were frequently broken. The range of mountains along the northern Silk Road, called the 'Heavenly Mountains', was rendered T'ien-shan in the old Wade-Giles romanisation system, Tien Shan by the Imperial Chinese Post Office (run by foreigners), which used a sort of 'modified Wade-Giles', and in the official pinyin transcription of the People's Republic of China, used since 1956, the mountains are the Tian Shan. But Ralph Cobbold, who went there to shoot bear and deer in the last years of the nineteenth century, fell somewhere between and used his own system to call them the Thian Shan mountains.

We have tried to use the most well-known of the names involved, adding variants in brackets for clarity.

FRANCES WOOD

- 1 -

'A ceaselessly flowing stream of life'

THE SILK ROAD, or Roads, is one of the most evocative of names, conjuring visions of camels laden with bales of luxurious brocades and diaphanous silks in all the colours of the rainbow. In his poem, 'The Golden Journey to Samarkand', James Elroy Flecker wrote:

> When those long caravans that cross the plain
> With dauntless feet and sound of silver bells
> Put forth no more for glory or for gain,
> Take no more solace from the palm-girt wells[1]

conveying the sense of distance and movement, as well as the exotic. Having not travelled further east than the Lebanon, he was probably unaware of the fact that there were hardy deciduous poplars rather than sub-tropical palm trees surrounding the Central Asian oases. His poem, however, expresses the timeless picture of camel trains trekking slowly along the Silk Road across deserts surrounded by snow-capped mountains, through oasis towns with bustling markets thronged with exotic inhabitants and travellers from all over northern Asia, buying and selling grapes, raisins, Hami melons, fat-tailed sheep and tough little horses. The romance of the Silk Road can be traced back to the medieval accounts of travellers such as Marco Polo who described the route from Baghdad to China.

Yet the romantic name, *Seidenstrasse* or Silk Road, was only coined in 1877 by the German explorer and geographer Baron Ferdinand von Richthofen. From the first century AD at least, the Chinese had their own terms for the northern and southern routes that led from the Chinese capital to the 'Western Regions' (about as far as the Oxus).[2] And though silk was transported along a series of routes across Central Asia to Europe, from China to Rome, though this complex of tracks can be described as one of the world's earliest highways, the very name 'Silk Road' is somewhat misleading. It suggests a continuous journey whereas goods were in fact transported by a series of routes, by a series of agents, passing through many hands before they reached their ultimate destination. The number of travellers who actually traversed the full length of the Silk Roads was always very small: in the early days they were mainly missionaries of various faiths, but from the nineteenth century they included explorers, geographers and archaeologists.

9

Huangshan mountains, Anhui province. The seventy-two peaks of this mountain range have long provided inspiration to poets and painters

Today many use the Silk Road as a portmanteau term covering not only a vast geographical area, marked by high mountains and deserts, but also a long cultural history. The civilisations of the Silk Road include long forgotten empires like those of the Sogdians and the Tangut or Xixia, and their centres range from Nisa and Merv (Chorasmia) through Bokhara and Samarkand (once the capital of Sogdia) to the old oasis towns of Kashgar, Bezeklik, Dunhuang and Khotan surrounding the Taklamakan and Lop deserts of Central Asia (now the Chinese provinces of Gansu and Xinjiang). Southwards, there were extensions of Silk Road trade routes into Afghanistan and Tibet. Even as late as the 1930s, the tracks across the desert were still clear. Missionaries Mildred Cable and Francesca French described a dawn departure on the Silk Road:

'A ray of the rising sun touched the scalloped ridge of ice-fields in the Tibetan Alps and threw a veil of pink over their snowy slopes, but the great mass of the mountain range was still in the grip of that deathlike hue which marks the last resistance of night to the coming day. The morning star was still visible, but it was grey dawn on the plain below, and light was gaining rapidly . . .

'At the foot of the mountain lay the old travel road, wide and deeply

A detail of a wall-painting from Dunhuang depicting the important Chinese Buddhist site of Mount Wutai with its numerous temples and pilgrim routes

marked, literally cut to bits by the sharp, nail-studded wheels of count-less caravan carts. The ruts parted and merged, then spread again, as the eddies of a current mark the face of a river. On this road myriads of travellers had journeyed for thousands of years, making of it a ceaselessly flowing stream of life, for it was the great highway of Asia, which connected the Far East with distant European lands.'[3]

Most maps depict the Silk Road as departing from Xi'an in China, though most of China's silk was produced further south. Formerly known as Chang'an, this city in the northwestern province of Shaanxi was the capital of China from 206 BC to AD 25, during the Han dynasty (206 BC–AD 220), when the Chinese emperors first expressed a considerable interest in the lands beyond their western frontiers and when Rome was equally interested in acquiring Chinese silks, and again from AD 618 to 907, when the Tang dynasty saw an extraor-dinary increase in contact with the Central Asian kingdoms and in Buddhist connections with India via the 'Silk Road'.

From Xi'an, the Silk Road ran westwards through Lanzhou and

then, following the westernmost spur of the Great Wall, through the
Gansu corridor to Dunhuang. This substantial oasis town was to
become one of the great Buddhist centres of China from the fourth
century to the tenth, when caves carved from a cliff on the eastern edge
of the Lop desert and the southern edge of the Gobi desert were excavated and filled with wall-paintings and stucco images by Buddhist
monks. In the fifth and sixth centuries, many famous Buddhist pilgrims, like the great Xuanzang, passed through Dunhuang on their
way to India, where they went to collect holy texts for translation into
Chinese. In a typically desert landscape of bare, rolling sand dunes, the
long cliff, carved with little dark cave entrances, is almost hidden by a
grove of tall poplar trees growing on the bank of the small stream that
runs along the foot of the cliff. In the centre of the cliff, rising above
the trees, is a multi-storeyed temple building with curved, dark-tiled
eaves standing above the sand.

Near Dunhuang, the desert routes split. The main northern route
followed the southern edge of the dark, snow-capped Tian Shan
mountains, running along the north of the Taklamakan desert and
passed through the oasis towns of Hami, Turfan, Korla, Kucha and
Aksu before reaching Kashgar. This longer route was less direct
but less arduous than the southern route, and came into its own in the
late fourth century. The southern route ran through the oases of

12

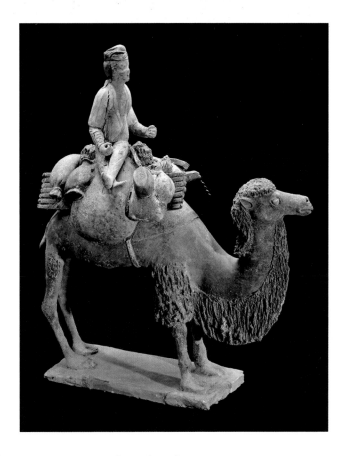

Tang dynasty terracotta figurine of a merchant on a camel loaded with trade stuffs

Charkhlik, Cherchen, Niya, Keriya, Khotan (Hetian) and Yarkand, and also ended in Kashgar. Buddhist monks might leave the main southern silk route at Yarkand to head through the Karakoram mountains to Leh and Srinagar and down into India. The southern route was most significant from the second to the fourth centuries.

There was a second, more northerly route that ran to the north of the Tian Shan mountains from Hami to Almalik, Balasaghun, Tashkent, Samarkand and Bokhara.

Travelling merchants and pilgrims avoided the central desert area on their way to Kashgar at the western end of the deserts. From Kashgar, there were a variety of routes westwards and southwards: Buddhist monks could travel through the Hindu Kush past Tashkurgan to the Buddhist kingdoms of Gandhara and Taxila, whilst traders could pass north of the Pamirs to Samarkand and Bokhara, or south of the Pamirs to Balkh and thence to Merv. From Merv, a variety of trade routes led to the Mediterranean via Baghdad to Damascus or Antioch or Constantinople (Istanbul), and to Trebizond (Trabzon) on the Black Sea.

Throughout two millennia, luxuries were transported along these difficult routes. Ruy Gonzalez de Clavijo, who led an embassy in 1403–5 to Timur in Samarkand, described how 'The best of all merchandise coming to Samarkand was from China: especially silk, satins,

13

musk, rubies, diamonds, pearls and rhubarb. The Chinese were said to be the most skilful workmen in the world . . . Cambalu, the chief city of Cathay, was six months from Samarkand, two of which were over steppes. In the year of the Embassy, eight hundred laden camels came from Cambalu to Samarkand.'4 (Rhubarb, which sits so oddly with pearls and diamonds, was exported from China as a valuable medicine, used as a purgative.5*)

Between oasis towns and the cities of the Mediterranean, the Silk Roads traverse extremely inhospitable terrain, and the difficulties of the route have greatly added to its romance. The great Taklamakan, Lop and Gobi deserts were bounded by mountains. The Kuruk Tagh and snowy Tian Shan to the north, the Altun Shan and Kunlun Shan to the south, and the Pamirs, Hindu Kush and Karakoram ranges to the west all created considerable natural barriers.

The vast area enclosed by these mountains was some two thousand miles from the east to the Pamirs, although, writing at a time when camel travel was still the main means of transport in the 'Central Asiatic steppes and deserts' along whose edge the Silk Roads ran, George Babcock Cressey suggested that, 'in place of stating its size in terms of distances, this region should be described as one which is six months from east to west and one month or more from north to south.'6

The northern and southern Silk Roads followed the lines of oasis settlements set near the encircling mountain ranges which supplied the oases with melt-water. Until the arrival of explorers in the late nineteenth century, few travellers ventured into the central area. Partly divided by the Tarim and Khotan Darya rivers, the area consisted of a series of deserts, with the Gobi desert to the east and the Taklamakan to the west. In the centre was an ancient lake, Lop Nor. The lake once supported a flourishing garrison settlement at Loulan and the remains of beautifully carved wooden railings, posts, doorways and furniture, as well as documents, discovered by Sven Hedin (in 1899–1902) and Aurel Stein (in 1906–8) indicate the relative wealth and comfort enjoyed by the inhabitants before the area was gradually abandoned after the third century.

The edges of the lake dried into hard salt-caked mud-flats and new lakes formed and dried within a few years, as the Tarim river shifted

---

* Medicinal rhubarb was commercially grown from 1777 in Oxfordshire. It had been valued as a purgative and laxative for many centuries: a bag of rhubarb was considered sufficiently valuable to have been listed in the will of Marco Polo, and in the mid-nineteenth century the Chinese official Lin Zexu, unaware that it was, by then, a familiar feature of the Victorian vegetable garden, threatened Queen Victoria with a complete ban on the export of rhubarb. His intention was to bring a constipated nation to its knees and thus to end British sales of opium in China.

The dried wasteland at Loulan and, below, the ruins of the ancient city of Gaochang

in its shallow, silted course. Across the salt marshes, the fierce wind sculpts the surface into hard, shallow waves, very different from the high rolling sand dunes of the Gobi and Taklamakan. Today the area is used for nuclear testing, displacing the nomadic fishermen that Stein encountered in 1907.

The climate of the Central Asian deserts and oases is extreme. The leaves of the poplar trees in all the oases turn from green to golden yellow in September, before they fall, announcing the start of a winter which lasts for some eight months. Beginning with frosts in September and the freezing of the few streams by October, temperatures descend to minus 40°C or lower. During the short, hot summer, temperatures can reach 38°C. Throughout the year, 'the winds blow strongly and lift clouds of dust and silt into the air, often giving it a yellow haze which persists for days.'[7]

Across most of the region the annual rainfall is a mere 200 mm or less, although inhabitants of the oasis towns bordering the deserts make clever use of the abundant snow-melt, leading the water through underground channels (to lessen evaporation) to their grape vines and wells. The system is thought to have been imported from Persia thousands of years ago. Mildred Cable and Francesca French described the ancient *karez* system in the 1930s:

'Standing at a height and looking over the Turfan plain, a traveller will see long lines of earth-works on the barren glacis which give the

16

impression of mounds flung up by gigantic moles. The mounds are hollowed in the centre, and closer inspection shows them to be openings leading to a deep underground passage. Far below is a water-channel which conducts the melted snow to the torrid fields which are waiting for irrigation, and the number of openings in one line may be as many as two hundred.

'The nearer to the mountain the deeper is the *karez*, and at its start the water may be fifty feet below the surface, but at its final opening it flows almost to ground-level, and is as cool as when it left the hills.'[8]

The cold of the desert was particularly uncomfortable for an early explorer, the missionary monk William of Rubruck who was sent on a papal mission to the Mongol capital of Karakorum (1248–54). He reported one day: 'That morning the tips of my toes froze so that I could no longer go barefoot. For the cold in those parts is extremely severe and from the time it begins to freeze it does not leave off till May. Even in May it froze every morning but thawed during the day in the heat of the sun. In winter, however, it never thaws, but whatever the wind, the ice remains . . . When we were there about Easter, the cold which came with the wind killed at the time countless animals.'[9]

Six hundred years later, the same winter cold affected the British Consul at Kashgar: 'Our Christmas lunch on the road between Yarkand and Kashgar was one of the chilliest meals I have ever eaten. Dismounting at a ruined farm-house, we collected some fragments of green thorn bush and tried with only partial success to make a fire behind a wall. When we came to "lay the table", we found that our drinking water . . . was frozen in the thermos, the hard-boiled eggs were also hard-frozen. D thought the first one she broke was bad and threw it away, the cold chicken emitted a ringing sound when tapped and the juicy Kucha pears had to be thawed before we could get our teeth into them.'[10]

Marco Polo (*c.*1254–*c.*1324), the most famous European to leave an account of the Silk Road, also described the cold on the approach

Marco Polo crossing the desert. A detail from the Catalan Atlas, 1375

to the Tarim basin: 'This plain, whose name is Pamir, extends fully twelve days' journey. In all these twelve days there is no habitation or shelter, but travellers must take their provisions with them. No birds fly here because of the height and the cold. And I assure you that, because of this great cold, fire is not so bright here nor of the same colour as elsewhere, and food does not cook well. Now let us pursue our course towards the northeast and east. At the end of this twelve days' journey, the traveller must ride fully forty days more east-north-east, always over mountains and along hill-sides and gorges, traversing many rivers and many deserts. And in all this journey, he finds no habitations or shelter, but must carry his stock of provisions.'[11]

Down on the edge of the Tarim basin he encountered 'a tract of sand . . . the road runs fully five days through sandy wastes, where the water is bad and bitter, except in a few places where it is good and sweet.'[12]

Despite the cold, William of Rubruck seems, unusually, to have preferred the sandy wastes. 'We journeyed eastwards, seeing nothing but the sky and the earth . . . As long as we were in the wilderness all went well with us, but the wretchedness I endured when we came to inhabited places I cannot express in words. Now our guide wanted me to go to each captain with a present and our supplies were not sufficient for that. Each day we were eight persons eating our bread – not counting chance comers who wanted to eat with us . . . the meat they gave us was not sufficient and we found nothing that could be bought for money.'[13]

For most travellers, more gregarious than William of Rubruck, the oasis towns were welcome sights. Marco Polo reported that Khotan was 'a province eight days' journey in extent, which is subject to the Great Khan. The inhabitants all worship Mahomet. It has cities and towns in plenty, of which the most splendid, and the capital of the province, bears the same name as that of the province . . . It is amply stocked with the means of life. Cotton grows here in plenty. It has vineyards, estates and orchards in plenty. The people live by trade and industry; they are not at all warlike.'[14] He noted the trade, the reason for the Silk Roads, for Khotan sent yak hair, fine horses and 'jasper and chalcedony' (he probably means jade) to China.

There is a stock quality to the medieval travellers' descriptions of the desert traversed by the Silk Roads as totally devoid of life. Marco Polo states of the Tarim basin: 'This desert is reported to be so long that it would take a year to go from end to end [twice as much as George Babcock Cressey's estimate] and at the narrowest point it takes a month to cross it. It consists entirely of mountains and sand and valleys. There is nothing at all to eat. But I can tell you that after travelling a day and a night you find drinking water – not enough to supply a large company, but enough for fifty or a hundred men with their beasts. And all the way through the desert you must go for a day

and a night before you find water. And I can tell you that in three or four places you find the water bitter and brackish; but at all the other watering places, that is, twenty-eight in all, the water is good. Beasts and birds are there none, because they find nothing to eat.'[15]

Lush fields at Gulmit contrast with the barrenness of the desert and mountains

The problem of water was one that still preoccupied the camel caravans that were crossing the desert in the early twentieth century, and the answer was tea, as Owen Lattimore explains:

'We began the day at dawn, by making tea. We had with us only brick tea, made of the coarsest grade of leaves, twigs and tea-sweepings from the warehouse compressed into solid blocks, from which we would chop off as much as we needed for each brew. In this tea we used to mix either roasted oaten flour or roasted millet, looking like canary seed – which in fact it was – stirring it into a thin slush and drinking it down . . .

'The reason we drank so much tea was because of the bad water. Water alone, unboiled, is never drunk. There is a superstition that it causes blisters on the feet. Our water everywhere was from wells, all of them more or less heavily tainted with salt, soda and I suppose a number of mineral salts. At times it was almost too salt to drink, at other times very bitter. The worst water was in tamarisk regions. The tamarisk is a desert tree, or rather shrub, sending down its roots to a

19

great depth to reach water. When the water is near the surface, the roots, rotting in the moist earth, turn the water a yellow colour. It is thick, almost sticky, and incredibly bitter and nasty.

'Sometimes we had water every day; usually we came to a well every two or three days, carrying a supply with us in flat-sided wooden butts, which could be loaded two on a camel. Our longest distance between wells was in the crossing of the Black Gobi, where we had one stretch of nearly 100 miles between wells. Our average march was 15 or 16 miles, but in forced desert crossings we could push the distance up to 30 miles.'[16]

Flecker's poetic evocation of camel bells may have come from one of Marco Polo's more inventive passages where he described the mysterious spirits that called out to the traveller at night, to 'loiter and lose touch with his companions, by dropping asleep or for some other reason, and afterwards he wants to rejoin them, then he hears spirits talking in such a way that they seem to be his companions . . . Often these voices make him stray from the path, so that he never finds it again. And this way many travellers have been lost and have perished . . . Even by daylight men hear these spirit voices, and often you fancy you are listening to the strains of many instruments, especially drums and the clash of weapons.' In order to avoid these hallucinations, 'bands of travellers make a point of keeping very close together. Before they go to sleep they set up a sign pointing in the direction in which they have to travel. And round the necks of all their beasts they fasten little bells, so that by listening to the sound they may prevent them from straying off the path.'[17]

Real bandits, rather than siren sounds, were a serious problem. In the sixteenth century, Anthony Jenkinson, an English traveller to Khiva and Bokhara, had his caravan set upon by 'theeves', a band of thirty-seven desperadoes who began an attack. At nightfall a truce was called and Jenkinson and his party 'encamped ourselves upon a hill, and made the

Brigands attack foreign merchants on the Silk Road. From a wall-painting at Dunhuang

fashion of a Castle, walling it about with packes of wares, and layde our horses and camels within the same to keep them from the shotte of arrows: and the theeves also incamped within an arrow shotte of us, but they were betwixt us and the water, which was to our great discomfort, because neither we nor our camels had drunke in two days before.' They were eventually compelled to pay the 'theeves' to leave them alone, but not before the Christian Jenkinson had had a personal narrow escape. In the Khanates of Khiva and Bokhara, sixteenth-century (and later) travellers who were not circumcised Moslems ran the danger of summary execution. Jenkinson was saved by his 'Caravan Basha' who declared 'that he had no Christians in his companie, nor any strangers but two Turkes which were of their Law'. After this narrow escape Jenkinson's Caravan Basha decided to make a detour in order to avoid the main caravan route, and they 'passed through a wildernesse of sand, and travailed four days in the same before we came to a well, the water being very brackish . . .'[18]

Though all accounts from the fourteenth to the twentieth century agree on the extremes of temperature and that water, where it could be found, was frequently brackish, medieval travellers stressed the lack of animal life. Mildred Cable and Francesca French, who spent years travelling in the Gobi in the hope of converting its inhabitants to

Two argali (Ovis poli) *sheep on a ridge at Tso-Kar, Ladakh, India*

Christianity, were, by contrast, struck by the wildlife of 'Gobi and Lop, the most desolate wilderness that the earth can show . . .

'The only animals found in such regions are those which, either by reason of their strength or their fleetness, are able to cover wide distances in search of food. Among these are wild camels, wild asses, antelopes, gazelles and wolves. The most striking animal of the desert, however, is the wild sheep, called by the Turki *argali*, and known to the West as the *Ovis poli* [after Marco Polo]. It is a beautiful creature, remarkable for the size of its horns, which often measure forty-five to fifty inches in length and fifteen to eighteen inches in circumference at the base and weigh thirty to forty pounds. It covers long distances with incredible speed, and leaps from crag to crag almost with the lightness of a winged being. Wolves, which are very numerous in the Gobi, devastate the herds of wild sheep, and though the *argali* itself is not very often seen, the horns are found in great numbers, scattered on the desert floor, wherever the lovely creature has been torn down and devoured.

'Bird life is scarce, but everywhere the approach to water is heralded by the water-wagtail, and there is a small crested, sand-coloured bird which is found at every oasis. The tern seems as much at home in the bird sanctuary of Gobi sands as on the sand-banks of the Norfolk coast . . . In certain low, bare, grey, wrinkled, volcanic hills huge vultures make a home, spying from afar the tired camel which will inevitably drop out of the caravan line and sink by the track not to rise

22

again, or the overladen mule or donkey which is losing strength in the howling blizzard and will soon be frozen to death.

'Far overhead the Golden Eagles and buzzards outline wide curves in the clear sky, and below them the sparrow-hawk hovers, ready to swoop on any small rodent which has ventured out into the open. Among the salt marshes, grey herons feed on lizards . . . There is a yellow burnished snake which lies in the hollow of the sand-ruts.'[19]

Cable and French also mention wild pigeons roosting in the sandstone cliffs and the nocturnal jerboas. Unless you count the sparrow-hawks' prey, they do not mention hamsters, which originated in the Gobi and which, nervous and nocturnal like the jerboas, make such disappointing pets.

Herds of double-humped camels with thick, soft, dark brown fur still graze the shrubby tamarisks near Dunhuang, galloping away from passing vehicles, although many such herds are not true 'wild camels' but lost herds of feral camels which may occasionally have interbred with the increasingly rare wild camels.[20]

Though the wildlife on the margins of the Silk Roads may be shy and rarely seen, even today one of the most striking aspects of the area is the variety of peoples still to be found in the bustling markets of the oases. They still gather for events such as the Sunday market in Kashgar, as they always have, despite the rise and fall of rulers and political upheavals. Amongst the dust kicked up by herds of goats, small tough horses and occasional camels, or in the narrow streets of the old town where pots and pans, saddles and harness and traditional musical instruments are made, and mutton kebabs and carrot and rice pilau tossed and cooked on street stalls, the commercial nomads of today can still be distinguished by some, if not all, of their clothes. Black velvet embroidered skull-caps are worn by the Uighurs, Uighur women still often wear dresses of striped and shaded ikat-weave silk, and the Kirghiz men wear black hats with upturned rims, sometimes lined with white, and knee-length black corduroy coats lined with brilliant silks or the red cotton splashed with giant pink roses sold by the Chinese traders for covering quilts.

In the 1920s, Ella Christie described men's robes, particularly the local ikat-weave silks, as seen in the bazaar at Samarkand: 'The older men wore nothing more sombre than red-striped khalats, and the younger members donned such gay ones, blue, pink, yellow in Bokharan rainbow designs. Vividly I remember the robe of one "knut", it had bold forked patterns in black and yellow crossed by broad lines of magenta!'[21]

She described the Kirghiz whose 'yellow skins and flat Mongol features are easily recognised in a crowd . . . in winter the men wear fur-lined cloth bonnets tied under their chins with ear-flaps' and the

Spice sellers in the Sunday market, Kashgar

'Tekle Turcomans, a fine-looking race in their dark-red striped khalats ... very similar in shape to a dressing-gown, a gaily-coloured sash-band tied around their waists, on the head a huge fur cap of either black or white astrakhan, and high soft leather boots.'[22]

C. P. Skrine, British consul-general in Chinese Turkestan between 1922 and 1924, produced a list to demonstrate the 'diversity' of the people he saw on the streets of Yarkand: 'Andijanis (Mussulman Russian subjects from Ferghana), Badakhshis (from Afghan Badakhshan); Baltis (from the southern valleys of the Karakoram); Bokharans; Chinese; Chitralis; Dulanis (aboriginals from the Yarkand river valley); Gilgitis (mostly freed slaves or their children); Kanjutis (men of Hunza and Nagar); Kashmiris; Kirghiz; Ladakhis (from Little Tibet); Pathans, Afghan and British; Punjabi Hindus; Punjabi Mussulmans; Shighnis (from Russia and Shighnan, Upper Oxus); Sindhis (moneylenders from Shikarpur); Tajiks (from the Chinese Pamirs); Tungans (Chinese Muhammedans from N. Sinkiang and Kansu); Turkis [Uighurs]; Wakhis (from Wakhan and the valleys of the Hindu Kush).' The rich variety must have left contemporary physical anthropologists aching to measure all those different skulls. Skrine elaborated: 'The Turkis form the great bulk of the population; the Chinese are comparatively few and are confined to the officials and their hangers-on, a few

24

Tientsin merchants and some petty shop-keepers; the Tungans are mostly traders, the Kirghiz and Tajiks come in from the mountains and the Dulanis from the down-river marshes.'

Skrine offered further information in another list, which hardly overlapped with the first, of the languages, 'apart from the dialects' that were 'spoken on the Gilgit road between Srinagar and Kashgar'. 'In British Indian territory generally, Urdu. In Gurais and Astore: Kashmiri. In Gilgit: Shina. In Hunza and Nagar: Burushaski. In Little Guyhal and again at Dafdar in the Chinese Pamirs: Persian (Wakhi dialect). In Sariquol: Toyuk. In Chinese territory generally: Eastern Turki.' His wife, Diana, gave a more impressionistic account of a walk through the Yarkand bazaar: 'Some of the types I saw were extraordinary – strange wild-looking men in square fur caps and ragged clothes, with Mongol faces and the eyes of people without minds! Shrivelled old men and women, mere heaps of rags crawling about the streets. Fat Begs, picturesquely dressed in black tunics and trousers and long boots with wonderful striped coats over all. Veiled visions with little fur-edged velvet caps, old Chinese men with brown walnut faces and terrific Chinese babies like small lumps of dough.'[23]

This profusion of peoples, costumes, religions and languages, this mixing in the bazaars of the oasis towns of Central Asia had been there for millennia, although one of the most interesting aspects of the history of the Silk Road is the rise and fall of different groups. When silk was transported from China to Rome, the Parthians held the key to much of the trade, despite customs barriers in China and official edicts in Rome; at the height of Silk Road trade in the eighth and ninth centuries, it was the Sogdians who were the major traders, still despite customs posts set up by independent kingdoms along the trade routes; by the time that the Skrines visited Yarkand, British imperial power stretched out from the south and the west as China lost control of its former empire.

- 2 -

Coiled dragons and filmy fleeces:
jade and silk

SOME SEVEN THOUSAND YEARS before the Silk Roads were first given that name, goods were traded between the oasis towns surrounding the Central Asian deserts and China. One of the earliest materials to have been transported from the Khotan area on the southern Silk Road was jade. Since jade is still transported by road from Khotan to China, it might have been more appropriate to use the term 'Jade Roads' rather than Silk Roads, were it not for the fact that, unlike jade, silk was traded over a far greater distance. It was once thought that all the neolithic jade carved in China came from this area, but other sources have since been discovered around Lake Tai in southeastern China.[1] The jade-carvers of the Xinglongwa and Chahai cultures (in western Xinjiang and southern Inner Mongolia) made ring-shaped pendants and long scoops from greenish jade from Khotan as early as 5000 BC. Jade-carvers of the subsequent Hongshan culture (*c*.4000–2500 BC) in the same area of northeastern China later described as 'beyond the Great Wall' – a traditional Chinese term for a non-Chinese or outlandish culture – carved hoof-shaped cups of translucent greenish jade, bird ornaments of yellow jade and little coiled dragons which were placed in graves.[2]

One of the most extraordinary aspects of the use of jade at this early period is its extreme toughness and consequent difficulty to work. These early pieces would have been worked with abrasive sands which were mixed into a 'sludge' which was ground into the stone with wooden tools or hemp cords. Holes were drilled by means of a wooden drill and abrasive sand. Polished and finished jade pieces were far more durable than ceramics and have survived for many millennia. These beautiful items were highly prized in early China. The tomb of Fu Hao, a Shang dynasty queen who died in *c*.1200 BC, contained more than seven hundred jades, some of which were already thousands of years older than she was.

Though jade was prized by many neolithic peoples throughout the world, it did not always retain its pre-eminent position after the arrival of metal-working techniques. In China, however, it remained a highly important material and acquired further significance in its symbolism. Confucius (550–479 BC) is supposed to have seen it as a paradigm of the human virtues that he most admired: 'Anciently superior men

Coiled dragon from a grave at Hongshan,
c.3000 BC

Women diving for jade, from a later Japanese edition of the seventeenth-century Tiangong kaiwu

found the likeness of all excellent qualities in jade. Soft, smooth and glossy, it appeared to them like benevolence; fine, compact and strong, like intelligence; angular, but not sharp and cutting, like righteousness; hanging down (in beads) as if it would fall to the ground, like (the humility of) propriety; when struck, yielding a note, clear and prolonged, yet terminating abruptly, like music; its flaws not concealing its beauty, nor its beauty concealing its flaws, like loyalty; with an internal radiance issuing from it on every side, like good faith; bright as a brilliant rainbow, like heaven; exquisite and mysterious, appearing in the hills and streams, like the earth; standing out conspicuous in the symbols of rank, like virtue; esteemed by all under the sky, like the path of truth and duty.'3

Such was the demand for jade that it continued (and continues to this day) to be transported from the rivers of Khotan (Hetian) along the southern Silk Road. Its mystery was increased by the belief that it had a special affinity for women, and fanciful seventeenth-century 'geographical' texts include illustrations of women divers who were sent to plunge into the icy melt-waters of the White Jade river and the Black Jade river. Needless to say, raw jade boulders are very heavy, and diving for jade would have been a perverse way of committing suicide.

Thus, the material that gave its name to the great east–west trade route was by no means the only artefact to be carried along it. Silk, however, does have enormous significance in trade between China and the Mediterranean, for it was known in Rome, certainly from the first

27

Part of a rare surviving altar valance from Cave 17, Dunhuang, eighth or ninth century. Such valances were very common in Buddhist temples

century BC, at a time when it could only have been produced in China.

According to Chinese legend, the creation of silk is credited to Xi Ling, the wife of the legendary Yellow Emperor who is supposed to have lived from 2698 to 2598 BC. Though legends usually place inventions back in the dim and distant past, recent archaeological discoveries in China have produced dates anterior to the supposed inventor. Weaving implements and dyed silk gauzes dated to 3600 BC were found in a neolithic site at Hemudu in Zhejiang province, which is still one of the major silk-producing centres in China. More complex woven patterns, including damasks dated to 2700 BC, have been excavated from another Zhejiang site.[4] These finds perhaps help to substantiate the claim made that a silkworm cocoon, found in 1927 at an earlier neolithic site dated to *c*.5000–4000 BC, had been artificially cut.

By the Han dynasty (206 BC–AD 220) silk was produced in a variety of weaves and treated in a variety of ways. The tomb of the Marchioness of Dai, who died soon after AD 168 near Changsha, included painted silk hangings, forty-six rolls of silk and silk dresses, skirts, socks, mittens, shoes, a pillow, scent sachets, mirror cases and wrappings (for other grave furnishings). There were plain silk taffetas and gauzes dyed brown, grey, vermilion, dark red, purple, yellow, blue, green and black. There were painted silks and figured silks with woven designs, both self-colour and polychrome.[5]

28

Despite the archaeological record, Xi Ling's contribution to Chinese culture and industry was commemorated in the Hall of Imperial Silkworms and the Altar of Silkworms that used to stand in Beihai park, part of the imperial complex of the Ming and Qing dynasties (AD 1368–1911) at the centre of Peking. Two stone altars were used for the examination of mulberry leaves which were then fed to the imperial silkworms kept in stone houses along the outer walls of the Hall. During the third lunar month, empresses came to make offerings to Xi Ling, the Goddess of Silkworms.

Chinese silk appears to have reached the Mediterranean during the second century BC and it was the first significant commodity to be exported from East to West. The Romans' knowledge of its origin was hazy: the 'Seres' or 'silk people' was a term applied, not specifically to the Chinese, but generally to inhabitants of remote East Asia. It is probable that silk in Rome was transported across the Silk Roads, probably in several stages, but some also arrived by sea. In the *Periplus Maris Erythraei* of *c.* AD 50, one of the descriptive itineraries ('voyages around', usually following a sea coast, listing places, products and local perils) which informed much early geography, there is a description of silk, in the form of floss, cloth and yarn, being imported through India to Egypt.[6] Strabo's *Geography* (first century BC) also describes silk as originating in India.[7] Despite the fact that there were

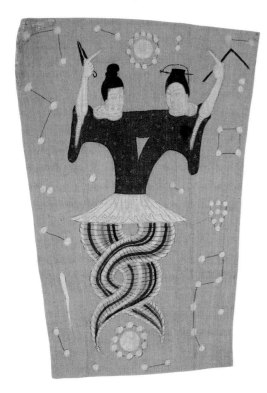

Silk gods Fuxi and Nugua entwined.
Right, silk-weaving, from a Ming vase

Scantily clad in silk, a Roman girl dances before a musician, from a mosaic of circus scenes, second or third century AD

wild silkmoths (a different species from China's domesticated *Bombyx mori*) in the Aegean, Mediterranean writers were very vague about the origin of silk. 'What filmy fleeces from leaves the Serians cull?'[8] Virgil's description of a silk harvest in the first century BC, with the threads being combed from leaves, reflected a widely held view which persisted for centuries. Strabo, as well as saying it grew in India, described silk as 'dried out of certain barks'.[9]

In both Greece and Rome, some writers associated silk with hedonism or, worse, decadence. Seneca the Elder was appalled by the transparency of fine silk: 'Wretched flocks of maids labour so that the adulteress may be visible through her thin dress, so that her husband has no more acquaintance than any outsider or foreigner with his wife's body.'[10] He exhorted women to greater modesty and warned of the inevitable consequences of going out 'naked hardly less obviously than if you had taken off your clothes'.[11] Despite the strictures of such critics and occasional attempts to curb its consumption for economic reasons, silk remained popular in Rome and the prices of silk garments and raw silk were listed in the Edict of Diocletian (AD 301), an attempt to curb inflation and fix maximum prices.[12]

Chinese silk is the thread produced by unravelling and joining the strands of cocoons made by the caterpillars of the moth *Bombyx mori*. The caterpillars feed on mulberry leaves for about five weeks (it takes about two hundredweight of leaves to produce a pound of silk) and grow from 1 mm to 70 or 80 mm before spinning their cocoons. The material for the cocoons is produced in two glands that run along the caterpillar's body and it consists of a protein substance called fibroin (which forms the fibre) and a gummy mixture called sericin or 'silk gum'. The caterpillar extrudes a little of the silk solution from a pair of holes on the top of its head, fixes it to a support and then draws its head back to stretch the fibroin out. Moving its head from side to side, the caterpillar lays its double filament in a figure-of-eight pattern,

forming a cocoon around itself as the sericin hardens. Left to itself, the caterpillar would turn into a chrysalis inside its nut-shaped cocoon and, after a week or so, a fat, hairy moth. The moth's exit from the cocoon would break the filaments so that they could not be reeled into a silk thread; thus the majority of the chrysalises are stifled by hot air or steam. Their cocoons are then placed in hot water which softens the sericin, making it possible to find the end of the filament and reel it. Five to seven filaments are reeled together to form a fine thread which can be woven into cloth.[13]

Though silk was produced in many parts of China, from Sichuan province in the southwest to Shandong (Shantung) province in the northeast, the Yangtze delta area was one of the most important. The combination of mulberry and silkworm production has affected both the economy and the landscape of the Yangtze delta area. Known traditionally as the land of fish and rice, it was criss-crossed by narrow waterways whose banks were often lined with stunted mulberry bushes. Though the wild mulberry grows to a height of fifty or sixty feet, the cultivated bushes are so constantly cut that they acquire the appearance of knobbly grapevines. Silkworms were reared on large flat basket-work trays within the whitewashed farm-houses of the

A painted silk robe from the tomb of the Marchioness of Dai, Changsha c. AD 168

31

area. There were ten rules laid down for their care: 'The eggs when on paper must be kept cool; after having been hatched they require to be kept warm; during their period of moulting they must be kept hungry; in the intervals between their sleeps they must be well supplied with food; they should not be placed too close together nor too far apart; during their sleeps they should be kept dark and warm; after they have cast their skins, cool and allowed plenty of light; for a little time after moulting they should be sparsely fed and when they are full grown ought never to be without food; their eggs should be laid close together, but not heaped upon each other. Wet, withered or dusty leaves are not to be given to them.' There were further recommendations: 'The greatest care is taken to keep the silkworms from noise, which they dislike; so far indeed do the silkworm carers take their precautions that they become superstitious, the silkworms at certain places being informed by their keepers of the arrival of travellers, and if this is omitted, any luckless wight, chancing on a village unannounced, will receive but scant courtesy, and be driven away with curses, if nothing worse.'[14]

32

Many children in China kept silkworms as pets. Chiang Yee, who lived in the Yangtze town of Jiujiang as a small boy in the early twentieth century, described his favourite hobby in considerable detail. 'Like other members of my family, particularly girls, I fed silkworms as a hobby . . . we never had more than a few hundred silkworms altogether, and I rarely tended more than ten or a dozen . . . One of my aunts, who lived in the country, kept a large number of silkworms, but we in the city learnt how to feed them only because Grandmother considered it good for us to understand country ways. From looking after silkworms we should acquire, it was felt, skilful hands and careful minds for dealing with bigger things.' In keeping with the tradition that silk was women's work, Chiang Yee's sisters were given more encouragement: 'We were . . . under no obligation to feed silkworms; girls were encouraged to do so more than boys, and some of my boy cousins, being uninterested, did not do it at all. Personally I found the job of tending them a nice quiet occupation.

'The task of keeping new-laid silkworm eggs from one year to the next was extremely difficult. At rearing time – about the middle of spring – my aunt used to bring eggs to us from the country. I always asked for just a few more than ten, lest some should fail to hatch out. She told us to watch for the new buds on the mulberry tree in our garden and then to place the eggs in a rather warm place. We did not have fires in our house after the Lantern Festival [fifteen days after the Chinese New Year] so I used to put my eggs under the mattress of my bed. At first the eggs were yellowish in colour, but after a few days they turned blackish-blue. I looked at mine every day. Soon creatures that looked like small black ants began to hatch out. I put these into a wooden box with some chaff on the top. Then I cut the new mulberry-leaf buds and put them in the box. Presently the ant-like silkworms climbed up the leaves and ate them. The chaff could then be cleared away. These young leaves only served as food for a few meals and had to be specially prepared. We dried them in the air for a few days in order to reduce the moisture they contained because too much water could easily make the silkworms develop disease. As the bodies of my ant-like silkworms grew, they turned greyish-white in colour and lost their ant-like appearance.

'At first our one small mulberry tree provided enough leaves, but as the silkworms grew, the supply became insufficient and some boy-cousins had to go out in search for more. Mulberry leaves could be bought, too, from farmers. We often heard stories of the mulberry-leaf pickers in Jiangsu and Zhejiang provinces, where silkworms were cultivated systematically and whole fields of mulberry trees had to be grown. The pickers went out to gather the leaves in groups, women and men, girls and boys, singing folk-songs. Romantic stories were

Sorting silk cocoons in a factory at Khotan. The fibres are loosened for removal from the inner shell of the cocoons by soaking them in boiling water. Below, the new silk sorted into two-kilo skeins

woven about them. Some of my cousins had not the patience to do the feeding work, but they were ready to go out searching for mulberry leaves. Not that they were concerned in those days, I think, with romance.

'At seven days old the silkworms were two-thirds of an inch long and gradually turning a brownish colour; the heads waved to and fro. After that they began to eat less and less and at last refused to eat at all. The head-waving also gradually declined to immobility. This was their period of sleep during which they changed their skins. The new skin grew beneath the old one. Then a reddish spot appeared near the head and the old skin broke at this point and the silkworms gradually emerged in new skins. After a couple of hours they began to eat fresh food again, much more of it than before. This, of course, resulted in rapid growth. They generally underwent four such periods of sleep

and changes of skin, each taking two or three days. Unfortunately not all the silkworms went to sleep at the same time, and this was a serious problem for those who fed them on a large scale. It did not worry me much. I kept a pair of new bamboo chopsticks with which I lifted out the sleeping silkworms and placed them in a bamboo sieve. All this time, the silkworms had to be kept in a warm room, free from draughts as well as flies. On waking from the last period of sleep they developed much larger appetites and ate considerable quantities of leaves. This generally placed us in a difficulty, the mulberry trees being by that time nearly denuded of leaves. We managed somehow.' Chiang Yee did not rear his silkworms in order to produce proper thread and unprofessionally saved the moths from being boiled alive. 'Eight or nine days after the last period of sleep, when the silkworms were as long as three inches, their bodies became transparent. They stopped eating and were ready to spin silk. I used to put a piece of paper on top of a small bowl and place one or two silkworms on that. They would crawl around paying out their silk until the paper was covered. If two could not manage to cover the paper, I added another. By the time they had finished, their bodies had changed from being long thin things to barrel-shaped objects with a point at each end. They remained like that for some days, then their eyes came out, they grew wings, and I put them out on the trees . . .

'I was always amazed at how beautifully the silk was woven, as though with a mechanical instrument. Some silks were pure white and some golden yellow. My sister used her small pieces to make powder puffs. She embroidered ordinary silk very well to make the outside of the puff and used this raw silk for the fluffy surface with which the powder was applied. Unlike me, she also made large pieces of silk, keeping hundreds of silkworms for the purpose. When the insects were ready to spin she would cover the surface of a table with large sheets of paper and let any number of silkworms spin on that until they had made her a sheet of silk large enough to use for wrapping up her embroidery silks. Coloured unwoven silks were very sticky and clung to the fingers, so it was necessary to use some smooth material to keep them in.

'These were the results of our careful labour. My sister and girl-cousins used to compete against each other to see who could produce the best piece of silk. My aunt judged the pieces when she visited us. I am sorry to say that among the members of my family belonging to the generation after mine, most have not even had a chance to see what a silkworm looks like!'[15]

- 3 -

From Greece and Rome to China
– and back again

BEFORE THE CHINESE set off towards Rome, Europe first penetrated the western end of the Silk Roads with the invasion of Alexander the Great in 334–323 BC. Alexander fought his way eastwards from his home in Macedonia to found an empire that stretched to Egypt, across Persia, from Samarkand through Sogdiana and Bactria down into Northern India: 'a single world stretching from Gibraltar to the Punjab' which effectively covered much of the western end of the Silk Roads. He set up a coinage system based on the silver standard of Athens which, with a relatively open trade and the use of a Greek lingua franca, considerably enhanced communication within his empire.

Ancient Bactria, which lay next to Sogdiana, on the other side of the Oxus (today's Amu Darya), was almost enclosed by the soaring Pamirs and Hindu Kush whose high peaks and passes were perpetually snow-bound. The open area to the northwest was part of the Central Asian desert traversed by the Oxus, which, with the other rivers of Bactria, swelled by melting snow, was subject to flash-floods in spring, though the desert areas were characteristically dry. The area around Tashkurgan, itself a major market place on the Silk Road, was lush and fertile, with orchards, nut-trees and vineyards. The combination of hot desert, fertile plain, semi-tropical valleys and frozen mountains led the historian Curtius (1st–early 2nd century AD) to remark, 'Bactrianae terrae multiplex et varia natura est'.[1]

In the mid-sixth century Bactria came under Persian rule, and the support of the Bactrians and Sogdians for Darius the Great was commemorated in the famous rock-carved inscription at Behistun which so fascinated Sir Henry Rawlinson of the British Indian government in the early nineteenth century because it provided the material necessary for deciphering Old Persian.

It was in 329 BC, in the reign of Bessus (who had murdered Darius III), that Alexander the Great crossed the Hindu Kush into Bactria. As Alexander had already conquered Achaemenid Persia, he could be seen as simply bringing Bactria back into the fold. Though he took Bactria without great difficulty, Sogdian uprisings were far more difficult to control, and it was not until the winter of 328–327 BC that he gained the upper hand.[2] In early 327, Alexander married Roxane,

36

daughter of one of the Sogdian nobles, and turned his attention to India and (today's) Pakistan, despite difficulties with his Macedonian troops who were not happy with disastrous forays into the deserts.

Alexander's conquest of Pakistan was as bloody as any of his campaigns and was written up enthusiastically by contemporary historians. In his campaign in 326 BC against Porus, ruler of the area bounded by the Himalayan foothills and the Chenab and Jhelum rivers, the territory conquered was described as 'a land of great cities' although it was only some 15,000 square kilometres and rather sparsely inhabited. In his attack on Porus' forces, Alexander's troops employed particularly vicious methods against the elephant cavalry (of which they already had had some experience in battles in India), using eighteen-foot pikes tipped with sickle-shaped cleavers designed to inflict maximum damage on their trunks. Alexander's troops also

A remarkably Greek-looking male portrait, from a third- or second-century BC woollen wall-hanging found at Sampul

37

*Alexander in battle at
Issus. A mosaic from
the House of the Faun
at Pompeii,* c. *first
century* BC

aimed for the mahouts and for the elephants' eyes, whilst another
phalanx attacked from the rear. Thus the panic-stricken elephants
retreated 'like warships backing water, no longer charging but emitting
a high-pitched squeal', and trampled their own troops underfoot.
Porus survived to be brought before Alexander, by whom, in an inter-
view through interpreters, described by the Indian sage Dandimus as
'like clear water passing through mud', he demanded to be treated as
a king (a statement Alexander asked him to clarify). He was eventually reappointed as ruler over his own territory but under Alexander's
sovereignty.3

Alexander was not insensitive to the geography and natural history
of his vast domains and was interested to discover lotus flowers on the
bank of the Chenab river bordering Porus' territory. 'He and his staff
were familiar with the plant from their stay [*sic*] in Egypt, where it had
been introduced, probably by the first Achaemenids, and become
known to the Greek world from Herodotus onwards as the Egyptian
bean.'4 Owing to Herodotus' helpful exegesis, and having seen croco-
diles when crossing the Indus earlier, Alexander apparently thought
for a brief moment beside the Chenab that he might have discovered
the upper reaches of the Nile. There was much confusion of information gleaned as a result of Alexander's imperial ventures: his boyhood
friend Nearchus, who wrote an account of Alexander's campaigns,
included mention of seeing not only a tiger skin in the Punjab but also
some fabulous ant skins. The skins were, Nearchus reported, those of
gold-digging ants which were 'somewhat larger than foxes and possessed an amazing turn of speed'. The Macedonians had heard about
these useful beasts from Herodotus and asked for more. The local Pun-

A damaged life-size statue of Kanishka, dating from AD 128. *The statue was completely destroyed in a raid on Kabul Museum under the Taliban regime*

jabi traders obliged with 'an array of hides which purported to be those of the outsize ants, spotted like leopard skins'. It was felt by the Macedonians that 'the material evidence of the ant skins guaranteed the truth of the mining operations and the ants were recognized as a reality, not more exotic and incredible than the Indian tiger.'5

The empire did not survive its founder and it is doubtful that anyone could have held such a vast territory together, but some of Alexander's legacy can still be seen in the extraordinary sculpture of Gandhara in the Peshawar valley. Though Hellenistic influence is indeed evident, scholars since the late nineteenth century have offered a range of possible influences, covered by terms such as 'Romano-Buddhist' (owing to the importance of sea trade between Alexandria and Palmyra and India in Roman times), 'Graeco-Iranian' (stressing the contribution of Parthian sculpture), culminating in 'Graeco-Bactrian', describing how 'there grew up in and around ancient Bactria modified Hellenistic or Graeco-Iranian artistic traditions that survived the extinction of Greek rule and developed under the Kushans who also adopted the Greek alphabet for their own language.'6

Buddhism had entered Gandhara less than a century after Alexander's conquests with a great missionary campaign supported by the Indian ruler Asoka (c.272–232 BC), himself a devoted Buddhist, but it was under the early Kushans that Gandharan art flourished. The

39

Kushans, who ruled Gandhara between the first and third centuries AD, may well have been Yuezhi, driven out of the Gansu area ('a weird environment of Central Asia', as one writer put it[7]) by the Xiongnu. The Kushan empire incorporated Samarkand, Bokhara and Ferghana, bordering on the Silk Road towns of Kashgar, Yarkand and Khotan. The main route from Central Asia into India, connecting India with the Silk Roads and the Mediterranean, ran through Gandhara. It was probably taken by the Kushans under Kujula Kadphises, who cast coins impressed with a copy of the head of the Roman emperor Augustus (27 BC–AD 14), but the best-known Kushan ruler was Kanishka, who lived *c.* AD 78–144. A life-sized sculpture of him survives showing a figure clad in a tunic covered by a pleated coat, holding two huge swords in decorated scabbards.* The head is, unfortunately, missing but he has the most enormous feet. Though his empire stretched down south to Benares, he was conscious of his Central Asian origins and sought to maintain the thriving trade with the Silk Road centres like Kashgar and beyond, sending an envoy to Trajan in Rome.[8]

Kanishka was a great patron of Buddhism, building a tall pagoda seen by the Chinese pilgrim Xuanzang in 630, when he described it as thirteen storeys high, topped with shining gilded copper discs.[9] It was during his rule that the first of the great Gandharan Buddhist sculptures were created, and over the succeeding centuries carvings were made over an area stretching from just east of Kabul in Afghanistan, along the Peshawar valley east into the Punjab and the great site of Taxila. Gandharan sculptures, depicting scenes from the life of the Buddha, groups of Buddhas and Bodhisattvas and single figures, were carved from stone, although some stucco sculptures survive, particularly from Afghanistan, and there are gold, bronze and steatite reliquaries, as well as gold coins cast at Kanishka's order with standing Buddha figures.

Relief panels in stone were made to adorn the walls of stupas and stupa courtyards. The stupa was originally a shrine, a mound made to cover the remains of the Buddha or his disciples or objects of veneration such as his begging bowl. Around the circular stupa stone panels were set, and elaborately carved stone gates marked the cardinal points. The Gandharan figures range from hieratic groups of Buddhas and Bodhisattvas sitting and standing, with stone flame haloes and elaborately pleated robes, to scenes from the lives of the Buddha, including his former existences as a Bodhisattva. As the historic Buddha was associated with sites in Eastern India, his connection with Gandhara was created through visits and events in previous lives, all

Gandharan Buddhist statue from the Peshawar valley, eleventh or twelfth century

---

* The statue, in the Museum at Kaset, was probably destroyed under the Taliban regime in 1998.

41

Opposite: In contrast to the Gandharan statue above, with its Romano-British-Hellenistic influence, this Tang dynasty head of a Bodhisattva from Mingoi shows a marked oriental influence

Stone relief panel of Buddha preaching, from Gandhara, second or third century

carefully recorded by Chinese pilgrims such as Faxian (in AD 400).

Panels depict the stories which tell how the Buddha, in a previous life, gave away for charity his lucky white elephant, his wife and his children, offered his body to feed a hungry tiger and donated his flesh to ransom a pigeon. In contrast with the contemporary Buddha images of the Mathura school in North India, where the strong, powerful Buddha images owe much to earlier religious icons such as the male nature deities or yaksas, the Gandharan Buddha image is depicted wearing the sort of robes seen on imperial Roman statues, accompanied by figures in senatorial stances and associated with such Graeco-Roman forms as vine-scrolls, cherubs carrying garlands, tritons and centaurs. Many of the Gandharan panels and images were stripped from their original sites from the nineteenth century onwards as archaeologists and collectors travelled up from British-ruled India.

In Pliny's *Natural History* (first century AD) there is a lengthy description of the Seres, though they are rather bafflingly sited: 'After leaving the Caspian Sea and the Scythian Ocean, our course takes a bend towards the Eastern Sea as the coast turns to face eastward. The first part of the coast after the Scythian promontory is uninhabitable on account of snow, and the neighbouring region is uncultivated because of the savagery of the tribes that inhabit it. This is the country of the Cannibal Scythians who eat human bodies; consequently the adjacent districts are waste deserts thronging with wild beasts lying in wait for human beings as savage as themselves. Then we come to more Scythians and to more deserts inhabited by wild beasts, until we reach a

42

mountain range called Tabis which forms a cliff over the sea; and not until we have covered nearly half of the length of the coast that faces northeast is that region inhabited. The first human occupants are the people called the Seres, who are famous for the woollen substance obtained from their forests; after a soaking in water they comb off the white down of the leaves, and so supply our women with the double task of unravelling the threads and weaving them together again; so manifold is the labour employed, and so distant is the region of the globe drawn upon, to enable the Roman maiden to flaunt transparent raiment in public. The Seres, though mild in character, yet resemble wild animals, in that they also shun the company of the remainder of mankind, and wait for trade to come to them.'[10]

The 'we come to' and 'our course' imply a personal experience that is clearly not the basis for this account. The 'deserts' thronged with thirsty wild beasts and cannibals may presumably stand for northwestern Central Asia, for the Greeks and Romans characterised the Caucasus as 'Scythia'. The picture of the Seres is an interesting one because, though trade was a despised occupation in later traditional China, the early Han emperors were keen to promote trade with the West and first sent an imperial envoy out to Ferghana in the second century BC. And one of the Han emperors, Lingdi (r. AD 168–89) was so taken with the idea of trade that he 'several times played the merchant game with his court ladies in the Western Garden. He asked the ladies to play the role of hostesses of private inns while he himself impersonated a travelling merchant stopping at every "private inn" to enjoy the entertainment of the "hostess".'[11]

The geographer Strabo (born *c*.64 BC) presented a very different approach to geographical description, laying 'little stress on geographical wonders'.[12] Following him, Ptolemy (second century AD) is said to have derived his information about Serica and Sinae from the journey of a man called Alexander in the first century AD, and a man called 'Maes, also known as Titianus' from Damascus, the latter familiar with the overland trade routes.[13] Not for him the cannibals and wild beasts but lists of towns and rivers. His maps, surviving in medieval editions which may have benefited from subsequent discoveries, are surprisingly informative. In his text, he refers to Serica, 'terminated on the west by Scythia beyond the Imaus mountains . . . on the north is unknown land to that parallel which extends through Thule' and it is bordered 'on the south by the remaining part of India beyond the Ganges'. This description appears to place Serica, the land of silk, in Central Asia, and his description of the 'northern part of Serica', where 'the race of the Anthropophagi pasture their flocks', is not inappropriate. His Sinae is adjacent to Serica and ends, to the east, in the 'unknown land', though it seems to sit rather inaccurately south of

The mysteries of the world beyond the borders, from the Shanhai jing. *The original text dates from some two thousand years ago*

Serica and due west of 'India beyond the Ganges'. Its main towns are listed as Acatharia, Aspithra, Coccoranagara, Sarata and Thyne metropolis. The last is the only recognisable term, the 'Thyne' or 'Thin' (as well as Sinae) thought to be derived from Qin, the name of the dynasty founded by Emperor Shi in 221 BC. The emperor is well-known today for his massive burial site outside Xi'an, complete with buried armies of life-sized terracotta warriors.

Oddly enough, the Chinese appear to have used the same name for Rome and the Roman empire in the East, calling it Da Qin ('Great Qin'), as if they sensed a parallel power at the other end of the Silk Road. Arguments over whether Da Qin definitely designated Rome have raged for centuries. Most Chinese writers thought it did mean Rome, and eighteenth- and nineteenth-century European writers like De Guignes, Bretschneider and Edkins concurred, but the early twentieth century saw a revision as scholars like Pelliot, Stein, Laufer and Maspero attempted a more scientific interpretation of the mass of

44

The many-headed wakwak tree, from an Indian manuscript, c.1500

وطول او مقدار یک بدست باشد واز فرود

تا بنا ف یک یک متصل

وبالاتراز ان علاحده

بمواجهه

یک یک

confused early texts, and decided that they referred only to the Roman Orient. A more recent study by Donald Leslie and K. J. H. Gardiner concludes that Da Qin did indeed encompass Rome itself as well as the Roman Orient.[14] They quote the nineteenth-century scholar Colonel Sir Henry Yule ('both cautious and shrewd') on this mirror image of Rome in China: 'We shall also find presently that the view entertained by the Chinese themselves of the Roman Empire and its inhabitants had some striking points of analogy to those views of the Chinese which are indicated in those classical descriptions of the Seres. There can be no mistaking the fact that in this case also the great object was within the horizon of vision, yet the details ascribed to it are often far from being the true characteristics, being only the accidents of its outer borders towards the East.'

The *Shanhai jing* (*Classic of Mountains and Seas*) is a mythical geography, parts of which were compiled before the Han dynasty (206 BC–AD 220, the period in which the first official Chinese explorers ventured into Central Asia) and which contained many illustrations of the barbarous monsters that inhabited the 'Western Regions' and beyond. Many of its strange beasts and people were incorporated into later encyclopaedic works and they often correspond with the mythical beasts found in Western writers like Herodotus and later medieval works on the 'marvels' of the East. The convention that the lands beyond one's known borders are inhabited by monstrous barbarians is apparently universal, but the similarities in the form and habits of these monsters are surprising.

There is the wakwak tree, full of talking heads, which appears in a romance of Alexander the Great and is illustrated in a Chinese encyclopaedia with the caption: 'There are trees in the mountains on whose branches grow flowers which are in the shape of men's heads. They do not speak but merely laugh when questioned. If they laugh too often they fall to the ground'; and there are the one-eyed people in both Herodotus and Chinese sources (living somewhere in Scythia or India), and the long-eared people also from India.[15]

The first Chinese to have, possibly, reached Rome, was Gan Ying, sent by the procurator-general Ban Chao from the Tarim basin across Parthia in AD 97. The *Hou Han shu* (*History of the later Han dynasty*, AD 25–220), compiled by Fan Ye (398–455), states, 'In the ninth year [AD 97] Ban Chao despatched his adjutant Gan Ying all the way to the coast of the Western Sea and back. Former generations had never reached any of these places, nor has the *Shanhai jing* given any details of them. He made a report on the customs and topography of all these states.'[16]

Though it is unlikely that Gan Ying actually reached Rome, he seems to have got further west than any other Chinese. On the basis, perhaps, of what he heard from other oral accounts, he gave a full description of Da Qin, setting it to the west of the sea. 'Its territory covers several thousand *li* [Chinese miles, about a third of an English mile] square. It has over four hundred walled cities. Several tens of small states are subject to it. The outer walls of the cities are made of stones. They have established posting stations.' This highlights another parallel with China and its impressive post system stretching out across the deserts. 'There are pines and cypresses . . . Their customs are as follows: they devote themselves to agriculture and plant a large number of silkworm mulberry trees. They all shave their heads but wear embroidered clothes. Their king rides upon a small carriage, surmounted by a white canopy. When he goes out and returns a drum is hit and flags, banners and pennants are hoisted. The city where he resides is more than a hundred *li* in circumference. In this city are five palaces which are ten *li* apart from one another. In all the rooms of these palaces, the columns are made of crystal glass, as are the utensils

46

in them.' The description of glass is interesting, for glass, which had been known in China for several hundred years, was mainly made into small beads and jewellery: imported glass vessels were much prized.

The Romans practised some form of democracy: 'As for the King he is not a permanent figure but is chosen as the man most worthy . . . The people of this country are tall and regular featured. They resemble the Chinese and that is why the country is called Da Qin . . . The soil produces lots of gold, silver and rare jewels, including the jewel which shines at night: the full-moon pearl, the rhinoceros which frightens chickens, coral, amber, opaque glass, red cinnabar . . . they sew embroidered tissues with gold threads to form . . . tapestries and damask of many colours, and make a gold-painted cloth and "cloth washed in the fire" [asbestos].' Gan Ying offers a confusing picture of silk in Da Qin: 'They have a delicate cloth which some say is the wool of sea-sheep, but which is really made from the cocoons of wild silk-worms. They mix all sorts of perfumes and boil the mixture to make storax. It is from this country that all various marvellous and rare objects of foreign states come.'[17]

The idea that Rome was a massive state with dependencies, and that it produced marvellous things, was not only a tribute to Roman power at the time but a reflection of China itself, a similar power, similarly productive of rare and valuable commodities, at the other end of the Silk Road.

As Leslie and Gardiner demonstrate, the similarities do not end there. Both Roman and Chinese texts refer to countries of pygmies lying between them and, just as Pliny described the Seres silently laying out their goods, the Chinese text mentioned countries to the west like Shizi, a neighbouring country to India which 'originally had no inhabitants, only devils and spirits and dragons lived in it, with whom the merchants of neighbouring countries came to trade. When the exchange of commodities took place, the devils and spirits did not appear in person, but set out their valuables with the prices attached. Then the merchants, according to their prices, bought them and carried them off.' Even further, 'on the Western Sea there are markets where the traders do not see one another, the price being deposited by the side of the merchandise; they are called "spirit markets".'[18]

- 4 -

A people abandoned by Heaven:
the Xiongnu and trade during
the Han dynasty

THE IMPETUS to explore the 'Western Regions' was to some
extent forced upon the Chinese by the activities of a marauding
group of nomads known as the Xiongnu. Nomadic shepherds
inhabiting China's northwestern borders, they led constant raids on
their Chinese farming neighbours and were so irritating that they provoked the construction of the first part of the Great Wall in Gansu, as
an attempt to keep them out of China.[1] Then, as ever, the Wall proved
ineffective. In 201 BC, the Xiongnu invaded Shanxi province and
defeated an imperial army near Datong. Similar raids deep into Chinese territory occurred in 182, 181, 177 and 169 BC, and in 166 BC
an army of 140,000 Xiongnu horsemen reached a point only three
hundred *li* from the Chinese capital.[2]

There is still considerable argument about the Xiongnu. The Chinese two-character name (literally meaning 'fierce slaves': the first part
being an accurate description, the second a pious hope) was applied
rather vaguely by the Chinese to various groups of nomadic herders
who inhabited the areas just beyond China's northwestern frontier.
Early Western writers on the area, such as De Guignes in the eighteenth century, often translated Xiongnu as 'Huns', but the problem
with this identification is the gap between the effective destruction by
the Chinese of Xiongnu power in the mid-second century AD and the
appearance of the Huns 'on the European horizon' two hundred years
later, with no evidence of any westward migration.[3] Though Luc
Kwanten describes the Xiongnu as 'speaking an Altaic language' (we
have no real evidence of this), he acknowledges that we do not know
what they eventually became (if anything), and whether they were
'proto-Turkic or proto-Mongol' is difficult to determine.[4]

Archaeological excavations in Mongolia have revealed Chinese
goods, of the type traded with and presented to the Xiongnu, as well
as architectural remains, which suggest that they moved northwards
and were, perhaps, 'proto-Mongol'.[5]

The fact that Chinese goods were known to be 'presented' to the
Xiongnu demonstrates their power over the Chinese. China's traditional relationships with the outside world have often been covered by

the term 'tribute relationship' and seen as a system by which China demanded obeisance through the ritual exchange of gifts and a ritual submission by foreign envoys. Some authorities consider that the tribute system began in the Zhou (1055–221 BC) and both the terms and conditions were certainly in place by the Han dynasty, although they were modified through succeeding centuries.[6]* During the Han, it

Possible present-day descendants of the Xiongnu – a group of Mongolian herdsmen at Jangothang in Bhutan

* The traditional picture is of China insisting upon its centrality as the 'Middle Kingdom' (the Chinese name for China) and its supremacy over 'external' states. In fact its significance and the operation of the system varied enormously at different times and naturally varied according to the standpoint of the observer. The concept is also confused by more recent history when truly foreign envoys, such as Lord Macartney who led the first British embassy to China in 1792–4, brought an entirely new approach to Chinese ritual, refusing to 'kowtow' (knock the forehead three times on the floor before the emperor) as this would imply disrespect for their own sovereign. It is interesting to note

49

could be seen as a method of balance. In an attempt to avoid frontier wars and skirmishes, the Han administration made arrangements with the Xiongnu, each side sending 'hostages' to the other. From the Han, these were mostly princesses sent in marriage; from the outside states, sons of rulers.

There was also a costly exchange of goods, which was one method by which the Chinese obtained essential goods such as horses from Central Asia, and the nomadic or semi-nomadic tribes obtained luxury goods such as silks, lacquer and metalwork from China. It is interesting to see that, despite the difficulties of their nomadic life, the Xiongnu set great store by the acquisition of silks and ornaments for the court. During the Han, this interest represented a serious drain on the national economy. In 25 BC, China sent out twenty thousand rolls of silk and twenty thousand pounds of silk floss, such 'gifts' amounting to some ten per cent of state revenues.[7] In the case of the Xiongnu, there were annual 'gifts' (the Chinese saved face by not describing them as 'tribute' to the Xiongnu) of silks, alcohol, rice and other foodstuffs.[8]

A contemporary Chinese account of the Xiongnu described their life as that of nomadic herders on the harsh steppe: 'The Xiongnu live in the desert and grow in the land that produces no food. They are the people who are abandoned by Heaven for being good-for-nothing. They have no houses to shelter themselves, and make no distinction between men and women. They take the entire wilderness as their villages and the tents as their homes. They wear animal skins, eat meat raw and drink blood. They wander to meet in order to exchange goods and stay for a while in order to herd cattle.'[9]

The first emperor of the Qin dynasty sent an army in 215 BC, which checked Xiongnu raids for some time,[10] but the problem reappeared after the fall of the Qin in 206 BC, eventually threatening the capital. The Wudi (Martial Emperor) of the Han (157–87 BC) presided over a considerable expansion in Chinese territory, taking the southern coastal provinces of Zhejiang and Fujian, bringing Guangdong and Guangxi in the far southwest under Chinese influence, if not quite into the empire, and despatching armies to drive the Xiongnu back to the Central Asian deserts. In 138 BC he sent an envoy, Zhang Qian (d. 114 BC), to try to enlist the support of another Central Asian nomadic group, the Yuezhi, in an alliance against the Xiongnu. Zhang Qian

---

that whilst Lord Macartney set great store by circumventing the 'tribute' system in his refusal to kowtow, the banners fluttering over the boats that carried his embassy throughout China bore the information (in Chinese) that this was a tribute-bearing embassy. The flag can be seen in a sketch by William Alexander in the British Library's Oriental and India Office Collections.

failed to achieve the alliance but he made two epic journeys to beyond the Pamirs, to Ferghana (in today's Kazakhstan) and Bactria (between the Oxus and the Hindu Kush).

His first trip lasted twelve years, during ten of which he was a prisoner of the Xiongnu, and took him north of the Gobi desert into Xiongnu territory in Mongolia and along the northern Silk Road to Kashgar, northwards to Ferghana and then around the western edge of the Pamirs to Bactria. He returned along the southern Silk Road.

Zhang Qian's biography in the *Han shu*, the official history of the western Han (206 BC–AD 8), describes how the Xiongnu had provoked the Yuezhi, thus encouraging the Han emperor to contemplate an alliance. 'At the time, deserters from the Xiongnu had said that they had defeated the king of the Yuezhi and made a drinking vessel of his skull. The Yuezhi had fled, but, furious as they were with the Xiongnu, there was no party with whom they could attack them jointly. As it happened Han [China] was wishing to start operations to eliminate the nomads; and hearing of this report wished to make contact with the Yuezhi by means of envoys; their route would perforce have to pass through the Xiongnu. A call was then made for persons to undertake the mission . . . Zhang Qian answered the call.'[11]

'Zhang Qian was a man of strong physique and of considerable generosity; he inspired the trust of others and the barbarians loved him . . . At the time when Zhang Qian started his journey, over a hundred men set out, but thirteen years later only two succeeded in returning. The states reached by Zhang Qian in person comprised Da Yuan [Ferghana or Sogdiana], Da Yuezhi [Bactria?], Da Xia [another term for Bactria?] and Kangju [anachronistic: Samarkand?] and those of whom he heard tell included five or six large states at their side. He told the Son of Heaven in full about the lay of the land and their resources, and his account is given in the chapter on the Western Regions.'[12]

Like the later pilgrim Xuanzang (602–64) who made the emperor quite forget that he had left China without imperial permission by telling him all he had seen in the 'Western Regions', Zhang Qian, though failing to effect a military alliance against the Xiongnu, nevertheless recouped his honour by the information he had gathered. 'The Son of Heaven was delighted and believed Zhang Qian's report.'

Chapter 96 of the *Han shu* is a 'Description of the Western Regions'. Presented to the emperor in AD 92, it incorporates Zhang Qian's account, material from an earlier 'comprehensive' history of China, the *Shi ji* (*Records of the Grand Historian*) compiled by Sima Tan and his son Sima Qian and presented to the emperor in 91 BC, and personal information. The compiler of the *Han shu*, Ban Gu (AD 32–92), had a brother, Ban Zhao, who served in the northwest and probably contributed. Ban Gu died in prison (demonstrating the danger of pronouncing upon history in China) and his predecessor Sima Qian was castrated on imperial orders after defending General Li Ling who had been forced to surrender to the Xiongnu in 99 BC.

The chapter begins with the geographical setting and a description of the 'northern' and 'southern routes' around the desert. Zhang Qian is credited with having 'for the first time opened up a way in the Western Regions', provoking the decline of the Xiongnu (by AD 92) and the establishment of four Han military commanderies, including that at Dunhuang. With the decline in Xiongnu power in the first century AD, the Chinese sent out agricultural colonists who, in the Gansu region, worked alongside the 'southern Xiongnu', who had accepted Han rule and a settled, agricultural way of life in the province.

The states and settlements of the Western Regions are set out one by one. The 'state nearest to Han is that one of the Qiang [a term applied to all the tribes living southwest of the Gansu corridor] . . . secluded in the southwest . . . not situated on the main route. There are 450 households, 1,750 individuals with 500 persons able to bear arms . . . In company with their stock animals the inhabitants go in search of water and do not apply themselves to agricultural work. For field crops they rely on Shanshan [Loulan] and Qiemo. The mountains produce iron and they make military weapons themselves. For military weapons they have bows, lances, short knives, swords.'[13]

Such descriptions reveal not only a preoccupation with the military potential of neighbouring states and their relations with other barbarians, but the Han Chinese bureaucracy at work. The earliest surviving census of China itself was made in AD 2 and the registration of the population for taxation was a vital underpinning of the economy. Registered males were eligible for military service and corvée labour (building roads or the Great Wall) as well as capitation tax and tax in the form of produce (silk, raw lacquer, grains).

More substantial settlements, such as that at Loulan (with '1,570 households, 14,100 individuals with 2,192 persons able to bear arms'), were described in census-like terms of population but also in terms of their historical relations with the Chinese. Loulan was a place where the Han emperor Wudi's envoys were constantly harassed; furthermore, its inhabitants 'frequently acted as ears and eyes for the Xiongnu, enabling their troops to intercept the Han envoys'. Punitive expeditions were despatched.

Relations between the Chinese, Xiongnu and Loulan were complex. Following the punitive expedition, Loulan surrendered to the Chinese and sent tribute gifts to the Han emperor. The Xiongnu, presumably suspicious of this potential alliance, proceeded to attack Loulan, 'whereupon the king of Loulan sent one son as a hostage to the Xiongnu and one as a hostage to Han'. Holding hostages and using

spare princesses to organise matrimonial alliances (in effect sending female hostages out into Central Asia) was a central feature of Han diplomacy. Zhang Qian had recommended sending a Chinese princess to the Wusun in the Ili valley. In the case of the prince of Loulan, the affair ended badly. When his father died in 92 BC, his countrymen asked for him back. Unfortunately, he 'had been indicted according to the terms of the Han laws and sent down to the silkworm house to undergo castration. For this reason Han did not send him to Loulan but affirmed in reply that "the Son of Heaven has become greatly attached to his attendant and is unable to send him away." '14 The imperial suggestion that they should enthrone the next eligible son was meekly accepted by the people of Loulan.

Some of the dangers of the Western Regions were described in the account of Wucha, west of Yarkand, sometimes identified as Tashkurgan. 'The inhabitants live in the mountains, and work the land that lies between the rocks. There is white grass and they pile up stones on one another to make dwellings.' The inhabitants apparently drank out of cupped hands. 'The land produces the short-pacing horse, and there are asses but no cattle. To the west there is the Suspended Crossing . . . what is termed the Suspended Crossing is a rocky mountain: the valley is impenetrable and people traverse the place by pulling each other across with ropes.'

The suspended crossing marked a considerable physical barrier and the *Han shu* noted that it kept the people of Zhibin (Kashmir?) out of reach. Beyond territories like those listed above that had fairly constant, if combative, relations with China, lay countries like Parthia (Persia) adjacent to Sogdiana in the north, where the emperor Wu's envoys acquired large birds' eggs and jugglers. Jugglers or acrobats, possibly sold as slaves in the markets of the Roman Orient, were 'often' presented as tribute to the Han court from Parthia and held their circus performances not only at court but in the squares of Chang'an.15

Much more important to the Han emperors were the horses of Central Asia, first reported by Zhang Qian. One of the most formidable aspects of the Xiongnu invasions of China had been their superior steeds and superior horsemanship. Major horse-breeding groups

The Kirghiz present horses to the Qianlong emperor, by the eighteenth-century Italian artist at the Chinese imperial court, Giuseppe Castiglione. His Chinese name was Lang Shining, pronounced 'Sherning'

included the Yuezhi, who had moved from Western Gansu to Bactria, the Wusun, nomads of the Ili valley, south of Lake Balkash, and the inhabitants of Ferghana. 'As soon as the emperor heard of the blood-sweating descendants of the Heavenly Horses, he sent envoys bearing a thousand pieces of gold and a golden horse with which to make a request for the fine horses of Yuan.'[16] This apparently simple request led to considerable bloodshed. The king of Yuan apparently demurred because Han was so far away; the Han envoys got cross ('spoke in unrestrained terms') and were beheaded. At this, 'the Son of Heaven sent General Li Guangli to take a force that amounted to over one hundred thousand men.' Four years of battle ensued until the king was beheaded by his own people who agreed to send 3,000 horses to China. Eventually things settled down, with the people of Ferghana offering to send 'two Heavenly Horses' per year. The Chinese also acquired lucerne grass seeds (to feed the horses) and grape seeds.

The passion for blood-sweating horses was driven by two problems. Austin Coates described one: 'The horse cannot be bred successfully in China due to the calcium deficiency in all organic matter including water.' The Chinese had imported horses from Mongolia but these were small, 'shaggy, furry little creatures, looking as much like dogs or bears as horses'.[17] They were quite unlike the splendid Arab steeds that could be found in the Western Regions. These more desirable beasts were required in a constant supply because of the difficulty of breeding from them.

They were also needed because of the discovery of the superiority of cavalry over infantry in war, devastatingly demonstrated by the Xiongnu. There were chariots and cavalrymen represented in the 'buried army' of the first emperor of the Qin (r. 221–206 BC), showing that the use of cavalry was known, but that it had not reached the level of superiority achieved subsequently during the Han. (Like the horses, chariot technology was originally a Western import, from Sumeria c.1500 BC.[18]) The king of the state of Zhao set up cavalry regiments during the fourth century BC and, in emulation of the nomadic horsemen that they faced, organised mounted troops of bowmen who could shoot from the saddle. The cavalrymen eschewed the cumbersome long robes of the Chinese, in favour of the short tunic and trousers worn by barbarian archers.[19] The importance of cavalry was emphasised by the humiliating failure of a large Han army, mainly composed of infantrymen, sent by the Gaozong emperor against the Xiongnu in 201 BC, but the difficulty of breeding horses was over-whelming.

After examining the purely military concern for more and better horses, Arthur Waley came to the conclusion that the quest for perfect horses was more spiritual than practical. In 101 BC, the emperor Wu was in the Chinese capital of Chang'an, awaiting the arrival of over thirty 'superior' horses after a successful military campaign against Ferghana, and he composed a 'hymn' as he waited:

> The Heavenly Horses are coming,
> Coming from the Far West.
> They crossed the Flowing Sands,
> For the barbarians are conquered.
> The Heavenly Horses are coming
> That issued from the waters of a pool.
> Two of them have tiger backs:
> They can transform themselves like spirits.
> The Heavenly Horses are coming
> Across the pastureless wilds
> A thousand leagues at a stretch,
> Following the eastern road.
> The Heavenly Horses are coming;
> Jupiter is in the Dragon.
> Should they choose to soar aloft,
> Who could keep pace with them?
> The Heavenly Horses are coming;
> Open the gates while there is time.
> They will draw me up and carry me
> To the Holy Mountain of K'un-lun.
> The Heavenly Horses have come
> And the Dragon will follow in their wake.
> I shall reach the Gates of Heaven,
> I shall see the Palace of God.[20]

The Chinese believed at the time that special horses issued forth from water, normally the home of the watery dragon of Chinese folk-lore, and they sometimes had wings, like dragons. Such winged horses, carved in stone, can be found lining the approach to the tomb of the Tang empress Wu Zetian (AD 690–705), and the 'sea horse', an apparently normal horse, sometimes depicted with fishy scales on its legs and sometimes shown galloping through waves, remained a popular subject for artists throughout Chinese history.[21]

The association of heavenly horses with dragons, more powerful mythical beasts, emblems of the emperors of China, carried with it the idea that the Son of Heaven, the emperor, would be transported to Heaven itself by a pair of these beasts. The legend of the Heavenly Horses was reinforced by the story of a strange horse found at Dunhuang, on the edge of the Gobi desert, in 113 BC. A Chinese soldier serving in the military outpost near Dunhuang captured the horse and sent it to the court at Chang'an. It was praised in another hymn which was subsequently used in court sacrifices:

> The Heavenly Horse comes down,
> A present from the Grand Unity.
> Bedewed with red sweat,
> That foams in an ochre stream,
> Impatient of all restraint
> And of abounding energy.
> He treads the fleeting clouds,
> Dim in his upward flight;
> With smooth and easy gait
> Covers a thousand leagues.[22]

Such arrivals at court must have delighted the emperor Wu who, according to an account of *c.* AD 200, had hoped for immortality through the miraculous arrival of a 'heavenly horse' that would carry him to Kunlun, the home of the immortals. The reference to bloody sweat is characteristic of all descriptions of Ferghana horses at the time. Professor Homer Hasenpflug Dubs ascribed the phenomenon to parasitic infection by *Parafiliaria multipupillosa*, though Arthur Waley quoted another story in which a heavenly horse, given by the emperor Zhang (r. AD 75–88) to his uncle, was said to bleed from a small wound, apparently interpreted as a sweat pore, in its leg. Emperor Zhang said, 'I had often heard the line in Emperor Wu's song about the Heavenly Horse in which it is said that it is "bedewed with red sweat", and I have now seen with my own eyes that this is actually the case.'

Opposing the standard stress on the better performance of these Ferghana horses in cavalry engagements, Arthur Waley stressed that, for the rulers of Ferghana, they were probably used more in ritual than warfare, in emulation of the magic horses that transported the infant Buddha; and for the Chinese emperors they served an equally magical purpose, symbolising transportation to the land of the immortals in the mythical Kunlun mountains. In a concretisation of myth, the name 'Kunlun' was applied to the mountain range that runs along the southern silk road, south of Niya and Hetian (Khotan).

The importation of horses from Central Asia, heavenly or otherwise, was a major feature of all Han treaties with the 'Western' lands. This practice continued throughout most of China's history, latterly, in the late nineteenth and early twentieth centuries, from the north-eastern end of Central Asia, as Mongol traders drove herds of shaggy little horses down to the Yangtze where they were snapped up by Treaty Port inhabitants keen to ride and 'shake up their livers'. During

Stone relief panel of a horse and general from the tomb of the emperor Taizong, seventh century

the Han dynasty, the barbarian Xiongnu also managed a thriving trade in donkeys, previously unknown in China but appreciated for their endurance and stamina (and much easier to breed in China itself).

The state of Wusun (tentatively thought to be situated in the Ili valley) also felt itself to be impossibly distant from China, but the visit from Zhang Qian immediately provoked the Xiongnu (who were everywhere) and, to cement links between Wusun and China, a marriage alliance, swapping a Chinese princess for a thousand horses, was arranged. Xijun, daughter of the 'incestuous, unspeakably cruel and perverted' king of Jiangdu, was sent to the elderly ruler of Wusun with a train of several hundred eunuchs and servants and imperial carriages. A palace (tent?) was built for her but she only met her elderly husband at a banquet once or twice a year and they had no common language. 'In her deep sorrow, the princess composed a song for herself, which ran:

> My family sent me off to be married on the other side of heaven.
> They sent me a long way to a strange land, to the king of Wusun.
> A domed lodging is my dwelling place with walls of felt.
> Meat is my food, with fermented milk as the sauce.
> I live with constant thoughts of my home, my heart is full of
>   sorrow.
> I wish I were a golden swan, returning to my home country.

Taking pity on this lonely Chinese princess, the Chinese emperor arranged that she should be sent a comforting parcel of brocades and embroideries – every other year . . .[23] She was later, according to a fairly common custom amongst the non-Chinese, married to her husband's grandson and bore him a daughter. This practice of passing the wife of the deceased on to another family member was rather shocking to the Chinese who believed in virtuous widowhood (not necessarily any more fun).

57

The *Han shu* account of the Wusun breaks down into caricature with 'the fat king' and the 'mad king'. The Chinese were involved in a plot to kill the 'mad king' and a Chinese deputy envoy who brought a doctor to attend him was punished, like the prince of Loulan, by being 'sent down to the silkworm house for castration'.

Whilst such high-level fact-finding and despatch of envoys, princesses and armies continued, trade between the various tribes of Central Asia and the Chinese was carried on at the lower level. Border fairs saw the exchange of animals with horses, both Heavenly and normal, and donkeys acquired by the Chinese, while iron tools, cloth, grain and Chinese luxuries such as silk, lacquer and jade ornaments were bought by their neighbours.

Apart from horses, the Han court was anxious 'to accumulate manifold resources. Having beheld rhinoceros horn, ivory and tortoise shell . . . allured by betel-nuts . . . learning of the horses of heaven and the grape', they made contact with the suppliers. 'From then on rarities such as luminous pearls, striped shells, lined rhinoceros horn and kingfisher feathers were seen in plenty in the empress' palace . . . dragon-striped, fish-eyed and blood-sweating horses filled the Yellow Gate, groups of elephants, lions, ferocious beasts and ostriches were reared in the outer park and wonderful goods of various climes were brought from the four corners of the world.'[24] Aside from zoo animals and luxuries, foodstuffs were amongst the most important imports along the Silk Roads, for they greatly enlarged the potential of Chinese cuisine. Though some of them preserve an indication of their foreign origin in their names (there is a particular Chinese character meaning foreign which is used in the name of the large-bulbed onion, for example), it would surprise many Chinese cooks to know that some of their basic ingredients were originally foreign imports. Sesame, peas, onions, coriander from Bactria, and cucumber were all introduced into China from the West during the Han dynasty.[25]

Grapes were first introduced to China by Zhang Qian. They were planted in Chang'an and grown, at that time, just for the table. They were small grapes, apparently of three types, yellow, white and black.[26]

With these quantities of materials being traded along the Silk Roads, the Chinese government did its best to control trade and movement. A system of customs posts was established during the Han dynasty to prevent smuggling and possibly to tax goods as they passed, and Chinese traders were controlled by means of passports which indicated the destination, the purpose of the trip and the goods carried.[27] Contact and trade with the world beyond China was concentrated on the northern and southern land routes across Central Asia but there was also a considerable volume of trade by sea. Pearls, tortoise-shells, ivory and rhinoceros horns almost certainly came by

59

sea and it is possible that Chinese silk first reached India by sea.[28]

There were alternative land routes too, by which Chinese goods were exported to India and northwards. The land route from Sichuan province (a major silk-producing centre) into Yunnan and then Burma may have been another route for Chinese silks destined for India; in fact Zhang Qian had been rather shocked to discover that merchants of Shu (Sichuan) had been plying their private trade along this route in the second century BC.[29] And although Zhang Qian was described as an honourable official, subsequent Chinese envoys to Central Asia were often characterised as corrupt, determined to make their fortune by private trade in local exotica, and this problem continued: in the eighteenth and early nineteenth centuries the ability of the local trade official to make his fortune whilst stifling opportunities for foreign traders in the port of Canton was one of the major reasons for the Opium War of 1840.

- 5 -

The spread of trade and religions:
Tocharians and Sogdians

THE TRADERS who carried luxuries and necessities in camel trains between the oases on the Silk Roads were very varied in physique, language, costume and culture. At different times during the thousands of years when the Silk Roads were the most significant trade routes, different peoples dominated the trade and the earliest Silk Road inhabitants were amongst the last to be discovered.

Almost a hundred years ago, Sir Aurel Stein discovered well-preserved mummies at desert sites on the edge of the shimmering salt Lop lake at Loulan. 'Several of the bodies were wonderfully well-conserved, together with their burial deposits. The peaked felt caps decorated with big feathers and other trophies of the chase, the arrow-shafts by their side, the coarse but strong woollen garments, the neatly-woven small baskets holding the food for the dead, etc., all indicated a race of semi-nomadic herdsmen and hunters, just as the Han Annals describe the Lou-lan people when the Chinese found them on their first opening of the route through the desert.

'It was a strange sensation to look down on figures which, but for the parched skin, seemed like those of men asleep . . . The characteristics of the men's heads showed close affinity to that Homo Alpinus type which, as the anthropometrical materials collected by me have proved, still remains the prevailing element in the racial constitution of the present population of the Tarim Basin.'[1]

Stein associated these people with other finds he made in the area and, as his mention of the Han histories suggests, assumed that they were about 2,000 years old, contemporary with the beginnings of Chinese exploration of Central Asia. Similar mummified bodies have since been found at the Cherchen site, also on the edge of the Tarim basin but south of Loulan. Subsequent expeditions to Loulan led by Sven Hedin in the late 1920s followed Stein's description of the graveyard. The nature of the site, with its shifting, wind-blown sands, meant that stratigraphic analysis was impossible and in the early years of the twentieth century there were no other scientific means of dating the finds, except by association. However, associated finds such as coins and documents were similarly unstratified and unstratifiable, subject to the same shifting sand and wind.

More recent analysis suggests that the Cherchen burials were made

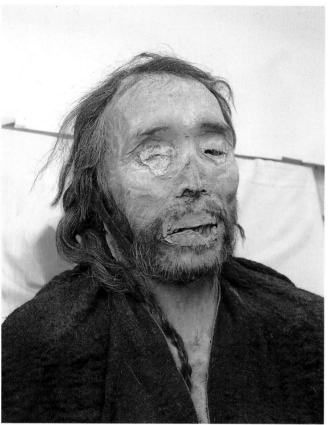

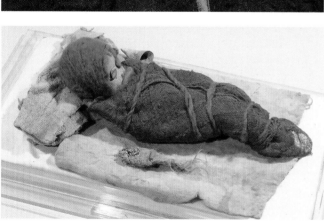

Top left, mummy of a red-haired and possibly Caucasian fifty-five-year-old male known as 'Cherchen Man', c.1000 BC. In a tomb nearby, below, was this mummy of a three-month-old infant, buried with blue glass stones across his eyes. His tie-cord suggests he is probably from the same household as Cherchen Man, and he is buried with a cow-horn cup and a sheep's-udder nursing bottle. The thirty-year-old male figure, right, buried at Yingpan, Urumqi, sometime between AD 265 and 420, was discovered more recently

about 1000 BC, whilst the Loulan graveyard bodies seem to have been buried as early as 2000 BC. Though the site is now barren, salty, sandy and windswept, the rings of dried tree-trunks surrounding the grave-yard, the bundles of ephedra twigs in the graves, and the arrows and baskets all point to a different environment thousands of years ago, enabling a semi-settled life. When the Chinese of the Han dynasty first set out into Central Asia, Loulan was still an important caravan stop with water and food in abundance. A disastrous flood in about AD 330 destroyed the town, and the Lop lake gradually dried up into salt flats, although, out of custom, many travellers still passed through the remains of Loulan on the northern route that offered no shelter or sustenance. From this time onwards the southern route was safer, though longer.

The mummies found at Loulan and Cherchen were strikingly European-looking. They had high-bridged noses, substantial beards, deep, round eye-sockets and often fairish or reddish hair. They were tall, if fully grown, and wore clothing of furs, woven woollen cloth, often in an interesting plaid pattern, leather and felt. The colours of their textiles remain remarkably fresh: a twisted skein of bright red and blue wool held the woven shawl of a baby in place; 'Cherchen

Flaming Mountains, Bezeklik

63

Man', a fifty-five-year-old buried about 1000 BC, wore a woven robe of deep red with white deerskin leggings but inside his leggings he had amazing felt socks of blue, red and yellow horizontal stripes. Some of their cloths were formed from rows of narrow plaited braids in blue, red and orange or yellow, some plain, some with large or small lozenge-shaped patterns. Their felt hats ranged from a bright blue felt bonnet with a red border (for the baby) to felt hoods adorned with large, jaunty feathers and tall felt witches' hats.[2]

The origins of these apparently European people are somewhat mysterious but it is thought that they may have migrated in about 2000 BC from somewhere east of the Caspian Sea, over the Tian Shan mountains down to Loulan. Though they left no evidence of a written script and we cannot know what language they spoke, documents found in the area (dated to about the third century AD) were identified in 1908 as Tocharian, a language which, one expert stated, 'had many affinities with Latin'.[3] These early inhabitants are, therefore, tentatively identified as Tocharians, speaking an Indo-European language, and are thought perhaps to have been the ancestors of the Yuezhi who lived in the same area during the Han dynasty and who moved, in part, westwards, to found the Kushan empire on the northwestern edge of India.[4]

Today, the area where the mummies were found is out of bounds, for it is near where the Chinese test atomic bombs in the open air.

Sven Hedin made a terrifying crossing of the desert of Lop in 1896 and Aurel Stein returned twice, in 1906 and 1913, both choosing to travel in winter with water transported in the form of blocks of ice, rather than risk near death from dehydration as Hedin had, in 1895, near Yarkand at the other end of the Taklamakan desert (west of the Lop desert). Stein's account of his crossing of the Lop desert is a fascinating juxtaposition of sand and camels with freezing weather and ice. Hedin returned to the Loulan area in 1934 and, as he had done previously, made much use of boats and canoes to reach the lake by means of the rivers that fed it. Just sixty years later, in pursuit of the increasingly rare wild camel, John Hare found arrowheads, coins and beads on the sandy surface which had still been under water when Hedin last passed. Hedin had described conditions that the Tocharians might have recognised: 'Tamarisks and reeds looked up out of the water. It was a delicious place! I sat with my sleeves rolled up and dabbled my hand in the water . . .' As his boat moved forward, he saw 'a wild hog, swimming from the mainland, to the reeds'.[5] There were ospreys, grebes, herons and a multitude of fish, all vanished as dams constructed by today's Chinese garrisons have blocked the water that once fed the Konche Darya and Kuruk Darya rivers that emptied out into Lop Nor.[6]

Road marking at Black Gobi, photographed by Hedin in 1934. Such grisly remains served as warnings or signposts to travellers on the Silk Road

Long after the Tocharians had apparently vanished, leaving only desiccated bodies behind, the town of Loulan enjoyed a position in the fourth century AD as a major staging post on the 'middle' Silk Road, a position attested by some of the 'Sogdian letters' (see page 67).

From the second century BC until the end of the Tang dynasty (tenth century AD), Sogdian merchants dominated much of the trade of the Silk Roads. Their homeland, the fortified city of Marakanda, now Samarkand, lay due northwest of the Silk Road. Even before they became known to the Chinese through Zhang Qian's explorations of the Western Regions, the Sogdians were known to the Greeks of the fourth century BC. Though they had been thought of as fierce warriors by the Greeks, the Achaemenid fortress at Marakanda, and the walled city, were taken by Alexander the Great on his eastwards progress in 329 BC. The capture of the city did not end local resistance, for one of Alexander's columns was ambushed just to the west and he embarked on an expanded campaign to subdue Sogdiana. Fortress after fortress was taken and the local population were massacred, enslaved

65

Loulan photographed by the Swedish explorer Sven Hedin in 1901. The remains of a reed house are visible on the right

or subjected to forced transportation. By the time the revolt was put down in 327 BC, the area was left with 'a large garrison of mercenaries and a network of new city foundations, in which a Hellenic military elite was supported by a native agrarian workforce – the invariable model for the dozens of Alexandrias he founded in the eastern empire'.7

The military power of the Sogdians never recovered and it was as travelling tradesmen that they subsequently became known all over Central Asia – the Khotanese called all merchants *suli* (Sogdian) whether they were or not. Their language, related to Aramaic, became the common language of trade along the Silk Roads and they were partly responsible for the movement of religions like Manicheism, Zoroastrianism and Buddhism eastwards along the Silk Road. Chinese stories of the Sogdians describe them as born to their trade: 'At birth honey was put in their mouths and gum on their hands . . . they learned the trade from the age of five . . . on reaching the age of twelve they were sent to do business in a neighbouring state.'8 The Buddhist pilgrim Xuanzang described them as farmers and traders, carpet-makers, glass-makers and woodcarvers. He rather approved of the fact that little boys in Samarkand were taught to read and write at the age of five, even if it was in the service of their commercial skills.

66

Our knowledge of Sogdian trading activities was enhanced by the 'Ancient Letters' found by Stein near a beacon at the end of the Great Wall. They appear to have come from a post-bag which was abandoned, for reasons unknown, at some time around AD 307–11. The letters were written by Sogdian merchants resident in Chinese Central Asia (two in Dunhuang) and the only one with an address was for Samarkand, whilst the others may have been destined for Loulan and other places on the route west to Samarkand. Though the letters are fragmentary and difficult to decipher, they refer to commodities such as gold, musk, pepper, camphor, flax cloth and wheat. There were calculations of weight, based on Chinese copper coins. They also suggest that there was a Zoroastrian temple in Dunhuang.

It appears from these, and other scattered Sogdian sources, that in the fourth century AD they may have managed a sort of triangle of trade, possibly a monopoly trade, between India and Sogdiana and India and China. By the seventh century, many Sogdian merchants had settled in China and assumed Chinese names (usually taking the 'An' surname also used by Parthians). By the middle of the eighth century, the Sogdians of Dunhuang were respected members of society, many having taken up agriculture, and they were sometimes given Chinese titles. The Sogdians of Turfan at the same period were still trading in silk and horses, but much more on a local basis than the grand triangular trade of the third century.

The Sogdians were responsible for the transportation to China of the grapevine and alfalfa (or lucerne grass) to feed the heavenly horses from Ferghana. They also carried the special mare's teat grapes from the oasis of Khocho (packed in ice in lead containers) and sold luxury goods from the west to the Chinese: Sassanian silverware from Persia which had a huge influence on Chinese silverwork, glass vessels and beads from Syria and Babylon, amber from the Baltic, Mediterranean coral, brass for Buddhist images, and purple woollen cloth from Rome. They themselves bought silk, copied the Chinese copper coinage and used Chinese paper. The establishment of paper manufacture in their native city, Samarkand, in the eighth century, led to the gradual transmission of paper-making to Europe. Legend has it that it was the capture of Chinese paper-makers during a battle on the Talas river in AD 751, when an allied army of Uighurs and Tibetans defeated a Chinese force under Gao Xianzhi, that led to the establishment of paper-making in Samarkand (where local hemp and flax and the abundant water from the *karez* provided raw materials in abundance).[9] The westwards transmission of this vital technology was probably more gradual, and part of various Sogdian borrowings. Chinese art, for example, especially that of wall-painting, had a strong effect on Sogdian art.[10]

In the ruins of a Sogdian city at Panjikent, Tajikistan, the remains
of fine wall-paintings have been found which vary the picture of the
travelling merchants. The frescoes show jousting and banquet scenes,
and the Sogdians depict themselves as having 'long thin faces, prominent noses, deep-set eyes and luxuriant beards'.[11] Similar faces can be
found in Manichean manuscripts, found at Khocho in the 1920s by
the German explorer and archaeologist von Le Coq. The illustrations,
probably produced by Sogdian artists, depict priests with neat, pointed
beards, long dark hair and rather corpulent figures.[12] They wore Phry-
gian felt hats with knee-length silk tunics, belted at the waist, over
narrow trousers and high leather boots, very like the dress of the
Kirghiz today.[13]

Panjikent was, like other Sogdian cities, built on a hill and surrounded by a wall. It stood above the Zerafshan river, in sight of the
snow-capped Pamirs. The surrounding wall, enclosing only about
thirty acres, meant that the city was very crowded. Houses were built
upwards, with upper storeys meeting over the streets, leaving them
narrow, dark and airless. The markets and caravanserai were outside
the walls.

The Sogdian capital, Marakanda, later Samarkand, which lies
between the Syr Darya and Oxus rivers, is a city that has been
destroyed and rebuilt countless times throughout its history. After
Alexander the Great captured it in 329 BC, Turks and Huns descended on it and each time it would be patched up. Xuanzang, who
passed through in the seventh century AD, described it as 'six miles or
so in circumference, completely enclosed by rugged land, and very
populous'. He noted the markets with many goods, brought from the
west and destined to travel further east: 'The precious merchandise
of many foreign countries is stored here. The soil is rich and productive and yields abundant harvests. The forest trees afford a thick
vegetation and flowers and fruit are plentiful. *Shen* horses are bred
there. The inhabitants' skill in the arts and trades exceeds that of
other countries. The climate is agreeable and temperate and the people brave and energetic.'[14]

Sogdian merchants and travellers were mainly responsible for the
spread of Zoroastrianism along the Silk Roads, eastwards to China,
although the initial contacts may have been earlier, for linguistic evi-

68

dence has been cited to suggest that there were Iranian soothsayers in China as early as the eighth century BC.[15] There is evidence of Zoroastrian temples in Lanzhou and in the secondary capital of Luoyang during the Tang, where magic shows were held in front of huge crowds.[16]

The dates of the prophet Zarathustra or Zoroaster are uncertain. Some place him in the thirteenth century BC, others in the sixth century BC, and his origins similarly are set as far apart as Azerbaijan and Mongolia. Rather as the Buddha reflected his own religious background in adapting various aspects of Hinduism, so Zoroaster's religion represented both an incorporation of existing Iranian belief in the sun as the visible manifestation of Ahura Mazda, and a rejection of other prevailing beliefs such as the sacrifice of bulls and ritual drinking sessions. Zoroaster elevated Ahura Mazda as the sole god to worship, thus placing him amongst the earliest monotheists, but his opposition of an evil deity means that Zoroastrianism is generally

Fragment of a wall-painting from Panjikent, Tajikistan, showing bearded demons with bows and arrows, first half of the eighth century

69

Sogdian silver plate, seventh century. The figures engaged in a duel bear some resemblance to those of the Panjikent murals

characterised as 'dualistic'. The association of Ahura Mazda with the sun and 'its earthly analogue, fire', included a general belief in the purifying potential of both, and paradise was seen as a place of light.[17]

Zoroastrianism was adopted by a number of Sogdians who carried it along the Silk Roads, into China where it was tolerated for a while during the Tang, and into India where it still survives.

Another major religion transmitted along the Silk Roads into China by Sogdian merchants and travellers was Manicheism, as the Sogdian letters demonstrate.

Manicheism began in Mesopotamia with the prophet Mani, born in AD 216 in a family descended from the royal house of Parthia. After two revelations when he was twelve and twenty-four, Mani set out to preach his message in Buddhist Kushan, in northwest India. His beliefs were a blend of Iranian and Semitic traditions, with additions from Buddhism and Christianity, and they were to survive in medieval Europe in the Cathar movement in Provence and amongst the Bogomils of the Balkans.[18]

Mani's ideas are generally characterised as gnostic, offering a dualist view of the universe where good is balanced against evil and where esoteric interpretations lead to salvation through knowledge.[19] Spirit was equated with light, matter with darkness, and good was seen as

Fragments from a Manichean manuscript found by Albert von Le Coq in Khocho. The first, right, shows priests at their writing desks. It has a panel of Sogdian writing. Below, the fragment shows the feast of Bema, an annual feast held to commemorate the martyrdom of Mani in March 276. It was mentioned by St Augustine, who was himself at one time a Manichean

particles of light struggling to escape from the dark matter in which it was trapped. Mani set forth a pantheon which incorporated previous prophets including Zoroaster, Buddha and Jesus, declaring himself a successor to these prophets, and spoke of an elite or 'elect' group which would lead the faith, wearing white, adhering strictly to a vegetarian diet and potentially ensuring the end of the faith through strict abstinence from reproduction. In a leaf from a Manichean book found in a temple of the eighth to ninth century in Khocho, a white-robed priest is shown surrounded by the Hindu deities Shiva, Brahma and the elephant-headed Ganesh. On the opposite part of the fragment is a depiction of the feast of Bema, commemorating Mani's martyrdom (he was crucified in 276 on the order of the Persian king Hormizd I). White-robed Manicheans with black beards and a variety of tall or turban-shaped white hats, sit on a carpet beside a gold tripod piled with a vegetarian spread of watermelons, grapes and honeydew melons.[20]

Mani believed that people (matter) contained a finite number of light particles and reproduction would divide their light particles increasingly sparsely amongst their descendants. Similarly, the preparation of food would divide the good light particles residing within all living things including vegetables. Thus, the elect ate vegetarian food prepared by others whilst reciting, ' "Neither have I cast it into the oven, another hath brought me this and I have eaten it without guilt." '[21]

From the Sogdian capital, Samarkand, a Manichean centre, the faith spread along the Silk Road. The scriptures, written in Syriac, Middle Persian and Parthian, were translated into Sogdian, Turkish and Chinese, and several texts, mostly dating to the eighth or ninth century, were discovered in the great Buddhist temple library at Dunhuang and at several sites in the Turfan area.[22]

The religion was adopted by the Uighur ruler Bugug Khan (759–80) and it remained the state religion of the Uighurs for some hundreds of years until the rise of the Mongols. There were also Manichean temples in China and, whilst the religion gradually lost adherents to Buddhism and Islam, one temple, at Caoan, near Quanzhou (Fujian province), still survives. Its courtyard contains an inscription with the words 'Mani the Buddha of Light' and its halls contain images which, to the expert, are clearly of Mani rather than the Buddha. But the faithful who worship there, 'pious old women', seem to be under the impression that the figures are Buddhist.[23]

A similar confusion over Manicheism apparently occurred in the late thirteenth century when Marco Polo, his father and his uncle visited Fuzhou in southeast China. They met a group of believers there, who were terrified of persecution for their faith. They were something of a mystery to the Polos: they did not worship fire so they were not

Opposite: Figure of a warrior of the Sassanian or Iranian type. The figure came from a shrine at Mingoi, decorated with reliefs of soldiers

Zoroastrians; they did not worship 'idols' so they were not Buddhists; and, according to a local 'Saracen' interpreter, they were not Moslems. The Polos studied their religious texts (one wonders what the language and script were), identified their holy book as a Psalter, and informed them that they were Christians after all, and that the Polos would intercede on their behalf with the Great Mongol Khan. Most modern scholars, aware of Mani's borrowings from Christianity, have identified the group as Manicheans, particularly since Fuzhou is in the same province as Quanzhou and Caoan, though well over 150 kilometres to the northeast; Marco Polo, as usual, getting things nearly right. The account of the meeting with the Manicheans occurs only in one manuscript of Marco Polo's *Divisament dou Monde*, found in Toledo in the 1930s and dated to the mid-fifteenth century; a manuscript which contains over two hundred passages not seen in other earlier versions, which leaves me (though few others) with some doubts. The story itself may reveal that there were, indeed, practising Manicheans in Fuzhou in the thirteenth (or fourteenth or fifteenth) century and, perhaps, that a description was incorporated by the copyist of the 'Polo' manuscript in the mid-fifteenth century.

Whether the Polos were right or not, the Manichean faith, in one confused form or other, persisted in China long after the Sogdian traders had been forgotten.

- 6 -

The fashion for all things Central Asian

CHINESE TRADE along the Silk Roads began to flourish during the Han dynasty. When the dynasty fell in AD 220 there was an end to Chinese suzerainty in Chinese Turkestan (it is easier to use a blanket term such as this, for borders shifted, non-Chinese states rose and fell in the 'Western Regions', and Central Asia is too large a term to signify the area over which China maintained some sort of control through its military outposts and customs barriers).

With the establishment of the Tang dynasty (618–907) the garrisons and customs posts in the area were reinstated. The Tang is often characterised as an outward-looking era, a cosmopolitan period when countless foreign traders set up shop in the capital, Chang'an, and the taste for 'all sorts of foreign luxuries and wonders began to spread from the court outward among city dwellers generally.'[1] The foreign inhabitants of Chang'an, Turks, Uighurs, Tocharians, Sogdians, Arabs and Persians, built their own temples (the mosque is still a fine and busy building but the three Zoroastrian temples have disappeared) and their affairs were controlled by a special government bureau, 'the Office of the Caravan Leader'.

There was considerable development of the sea trade routes but the old Silk Roads were still used, despite the horrors of the direct route from Dunhuang to Turfan across the salt crust of Lop Nor and the persistent threat of sand-storms, described in a seventh-century history: 'When such a wind is about to arrive, only the old camels have advance knowledge of it, and they immediately stand snarling together, and bury their mouths in the sand. The men always take this as a sign, and they too immediately cover their noses and mouths by wrapping them in felt. This wind moves swiftly, and passes in a moment, and is gone, but if they did not so protect themselves, they would be in danger of sudden death.'[2]

The two-humped Bactrian camel had been the main beast of burden in Turkestan for thousands of years and became quite a common sight in northern China right up until the mid-twentieth century. The novelist Ann Bridge, who lived in Peking as a diplomatic wife in the late 1920s, noted how they moulted messily and the carters, anxious not to lose any of the precious camel hair, tied them up with string so that they looked like 'badly done up brown paper parcels'.[3]*

* I remember them on the outskirts of Peking and Shijiazhuang in 1976, pulling coal carts. They were memorably large and just as Ann Bridge

One of a series of paintings of dogs by Castiglione, court painter in China in the eighteenth century. The earliest known depictions of 'Roman' dogs in Chinese art date from the tenth century

During the Tang, demand for camels was enormous, not just as beasts of burden, and not just for the cloth that would be woven from their hair, but even as food: the Tang poet Du Fu (712–70) praised 'the hump of a purple camel emerging from a blue cauldron'. The Uighurs and the Tibetans sent camels to Tang, Khotan sent a 'wind-footed wild camel', and they could be obtained in the city-states of the Tarim.4 Special white camels were acquired for the 'Emissaries of the Bright Camels', super-postmen who took imperial messages out to the border settlements and gave early warning of border problems. 'Flying Dragon Camels' were kept in the imperial stables.5

Amongst the other animals that were brought to China along the Silk Roads were yaks, presented to the court as tribute from Tibet and the Kokonor, and 'zobos', crosses between male yaks and female zubus, smaller animals, better able to tolerate 'the oppressive low-lands'.6 Though they heard stories of fabulous sheep, the most fabulous being the earth-born lambs of Rome, others including the fat-tailed sheep of Samarkand, the blue sheep with kingfisher tails (*bharal*) of the Kunlun mountains and the huge *Ovis poli* (later named 'Marco

described them although mysteriously without the string. Perhaps the bottom had dropped out of the camel-fluff market.

Tang terracotta figures. The fashionable Chinese silhouette changed with the popularity of Yang Guifei, the 'fat concubine'

Polo sheep') of the Pamirs, the Tang emperors refused sheep offered in tribute. They accepted dogs, from Tibet, Persia, Samarkand and Kucha. It was said that the seventh-century master Yan Liben painted a Tibetan mastiff, and it is probable that the dogs from Samarkand and Kucha were hunting hounds for the imperial kennels, and that the spotted dogs from Persia were also hunters. But there were lap-dogs too, tiny long-haired, pointy-faced beasts, presented to the emperor by the ruler of Khocho in the early seventh century and described as 'Roman dogs'. What they actually were is difficult to say, since the earliest known depiction of such dogs is said to date from the Song dynasty (960–1279), but they were certainly indulged at court. There is a story about the Xuanzong emperor (r. 712–56) and his favourite concubine Yang Guifei which tells how when the emperor was playing Go (*weiqi* – a chess-like game played with black and white counters) with a prince and was about to lose a lot of men, Yang Guifei dropped a tiny dog from Samarkand on the board, scattering the pieces. 'His Highness was greatly pleased.'[7]

Yang Guifei (d. 756), the 'fat concubine', 'the most famous femme fatale in Chinese history',[8] was perhaps partly responsible for the fashion for all things Central Asian that swept the Chinese court in the eighth century. Despite being stout, she is known in China as one of

玉勒雕鞍寵太真年,秋後幸華清
開元四十萬疋馬何事驕驟蜀道行
吳興錢選春拳

Yang Guifei was the inspiration for many stories and paintings. In this thirteenth-century scroll painting she is shown mounting a horse

the 'historical beauties' singled out from the distant past. The daughter of an official, she became a concubine of the eighteenth son of the Xuanzong emperor, but when his own favourite concubine died, the emperor took her into his own harem. The only 'fat' lady amongst the historical beauties (for slenderness to the point of fragility has been the norm for both men and women throughout most of China's history), her shape and its influence can be seen in the pottery figures of women made to place in the graves of Tang nobles.

In the seventh century, the female figures were small and slender, wearing dresses with high, narrow bodices and long, narrow sleeves. Tomb figures of women of the mid-eighth century reveal a remarkable change in form, not only reflecting the shape of the fat concubine, but also her adoption of Central Asian fashions brought in along the Silk Roads. She wore large, padded turbans over her hair, in contrast with the neat little hatless heads of the seventh-century beauties, and long, loose gowns that flowed over her generous form. She also wore upholstered slippers with high, padded toes of a form that has been found in excavations along the Silk Road.

Yang Guifei was susceptible not only to Central Asian fashions but also to Central Asian gentlemen. Her passion for the general, An Lushan (d. 757), almost brought the Tang dynasty to a premature end. One of the villains of Chinese history, An Lushan was of Sogdian descent, not an unusual thing during the Tang when one of China's most famous poets, Li Bai (or Li Po), was born in Central Asia.9 Folklore has it that An Lushan's mother was a witch and when he was born, 'the beasts of the field cried aloud'. He was clever, speaking 'various frontier dialects well; a point which once saved his head when condemned to death for sheep-stealing'. He gained a reputation for repressing frontier raids and the emperor grew fond of him, though

78

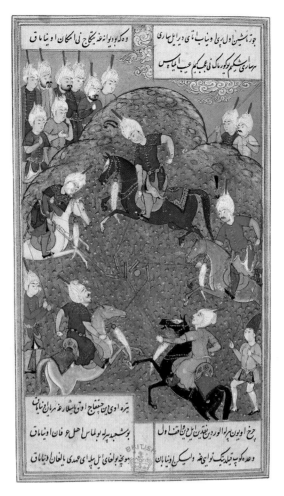

A game of polo, by a Turkish artist, c.1520

not as fond as Yang Guifei. After gaining control of an army of 160,000, An Lushan finally led an uprising against the emperor, which forced the court to flee from Chang'an. Many of the nobles who left with the emperor buried their valuables first. Whether their owners forgot where they had left their silver and gold, or whether they died on the flight, a number of these hoards have since been excavated, and reveal that, even in their homes, Tang nobles favoured imported vessels of Central Asian silver and gold or semi-precious stones.

An Lushan was assassinated by his own son and the Tang dynasty was restored, but not before the death of Yang Guifei. Fleeing from the capital with the emperor, his own bodyguard, considering her largely responsible for the uprising, insisted on her death. Some say she was strangled, others that she was hanged from a peach tree. The emperor, though restored to his throne, never recovered from her death. The flight from the capital, with its tragic end, and the misery of the emperor, inconsolably wandering through the palace, have remained favourite subjects for painters and poets ever since, the most famous example being the poem by Bai Juyi (Po Chu-I), 'Everlasting Remorse'.[10]

The Tang continued to import horses and discovered new, exotic aspects to them, as well as new uses. The game of polo was introduced from Persia early in the Tang dynasty and became so popular that there was a special polo field in the palace and the game was played by women as well as men. It is clear that certain horses were better suited to the game and there is a record of the presentation of two polo ponies from Khotan in 717. There was also a new fashion for 'dancing horses'. Tibetan envoys were entertained by horses that could follow music most gracefully, lie down and get up again, all the while decorated with unicorn heads, phoenix wings and caparisoned in silver and gold. The Xuanzong emperor had a hundred dancing horses which performed with precious stones woven into their manes, embroidered trappings with fringes of silver and gold, and attendants in yellow shirts with jade belts. The horses 'danced their intricate manoeuvres, with tossing heads and beating tails . . . they could dance on three-tiered benches.'

Perhaps the most famous individual horses of the Tang were the six chargers of the Taizong emperor, founder of the Tang dynasty, which had carried him throughout his campaigns against his rivals. He had the court painter Yan Liben draw them and the portraits were then carved in high relief on stone panels that were installed in his tomb. The group of panels was subsequently removed from the tomb and only four remain in China, one cut into pieces preparatory to transportation to America, where two panels are now in the museum of the University of Pennsylvania.[11] (See page 217.)

Hawks and falcons were kept next to the imperial hunting kennels. They mostly arrived as tribute from Manchuria or Turkestan. It is recorded that in 866 the governor of Dunhuang sent a tribute package of four 'green-shank' goshawks, two horses and a pair of Tibetan women. The Chinese would have fitted the birds with tail bells of jade, gold and chased metals, jesses of green silk or 'clouded brocade', and leashes with jade swivels, and would have kept them in carved and painted cages with gilded perches.[12]

Less useful exotic birds, which nevertheless came to occupy a privileged position in Tang imagery, were ostriches, first sent as a gift by the Parthians in AD 101. The males had red necks, black-feathered bodies and large white tail-feathers. They were probably Tocharian ostriches, related to the ostriches which became extinct in the Syrian and Arabian deserts in 1941. Two Tang tombs, including that of the Gaozong emperor (r. 618–26), include great, long-legged stone birds with luxuriously curled tail-feathers in the procession of stone figures lining their spirit ways.[13]

Animal products imported into China along the Silk Roads included horse hides from the Ordos, used for making saddle-cloths,

Young man with a falcon, by an Iranian artist, early seventeenth century

coracles and leather armour, and furs of all sorts from similarly northern states.

Amongst the plants introduced into China from the west was saffron (from India, Bokhara and Kapisa, brought in both dried and in plant form). It was used as an aromatic, to perfume clothes and hair and to flavour wines. The poet Li Bai, whose best-known poem describes how he asked the moon to join him so that he would not, technically, drink alone, spoke of

> Best wine of Lanling, with saffron aromatic,
> Comes in brimful cups of jade, amber shining.[14]

The introduction of the narcissus remains somewhat mysterious but the flower has its origin in the west, despite its contemporary association with China. It is a favourite subject for painters and has been one of the most important house-plants for centuries, mainly because, if carefully nurtured, it flowers at the Chinese Spring Festival (late January to early February), perfuming as well as decorating the house. The Chinese now grow 'paper narcissi' in water on carefully selected stones which shine in different colours in the water and there is a school of 'flower sculpture' whereby the bulbs are divided and forced to create a mass of intertwined flowers.

Foodstuffs continued to be significant imports along the Silk Road. During the Tang, kohlrabi appeared via the Gansu corridor, sugar beet (known by a Persian name) may have been introduced by the Arabs, and a group of 'fancy exotics' were sent in 647 from the king of Nepal. These were not of Nepalese origin and included a new kind of scallion or leek, something resembling lettuce, a 'Western celery' and spinach. Spinach (possibly of Persian origin) was regarded as a useful medicine by Daoist adepts. They were prone to eating various poisons in order to try to achieve bodily immortality (which they saw as a prerequisite for spiritual immortality), most particularly cinnabar.

81

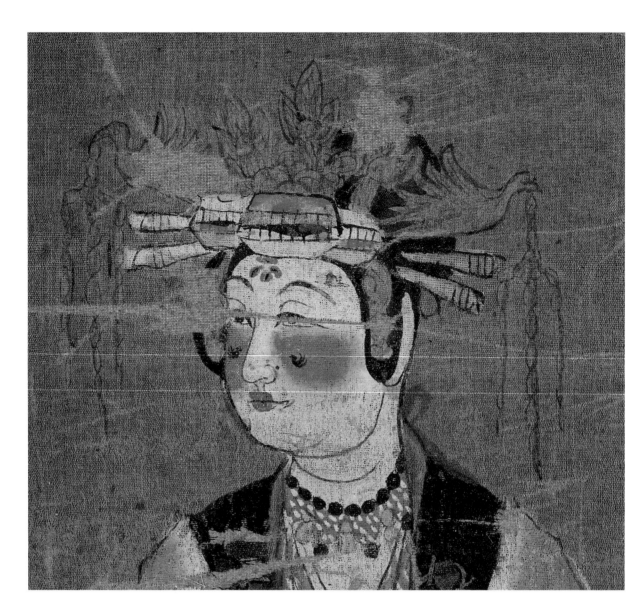

A lady with 'moth' eyebrows. A detail of a female donor, from a painting at Dunhuang

Spinach was recommended as an antidote in case of an overdose of cinnabar (and also in case of hangovers).[15]

Persian pistachios, fagara pepper from the 'Western Regions', 'mustard of the Westerners' (originating in the Mediterranean area), scented resins like storax, imported from Rome and Parthia, and Parthian 'gum guggul' were more of the foreign imports. In the case of gum guggul, an aromatic, 'a widely used adulterant of frankincense', the source is sometimes difficult to disentangle though it appears to have been in Syria and Persia. Gum guggul was originally associated (not entirely accurately) with Gandhara and with Buddhism, and was used by the fourth-century Buddhist priest Fotu Deng in rain-making ceremonies. It is probable that such Buddhist aromatics were traded through Gandhara from their nearby countries of origin, gaining in value and religious significance by the association. It appears that Parthian gum guggul was soon replaced by Indonesian benzoin, brought by the sea route.

The Chinese pharmacopoeia was also greatly enriched by trade along the Silk Roads. Asafoetida, imported as sun-dried cakes or roots, used to conceal foul odours, as an anti-helminthic and anti-demoniac, was imported from Persia and Beshbalik (where there was a Chinese garrison); castor oil beans from Persia were also used as a medicine. One of the most important animal medicines was bezoar, 'a concretion found in the fourth stomach of many ruminants',* used as an antidote for poison. Such lumps formed an important two-way trade along the Silk Roads: Chinese 'ox yellow' bezoars (mainly from Shandong) were highly prized as far away as Persia whilst a 'serpent yellow' lump was sent to China from Ferghana in 761.[16]

Palace women of the Sui dynasty (581–605) apparently used Persian 'snail kohl' to outline their 'moth eyebrows' (light fluffy marks, placed high above the real thing, a fashion most widely seen in Japanese paintings) and indigo was imported from Persia and Ferghana where it was used not only as a dye but also as an eye-shadow, a fashion that was followed in China. The poet Li Bai described

> A houri of Wu, just fifteen, borne on a slender horse,
> Eyebrows painted with blue kohl, and red brocade boots
> At a feast on tortoise-shell mats.[17]

Imported dyestuffs used for non-cosmetic purposes included oak galls from Persia and yellow orpiment. Imported chemicals included salt from the dried-up Lake Kokonor, mysterious 'black salt' sent as tribute from Kapisa in 746 and from Khawarizm, south of the Oxus, in 751 and 753. Alum, used to make animal skins soft and easy to work and to set dyes, was a major import. Some of the finest paper of the Tang was burnished with the highest-quality alum imported from Khocho. Metalworkers relied upon sal ammoniac from Kucha, which they used as a flux, whilst doctors used it sparingly to relieve bronchial congestion; another metalworkers' flux was borax from Tibet. From the dried lakes of Central Asia, potassium nitrate was used to make the famous fireworks, 'flame flowers', 'silver flowers' and 'peach blossoms', and Epsom salts were used as purgatives. Skin diseases were cured by realgar and litharge from the west.[18]

Though many of the foodstuffs that were introduced were quickly incorporated into Chinese agriculture, the chemicals were continuously

* A popular cold remedy in China today includes 'toad bezoar' (which must be quite a problem to extract).

Side street in the pottery district, Kashgar. Below, a man riveting Chinese pots

imported, even if there were Chinese sources, often because the imported materials had specific qualities. They must have required considerable camel caravans. Precious materials like carnelian and rock crystal from Samarkand, and lapis lazuli from Khotan (the market, not the original source which was Badakhshan) also weighed down the camel trains.

Apart from raw materials, luxury items also made their way along the Silk Roads. Though China was still exporting silk, other textiles from Central Asia travelled in the opposite direction. Central Asian felts, white from the Ordos and red from Kucha, were used for tents, draperies, curtains, mats, saddle covers and boots, and there was a fashion for black felt hats for men in the early seventh century.[19]* Though felt was imported to be cut and worked in Chang'an, other woollen goods appear to have been imported ready-made. Rugs and carpets were imported from Bokhara, Kapisa and Persia, and also asbestos cloth, which was used for 'dance mats' and, apparently, clothing. Linen was imported from the Ordos (though China produced its own) and cotton was introduced (to become a Chinese crop) from India via both the land and sea routes. The taste for exotica was also responsible for the importation of fancy silk textiles, often incorporating gold threads in damasks and brocades, from Persia, Kapisa and Byzantium.[20]

Jet from Khocho, amber from the Baltic region, red coral from the Mediterranean, and pearls, imported via the Western Regions, all added to the range of the Chinese jeweller, and ornamental glass, sculpted, moulded or blown into bowls, glasses and other decorative items, was first imported from Persia and beyond and then copied in China. The taste in glass objects is best demonstrated by the hoard in the Shosoin in Japan (a treasure collected in the seventh century that reflects the range of decorative articles available in China and equally admired in Japan). There are 'dark green fish-pendants with eyes, mouth and gills in gold . . . a shallow green cup with wavy edge; a shallow brownish dish with a foot . . . a four-lobed red-brown pedestal cup, with raised floral design and scrolls . . . derived from Sassanian silver work; a greenish white bracelet in the form of two confronting dragon heads holding a pearl'.[21]

One surprising import brought along the Silk Roads, which transformed the dress, architecture and life-style of the Chinese, was the chair. The fact that the Chinese sat on mats placed on the floor can be deduced from the continuing Japanese custom, based on the fact that 'seventh-century Japan took Tang China as a model of fashion and culture'.[22] Many aspects of late traditional Japan have their origins in

* I wonder if the Chico Marx black felt hats still worn by men in Shaoxing are descended from the Tang hats.

A Chinese evening tea party c.970, with the host seated in the traditional oriental manner on a Western-style chair, from a handscroll. Opposite: William Alexander's sketch of a Chinese official seated in the same manner eight centuries later

Tang China, because a wholesale borrowing of cultural forms, from architecture to the adoption of the Chinese script, took place at that time.[23] Though the kimono has evolved since then, the basic high-waisted, tight-bodiced shape recalls seventh-century Chinese dress (rather than the fuller, loose-waisted Central Asian styles popularised by Yang Guifei or the later loose cross-over robes of the Song), and Japanese traditional architecture reflects the lower (floor-based) focus of Chinese building at the time. Most interesting is the way that the Chinese language still reflects the floor-based arrangements of the past: Mao Zhuxi, usually translated as Chairman Mao, actually means 'Chief Mat Person Mao', indicating that he, the 'Chairman', actually sat on the principal mat.

Chairs must have come to China from beyond areas like Persia and Arabia where cushions and divans were used, from the borders of the Roman or Byzantine empires in Asia Minor. The first chair to enter China was a folding chair which was known as the *hu chuang*, meaning 'barbarian bed', the word 'barbarian' being a term which made its alien origins explicit. It was first mentioned in Chinese literature in the second century AD, although at this time it seems to have been used out of doors rather than in a domestic setting. The first literary description of such a 'barbarian bed' occurs in a poem by Yu Jianwu, written in about 552, and shows that even when the chair had moved into the house, it still retained its outdoor, military associations:

> By the name handed down [we know that] you are from a
>   foreign region,
> Coming into [China] and being used in the capital.
> With legs leaning your frame adjusts by itself,
> With limbs slanting your body levels by itself.
> You give audience in the Hall, facing the [foreign] guests.
> You order the preparation of the army, haranguing the troops
>   for the start of a military operation.
> You would rather live in the residence of an off-duty Minister,
> To be always kept to serve wise and enlightened worthies.[24]

86

Another type of chair, the frame chair known as *yi*, which means 'to lean', indicating the presence of a back on which the sitter could lean, was first used in China during the Tang period.[25] Paintings of the period show how the chairs were used. The frame chair, in particular, changed the form of Chinese furniture and architecture. Where earlier Chinese houses had a low focus, with long windows reaching almost to the floor, from the Tang, the outer walls beneath the paper-covered window lattice were raised to waist height. Where once the only piece of furniture raised on legs was the low bed, surrounded by a wooden rail and often curtains, used both for sleeping and as a day-bed on which people sat cross-legged, having removed their shoes, now Chinese houses contained high tables and chairs. Some of the frame chairs were quite broad and it is clear that people did not necessarily sit with their legs hanging down (and their shoes on); they sometimes sat cross-legged on the chair, adapting the ancient Chinese custom to the barbarian bed.[26] Moreover, this habit persisted and the stance can be seen in one of William Alexander's sketches of late eighteenth-century China.[27]

- 7 -

The Caves of the Thousand Buddhas:
Buddhism on the Silk Road

THE MOST IMPORTANT of the desert oases is that of Dunhuang and the nearby cliff known as Qianfodong – the Caves of the Thousand Buddhas. Dunhuang was a large oasis settlement, supporting a considerable population and many temples to various faiths. Cotton fields flourished and sheep and goats grazed on the extensive pastures. Some ten miles away out in the desert, a small river with narrow poplar trees on its banks runs beneath a long conglomerate cliff that juts up from the surrounding sand. Beginning in the fourth century AD, caves were hollowed out in the cliff, and over the succeeding seven centuries the caves were gradually filled with clay sculptures of Buddhist deities, and with wall-paintings influenced by earlier Buddhist sites such as Bamiyan and Gandhara. The cliff is still a magnificent sight behind its clean, green poplar hedge. Layer upon layer of dark caves cover the cliff and a rickety pavilion concealing a giant Buddha stands in the centre of the cliff, its dark-tiled, curled roof rising above the cliff-top. Inside the caves, the walls are covered with sea-greeny terracotta-coloured paintings of large deities with floating ribbon-like robes, scenes from the life of the Buddha, and the Jataka stories of the Buddha legends, any unfilled space being crammed with repeated rows of tiny Buddha images. In the centre of most of the caves is a pillar, against which stucco figures stand or sit on lotus thrones with attendants and flaming haloes.

A large community of monks lived in smaller caves to the right of the long cliff, working on the caves, painting them, creating the sculptures on wooden armatures, painting banners on hemp, paper and silk to be carried in processions and to decorate special caves at festivals. They copied sutras on long rolls of yellow paper for local believers and the numerous local temples, and painted images of the donors at the bottom of their banners.

In Cave 16 was a stone figure of Hong Bian, an eminent ninth-century monk from the Hexi region, west of the Yellow River. The sculpture of the monk, seated cross-legged in meditation, concealed a hidden door. In 1900 a Taoist monk, poking around the sand-filled caves that had been abandoned a thousand years before, opened the concealed door to find a smaller cave completely filled from floor to ceiling with rolled-up scrolls and paintings.

88

Abbot Wang had uncovered the world's earliest paper archive, a mountain of texts dating from about AD 400 to about 1000. Most of the texts and paintings were Buddhist and most were Chinese but there were also texts in Sanskrit, Uighur, Tibetan, Khotanese, Kuchean, Sogdian and Hebrew. There were Manichean, Nestorian and Jewish texts, there were Taoist and Confucian texts, and a considerable quantity of secular texts relating to the economy, history and social organisation of the area.

The whole life of the Silk Roads of the past was illuminated by this chance find, but the reasons for the accumulation of documents in the tiny cave are not certain. Some suggest that the documents were sealed and concealed when the area was threatened by the Tanguts, who established the Xixia kingdom in the area in 1038, but recent research suggests that the cave was probably closed slightly earlier, perhaps in the first decade of that century. The care with which the entrance was hidden also implies that this was a planned operation, not carried out in a rush during an invasion scare. The Hong Bian figure had originally been installed in a cave higher up the cliff which was consecrated soon after his death in the mid-ninth century, just after Dunhuang had been returned to Chinese rule after a period of Tibetan occupation. The sculpture was moved down to Cave 16 and accompanied by a wall-painting of attendant figures beneath a tree, with a leather pil-

Guardian lion. A Tang dynasty painting found at Dunhuang

grim's bag and water bottle hanging from the leafy branches. The small side-cave's door appears to have been painted over for further concealment.

In fact, the reasons for accumulating this hoard of documents were probably several. Fear of military action may have been one. Many of the Buddhist scrolls may have formed part of the temple library at the caves themselves; a large number of these canonical works have inscriptions which indicate that they originally belonged to other temples in the area and had, perhaps, been moved to the caves for storage when worn. Some of the paper may have been stored for use in conservation, for a number of the well-used sutra scrolls were mended with paper patches. There was also a long tradition in China of preserving paper with writing on it, called *jingxi zizhi* (respect writing and paper), intended to prevent such material being used for 'base ends'.[1] Secular documents such as wills and contracts may have been deliberately stored in Buddhist temples for safe-keeping (in the absence of banks and safe deposit boxes). Particularly in the Tang dynasty, when the religion was at its height in China, Buddhist temples, like medieval cathedrals, were focal points for much local social organisation. Brought into China along the Silk Road, Buddhism was enthusiastically adopted and flourished for many centuries.

Buddhism was founded by Siddhartha Gautama, of the Sakya tribe in the Nepalese Terai, who lived *c.*563–483 BC. It is now impossible to disentangle the events of his life from the legends that surround him, but he taught a way to salvation expressed in a vast body of scriptures which, though often attributed to him, were composed over a period of several centuries.

Buddhism developed against a background of many other religious movements in India, most notably Hinduism. The tenet of rebirth, the view of a life as one of a series, each affected by the moral conduct of its predecessor, was widely held in India at the time, and was accepted as part of the Buddhist tradition. Buddhism differed from hierarchical Hinduism, however, in setting no store by caste, and also by down-playing ritual and the worship of gods in the hope of salvation. The Buddha had preached the 'Four Noble Truths', the first being that, in life, 'everything is suffering: birth, old age, sickness and death; contact with what one dislikes, separation from what one desires, not obtaining what one wishes. The second Truth defines the causes of suffering: desire for what is void of reality, for pleasure, for existence, all leading from one life to another. The third Truth is the suppression of desire and the end of suffering, and the fourth is the means by which that is achieved . . . The fourth Truth, the Noble Eightfold Path to the destruction of suffering, consists of right speech, right livelihood, right effort, right mindfulness, right concentration, right opinion and right intention.'[2]

The spiritual exercises necessary to follow the Eightfold Path (which was further sub-divided into three divisions of 'morality, concentration and wisdom') were best practised within the monastic setting. The lay Buddhist could hope to acquire merit, and hence better rebirths, by supporting the monks and their institution, providing money, food and clothing, and following instruction in the Buddhist doctrine as far as possible.

The rules governing monastic discipline were developed during the historic Buddha's lifetime. Admission to a monastery was allowed from the age of eight, as long as the applicant could prove he was 'male, not a criminal, free from physical deformity and illness, not a soldier, a slave or acting without parental consent'. The applicant made declaration of belief in the Three Jewels: the Buddha, his doctrine and the order; and vowed to follow the Ten Abstentions: 'from murder, theft, unchastity, untruth, fermented drink, eating after noon, entertainments, ornament, luxurious beds, and gold and silver.' His head was shaved, he assumed monk's clothing, ate only food that had been begged and, ideally, lived under a tree with the eight articles he was allowed to possess: a begging bowl, 'three pieces of clothing (an upper and lower garment and a cloak, coloured red or yellow), a belt, a razor, a needle and a water filter, and 'taking only cow's urine as medicine'. Later, the list of possessions was increased to include a raincoat, fan, wooden toothpicks, sandals, a staff and a rosary.[3]*

---

* These simple possessions entered the Buddhist tradition early and still persist. On the Chinese Buddhist mountain of Jiuhuashan in Anhui province, dedicated to the veneration of the Bodhisattva Ksitigarbha who presided over the underworld, judging the dead and determining their rebirth, there was a tiny little pavilion perched on the end of a narrow cliff. In 1981, this was inhabited by an ancient monk, a tall upright man who came down from his pavilion every morning to the main temple to collect his food for the day. He carried a small basket and the characteristic tall staff with a bronze leaf-shaped finial and a couple of rings below it. In the little Bell Pavilion, he sat with his possessions around him which included bottles of condiments, a pair

There is little known about the first entry of Buddhism into China though there are various legends about its arrival. One states that King Asoka, Maurya emperor of India (273–*c*.232 BC), the greatest patron of Buddhism, sent a deputation of monks, led by the teacher Shili-fang, to present a number of sutras to the first emperor of the Qin (r. 221–206 BC). He was unimpressed and immediately imprisoned them. But a giant golden man, said to be sixteen feet tall, broke down the prison doors and released them, whereupon the emperor treated them with considerable politeness. The confusion of dates (with Asoka dead before Qin Shi took power) is repeated in another famous story of the introduction of Buddhism, that of the dream of the Ming emperor of the Han (r. AD 58–75). Inspired by his dream of a great golden figure which was explained to him as being the Buddha, he sent a mission (in some versions this was led by Zhang Qian who had died in 114 BC) to the country of the Yuezhi, to acquire sacred texts. The envoys returned, it is said, on white horses and accompanied by the first two Buddhist missionaries, Kasyapa Matanga and Dharmaratna, for whom the emperor built the White Horse temple outside Luoyang (his capital). Two stone horses, possibly Song in date (960–1279), stand outside the temple which, though founded in AD 68, and still occupying the same site, has been rebuilt completely many times since.

Buddhism actually appears to have arrived in the first half of the first century BC, and it is assumed that it came in gradually, along the Silk Roads, and that the first real practitioners of Buddhism were 'foreigners' from Central Asia who were living in China as merchants or envoys or perhaps refugees and hostages taken during the successive Chinese campaigns against the nomads of Central Asia. The importance of 'foreigners' and Central Asian middlemen to the spread of Buddhism in China was enormous, for the vast collection of Buddhist texts, the *Sutrapitaka* (sermons of and attributed to the Buddha) and the *Vinayapitaka* (the monastic rules) and other texts all had to be translated into Chinese – it seems that no Chinese learnt any Sanskrit until the late fourth century AD.[4]

Significant foreign figures in early Buddhism were recorded: the Parthian merchant known in Chinese as An Xuan arrived in Luoyang in AD 181 and eventually joined a monastery headed by one of the most important translators of Buddhist texts, another Parthian, An Shigao.

---

of wellington boots (Central China is not India, after all), and an alarm clock. The latter was essential to his work, for he rang the bell, heaving on a huge rope which swung a log against the great bronze bell that hung above his head, at regular times throughout the day. He wasn't necessarily the best person to set your own clock by for he would also ring the bell when moved, as by the information that there were even Buddhists in England.

Kang Mengxiang (end of the second century) was of Sogdian descent, and Kang Senghui was born at the beginning of the third century to a Sogdian merchant resident in China. He was described as having the face of an Indian, with deep-set eyes and a protruding nose, despite his Chinese speech.

In the sinicisation of names like Kang Senghui or An Shigao, the groupings are evident: *kangju* was the term for Sogdians so they were usually given the 'Chinese' surname Kang, and Parthians were given the surname An from the Chinese name for Parthia, Anxi. The organisation of these translations of names was also reflected in the translation of many specifically Buddhist names, especially place names and terms. These specific characters, used to transliterate foreign (Central Asian) names in secular texts like the official histories of the Han and the *Xiyuji* (*Record of the Western Regions*), were also applied to Buddhist translation and may have been officially sanctioned by the Department of Foreign Relations.[5]

Many Yuezhi refugees who had turned back along the Gansu corridor into China rather than flee westwards from the Xiongnu were significant contributors to Buddhism. Zhi Qian's grandfather was a Yuezhi who had come to settle in China during the reign of the Ling emperor (AD 168–90). Zhi Qian's activities reflected the very heterogeneous nature of early Chinese Buddhism: 'He realized that although the great doctrine was practised, the scriptures were mostly in "barbarian" language, which nobody could understand. Since he was well-versed in Chinese and in "barbarian" language, he collected all these texts and translated them into Chinese.'[6]

Buddhism in its homeland had split into two distinct major schools: the Mahayana or 'Great Vehicle' which stressed the selfless ideal of the Bodhisattva who, although qualified for nirvana (non-being, a state beyond the sufferings of life and beyond the cycle of painful rebirths), stays in the world and helps others to be transported to nirvana; and the more orthodox Hinayana or 'Lesser Vehicle' (a disparaging term applied by Mahayana followers) which still stressed the ideal of becoming an *arhat* ('saint') and achieving personal nirvana. There were other sects, too, and Buddhism entered China not as a reflection of one of these but as 'a bewildering variety of Mahayana and Hinayana sutras, monastic rules, spells and charms, legends and scholastic treaties of different epochs and schools'.[7]

It was in about AD 260 that the first Chinese Buddhist monk ventured out along the Silk Road to collect Buddhist scriptures for translation into Chinese. Zhu Shixing came from Henan province in Central China, from a town called Yingquan where the Buddhist community had some connection with Kang Senghui (of Sogdian origin). Zhu Shixing appears to have been searching for a specific text and he

only had to travel along the southern Silk Road as far as Khotan (Hetian) where he obtained a copy of the *Prajnaparamita* in 25,000 verses. Khotan, when he visited it, was the dominant kingdom of the western part of the southern Silk Road, its influence stretching from Niya to Kashgar. Most Khotanese Buddhists of the period adhered firmly to Mahayana Buddhism (with Hinayana dominant in the northern Silk Road centre of Kucha). There were some Hinayana adherents in Khotan who seem to have opposed his taking the Mahayana text to China, going so far as to try to enlist the support of the king. In order to overcome their objections, Zhu Shixing is said to have asked for an ordeal by fire: the text was thrown into a fire but survived intact.

One of the most prolific of the translators of the Buddhist scriptures was Dharmaraksa or Fahu (born *c.*230) who came from a Yuezhi family long resident at Dunhuang. His biography provides the first mention of Buddhism in Dunhuang, the oasis at the western end of the Chinese empire which was to become one of the greatest centres of Chinese Buddhism during the fourth to the eleventh centuries. Dharmaraksa is thought to have come from a wealthy family and to have received a thorough Chinese education, for he is said to have been familiar with the Confucian classics and the Hundred schools of

Buddhist monks with red hats and parasols at a horse festival at Naru, Tibet

95

Chinese philosophy. When he set off to the west to collect scriptures, he is said to have acquired 'a reading knowledge of thirty-six languages' (a Chinese way of saying 'all the languages of Central Asia').[8] Though he worked on translations of the texts he had collected (up to 165, of which 72 survive) at Chang'an, he frequently returned to Dunhuang and maintained contact with Buddhists he had met on his travels to the west, such as a Kashmiri who brought him a copy of Sangharaksa's *Yogacarabhumi* which they translated together. A Kuchean envoy gave him the *Avaivartikacatrasutra* there in 284 and other monks from Khotan and Kashmir also brought him texts. He worked on his translations with a Chinese, Nie Chengyuan, with Indians, Kucheans, a Sogdian, a Khotanese and another Yuezhi, and he seems to have been a widely successful fund-raiser, attracting donations from Chinese and non-Chinese in the Dunhuang area and acquiring such vast funds that he could impress the aristocrats of the capital by his loans.[9]

A sinicised Indian monk of considerable eccentricity was Zhu Shulan of the late second to the early third century. Born in Luoyang, he received a good Chinese education but, coming from an Indian family long settled in China, also knew Sanskrit, and he made a translation of the *Vimalakirti nirdesasutra* despite being famous for drunkenness. He used to get so drunk that he passed out in the street and he was once arrested for breaking into the local prefect's office and creating havoc.

A more sober contributor to the Chinese Buddhist canon was Kumarajiva (350–413) who spent his early life in the Buddhist centres of Kuqa (Kucha) and Kashgar. His father, of Indian origin and coming from a long line of highly placed officials who had served in Kuqa, had wanted to renounce the world and become a Buddhist monk, but the king of Kuqa persuaded him against it and gave him his sister in marriage. Their son Kumarajiva was taken by his mother to Kashmir to study Indian literature and Buddhism. He also studied in Kashgar and was living in Kuqa as a highly respected Buddhist scholar when, in 382 or 383, he was carried off to the Chinese capital by the Chinese general Lu Guang who had invaded Kuqa.[10] In Chang'an he directed a translation bureau of several thousand monks who produced translations of thirty-eight texts. Despite devoting his life to this work, he is supposed to have said that reading the sutras in translation was like eating rice that someone else had already chewed.

Though many went on long journeys to collect sutras, an activity that was to continue through to the seventh century in the journey of Xuanzang, these early Buddhist travellers were not strictly pilgrims because they did not travel to see religious sites, or to join in worship. The first 'pilgrim' to set off along the Silk Road was Kang Falang (presumably of Sogdian origin) in the third century; the first true Chinese pilgrims were Yu Falan and Yu Daosui who started out for India sometime between 325 and 335. They both died in Indochina without reaching their destination, and, as the site of their death implies, they were travelling not by the well-trodden Silk Roads but by the southern route, and largely by sea.[11]

The first full account of pilgrimage was made by Faxian, who set out across the Silk Road in 399, reached the holy sites in India, Sri Lanka and Java, and returned to China by sea in 413, where he translated the texts that he had collected and wrote an account of his travels, *Foguoji (Record of the Buddhist Countries)*.*

Faxian was moved to make his pilgrimage because he was 'distressed by the imperfect state of the Buddhist "Disciplines" ' or vinaya texts, which laid down the rules for monastic life, and he 'entered into an agreement with Huijing, Daocheng, Huiying, Huiwei and others to go together to India and try to obtain these "Rules" '. The group of monks was joined by others in Gansu province and they travelled together to Dunhuang where they stayed in the monasteries for a month. They were well supported by local monks and dignitaries: 'The Governor of Dunhuang, by name Li He, gave them all the necessaries for crossing the desert of Gobi. In this desert there are a great many evil spirits and also hot winds; those who encounter them perish to a man. There are neither birds above nor beasts below. Gazing on all sides as far as the eye can reach in order to mark the track, no guidance is to be obtained save from the rotting bones of dead men which point the way.'[12] The party travelled just south of Lop Nor where 'the land is rugged and barren', but they were again sustained by the local ruler who had 'received the Faith'. After travelling west for fifteen days, the party divided, with three monks returning to Turfan for further funds and Faxian and the others proceeding 'forthwith on their journey towards the southwest. Along the route they found the country uninhabited; the difficulty of crossing rivers was very great; and the hardships they went through were beyond all comparison. And being on the road a month and five days they succeeded in reaching Khotan.'

* Faxian's Record has been translated several times, notably by Rémusat, Klaproth and Landresse in 1836, a version that 'ran to 420 large quarto pages, mostly consisting of elaborate notes, and of course failed to attract a wide circle of readers', as described by Professor Herbert Giles in the 'Bibliographical Note' to his own translation, which I have used. Giles, who always took exquisite pains to rubbish the opposition, was similarly dismissive of the Revd S. Beal's attempt, in which 'he reproduced all Rémusat's mistakes while adding many more of his own', and that of Dr Legge, 'in which he borrowed largely, without acknowledgement, from my corrections of Beal, and managed to contribute not a few mistakes of his own'.

Khotan was, at the time, a flourishing oasis with a large Buddhist community, supported by the king. The monks moved on separately: one went towards Kashmir; Faxian and the others through Karghalik and Tashkurgan to Kashgar where a great Buddhist 'quinquennial assembly' was in progress with special tents for the visiting monks filled with gold canopies, streaming pennants and seats covered with silk embroidered with lotus flowers in gold and silver. Their pilgrimage began when they admired a 'spittoon which belonged to Buddha . . . made of stone and of the same colour as his alms-bowl', and one of his teeth, 'for which the people have raised a pagoda'. They travelled on through 'mountainous and cold' terrain towards the Bolor-Tagh range where snow lay all year round. 'There are also venomous dragons, which, if provoked, spit forth poisonous winds, rain, snow, sand and stones. Of those who encounter these dangers not one in ten thousand escapes.'[13]

Faxian visited Bamiyan to admire the two massive Buddhas carved into a cliff face in the third century AD, the taller image 175 feet or 53 metres tall. They were covered with gold paint and studded with jewels and surrounded by caves hollowed out of the cliff and filled with Buddhist wall-paintings. To Faxian, they were marvels, but a later visitor, faced with 'an enormous wasps' nest . . . the myriad caves of the Buddhist monks clustered about the two giant Buddhas', complained, 'I should not like to stay long at Bamian. Its art is unfresh.'[14] Robert Byron (1905–41) continued his criticism of the Bamiyan Buddhas: 'Neither has any artistic value. But one could bear that; it is their negation of sense, the lack of any pride in their monstrous flaccid bulk, that sickens. Even their material is unbeautiful, for the cliff is made, not of stone, but of compressed gravel. A lot of monastic navvies were given picks and told to copy some frightful semi-Hellenistic image from India or China. The result has not even the dignity of labour.'

By the time that Byron visited Bamiyan, the larger Buddha had lost half a leg above the knee and suffered some damage to the other, below the knee. The area had seen considerable waves of devastation. Islam had arrived in the area in the eighth century but it was not until the reign of Mahmud (998–1030) that the sculptures were first deliberately attacked. Mahmud, 'not an enlightened despot', enjoyed a reputation as 'the hammer of the heretical Ismaeli Shi'ites'[15] as well as of Hindus and Buddhists, and, as he conquered, he plundered, collecting temple treasures to adorn his own mosques and palaces and gardens. The town of Bamiyan was completely destroyed and its inhabitants massacred by Genghis Khan in 1221. The area was also subject to earthquakes but the Buddhas, knees upwards, survived all these until March 2001 when they were destroyed. Officers of the Ministry for the Prevention of Vice and the Promotion of Virtue in

*The great Buddha at Bamiyan.
The ancient Buddhas were
destroyed by the Taliban in February 2001. Below, a long view
of the Bamiyan site shows the
immense scale of the Buddhas.
Both photographs were taken by
Robert Byron in 1934*

Kabul were sent out with explosives to finish what Mahmud had begun, the destruction of images.[16]

In India, the monks separated to visit different holy places, inspecting the Buddha's footprint and the pagodas at the place where he 'sacrificed his eyes for a fellow creature' and where he 'gave his body to feed a hungry tiger'. Faxian went on alone 'towards the place of the Buddha's skull-bone'. He managed to acquire his vinaya texts and set sail to return home by sea to Canton. During a storm, the terrified merchants on board, 'fearing that the vessel would fill . . . promptly took what bulky goods there were and threw them into the sea. Faxian also took his pitcher and ewer, with whatever else he could spare, and threw them into the sea; but he was afraid that the merchants would throw over his books and his images and accordingly fixed his whole thoughts upon Guanyin, the Hearer of Prayers, and put his life into the hands of the Catholic Church of China [*sic*], saying, "I have journeyed far on behalf of the Faith. Oh that by your awful power you would grant me a safe return from my wanderings." ' Guanyin eventually responded, for after thirteen days and nights of gale, they were able to find a safe anchorage and patch up the ship for its return to China.

The next great Buddhist pilgrim was Xuanzang (602–64). Not only did he leave his own (surviving) account of his travels along the northern Silk Road to Tashkent and Samarkand, down into Kashmir, around India and then back to China on the southern Silk Road, but his disciple Huili, described by one commentator as Xuanzang's 'Boswell',[17] also left an account of his life. Xuanzang's own account of his epic travels, the *Xiyuji* (*Record of the Western Regions*), which included imprisonment, almost fatal dehydration and terrible battles against the elements, also inspired the great sixteenth-century novel *Xiyouji* (*Journey to the West*), better known in the West as *Monkey* in Arthur Waley's translation.

In the novel, the monk, Tripitaka (the name given to the collection of holy books), is accompanied on his pilgrimage by a pig, who represents the human passions and is, predictably, always thinking of food or chasing pretty girls, and a monkey who is a more complex character. The monkey is naughty to the point of wickedness, always up to dangerous tricks like stealing the peaches of immortality from the Queen Mother of the West and provoking dangerous characters, yet, in his cleverness, he can also argue doctrinal points. The novel represented a long folkloric tradition in China and is still a major source of reference, jokes and children's stories.

Very different from the fictional *Monkey* is Huili's *Life* of his master, Xuanzang; indeed it is not entirely free of hagiography. First he introduces Xuanzang's father, himself a pretty distinguished figure. 'His father Hui was distinguished by his superior abilities, the elegance

Xuanzang, the travelling monk, in a ninth-century
painting from Dunhuang

of his manners and his moderation . . . in figure he was eight feet in
height with finely lined eyebrows and bright eyes.* He wore his dress
large and his girdle was full, loving to be recognised as a scholar. Born
in those times, and a man of a remote district, he was simple in his
manners and contented – and sought neither honour nor preferment.
Anticipating the decay and fall of the Sui dynasty, he buried himself in
the study of his books. Many offers of provincial and district offices
were pressed upon him, which he persistently refused; he declined all
magisterial duties on the plea of ill-health; so he remained in retirement, much to the admiration of his acquaintance.'[18]

Xuanzang is, naturally, presented as an exceptional child. 'Even
when a child he was grave as a prince . . . When he was eight years old
his father sitting near his table was reading aloud the *Xiaojing* (*Classic of Filial Piety*), and coming to the passage where Zangzi stands
before his master, suddenly the boy arranged his dress and got up. His
father asking him why he did so, he replied, "Zangzi hearing the command of his master, rose up from his seat; surely then Xuanzang dares
not sit at ease whilst listening to the loving instruction of his father."

* The translator, Beal, notes that, at the time, a 'foot' was about nine and a
half inches, so Xuanzang's father was still over six foot, which must have been
pretty unusual.

His father was much pleased with this reply, and perceived that his child would become a distinguished person.' The priggish child would not look at a book 'without elegance and propriety . . . he would have no intercourse with those whose ways were opposed to the teaching of the holy and wise. He did not mix with those of his own age, nor spend his time at the market-gates. Although cymbals and drums, accompanied by singing, resounded through the public streets, and girls and boys congregated in crowds to assist in the games, singing and shouting the while, he would not leave his home. Moreover when he was young he applied himself with diligence to the duties of piety and gentleness at home.'

Apparently reaching the same towering height as his father, Xuan-zang was ordained a Buddhist monk at the age of twenty. Whereas Faxian wanted to collect monastic discipline, Xuanzang was concerned at the varying quality of the translations of the Buddhist sutras and their exponents: 'each followed implicitly the teaching of his own school; but on verifying their doctrine he saw that the holy books differed much so that he knew not which to follow'. So he 'resolved to travel to the Western world in order to ask about doubtful passages'.[19] There were, at the time, many lacunae in the Chinese translations from the Buddhist sutras, as well as many conflicting interpretations. A number of texts were translated several times, some versions being much better than others, and the confusion of texts was compounded by hand-copying, for they were probably only circulating in manuscript at that time.

A problem faced this would-be pilgrim: an imperial edict from the Taizong emperor (r. 626–49) forbidding travel abroad. Altogether the conditions of his journey were more difficult than that of Faxian, who generally met with official support, and was able to travel with a group of monks. In order not to attract attention, and to spare others from imperial anger, Xuanzang determined to travel alone and leave in secret, but first he waited for a 'happy omen'. 'He dreamt that he saw in the middle of the great sea the Mount Sumeru [the central mountain of the Buddhist universe], perfected with the four precious substances – its appearance supremely bright and majestic. He thought he purposed to scale the Mount but the boisterous waves arose and swelled mightily. Moreover, there was neither ship nor raft; nevertheless, he had no shadow of fear, but with fixed purpose, he entered. Suddenly he saw a lotus of stone burst as it were exultingly from the deep [Beal notes, 'this passage is very obscure']; when he tried to put his foot on it, it retired; whilst he paused to behold it, it followed his feet and then disappeared; in a moment he found himself at the foot of the Mount, but he could not climb its craggy and scarped sides; as he tried to leap upwards with all his strength, there arose a mighty whirlwind which raised him aloft to the summit of the Mount. Looking around him on the four sides from the top he beheld nought but an uninterrupted horizon; ravished with joy he awoke. On this he forthwith started on his journey.'

He started out from Chang'an along the Gansu corridor towards Lanzhou where he met some military officers who were returning to Liangzhou (Wuwei). There must have been a substantial monastery or monasteries there because he stayed for over a month. At the invitation of the local monks, he lectured on the perfection of wisdom and the nirvana sutra and was the great attraction at a 'Religious Conference' which drew crowds of 'people dwelling to the West of the River . . . merchants belonging to the borders of Tibet and countries to the left of the Congling mountains'. These merchants and visitors from distant countries 'were prepared with joyful heart to entertain him on his arrival, with magnificence . . . they offered him in charity abundant gifts, gold and silver money, and white horses without number.'

Drawing such crowds, Xuanzang attracted the attention of the local governor, the emperor's representative in Liangzhou, who tried to enforce the imperial prohibition, urging him to return home. Xuanzang was not to be dissuaded but 'from this time he dare not be seen in public – during the daytime he hid himself, at night he went on'. Despite this precaution, he was still travelling within Chinese territory, along the westernmost end of the Great Wall. At the Yumen (Jade Gate), a barrier across the Hu river, he still had to pass by five Chinese signal or beacon-towers, 'in which officers charged to watch, dwell – they are one hundred *li* apart. In the space between them there is neither water nor herb.' Xuanzang doubted his ability to pass them; what was more, his horse had died and he had to obtain another. He managed to find a guide, 'a foreigner' who brought along 'an old greybeard, likewise a foreign person, riding on a horse of a red colour'. The greybeard was introduced as an expert guide, although his description of the way ahead was not promising: 'The Western roads are difficult and bad; sand streams stretch far and wide; evil sprites and hot winds, when they come, cannot be avoided; numbers of men travelling together, although so many, are misled and lost; now much rather you, sir, going alone! How can you accomplish such a journey?'[20] The old man, apparently declining to serve as a guide, offered Xuanzang his horse: 'He has gone to and from Yigu fifteen times; he is strong and knows the road; your horse, sir, is a small one and not suitable for the journey.' Xuanzang conveniently remembered that a diviner had foretold that he would make a great journey on 'an old red horse, thin and skinny; the saddle is varnished, and in front it is bound by iron' exactly like the red horse in front of him. He continued with only the young foreigner as a guide. He crossed the river unseen at

Yumen, thanks to the young man's help, but that evening the young 'guide took his knife in his hand, and rising up, approached towards the Master of the Law [Xuanzang]; when about ten paces off, he turned round. Not knowing what his intention was, and being in doubt about the matter, the Master rose from his mat and repeated some scriptures and called on Guanyin Bodhisattva. The foreigner having seen this, went back and slept.'[21]

Constantly threatened by this sinister guide, Xuanzang ordered him back and, 'alone and deserted, he traversed the sandy waste; his only means of observing the way being the heaps of bones and the horse-dung'. He was tortured by a hallucination of a vast army, 'the soldiers clad in fur and felt . . . camels and horses . . . the glittering of standards and lances met his view.' He heard 'in the void sounds of voices crying out, "Do not fear! Do not fear!" ' As he approached the first watchtower, he waited till night. Finding water nearby, he knelt down in the dark and washed his hands. 'Then as he was filling his water-vessel with water an arrow whistled past him and just grazed his knee, and in a moment another arrow.' Fortunately for Xuanzang, the bowmen were not Chinese but Xixia (a tribe related to the Tibetans who took Dunhuang in the mid-Tang and established an empire around Gansu and Ningxia in the tenth to twelfth centuries), so he was spared, once he had explained who he was.

Further on in the desert he drove away 'all sorts of demon shapes and strange goblins' by invoking the name of the compassionate Bodhisattva Guanyin and reciting the Guanyin sutra: and he interpreted the sudden appearance of grass and water after four days with 'not a drop of water . . . his stomach racked with burning heat'. It was not only hallucinations and shortage of grass and water that threatened his progress once he moved beyond the long arm of the Chinese empire. The king of Kharakhoja (Gaochang) had been looking forward to his arrival and hoped to detain him as a spiritual adviser, preferably for ever. The king's pressure was such that Xuanzang was forced to go on hunger-strike for four days before the king agreed to discuss a compromise by which Xuanzang would stay for a month and lecture whilst the king had travelling clothes made for him. Whilst 'thirty priest's vestments' and special garments for the cold weather – 'face-coverings, gloves, leather boots' – were being made, and 'a hundred gold ounces and three myriads of silver pieces with five hundred rolls of satin and taffeta . . . thirty horses and twenty-four servants' were being assembled, Xuanzang sat behind a brazier containing incense in a specially prepared pavilion which seated three hundred and lectured on the diamond sutra.

With his horses, satins and servants, dressed in cold-weather face-coverings and boots, Xuanzang made his way south from the Silk

Road and down into India. His journeys there were not without incident, and he was unlucky enough to lose his elephants and all the books he had collected in a river, but, with his usual persistence, these losses (of books, though not elephants) were made good and he arrived back in China after an absence of some sixteen years with a considerable collection of religious luggage.

He carried six Buddha figures, of gold, silver and sandalwood, and 'the books of the Great Vehicle', which he had brought from the west, including 224 sutras, 15 works of the Sthavira school, including sutras, vinaya and sastras, the same number belonging to the Sammatiya school; 22 works of the same character belonging to the Mahisasaka school; 67 books of the same character belonging to the Sarvasatavadin school; 17 works of the same character belonging to the Kasyapiya school; 42 works of the same character belonging to the Dharmagupta school; 36 copies of the *Hetuvidya sastra*; 13 copies of the *Sabdavidya sastra*; altogether 520 fasciculi, comprising 657 distinct volumes, carried upon twenty horses. He also brought back 'one hundred and fifty particles of flesh [relics]'.

His entry into Chang'an 'with flags and banners' was very different from his departure and he was even welcomed back by the emperor, who was interested to know why he had disobeyed the edict but forgiving. Xuanzang devoted most of the rest of his life to translation, working on the materials he had struggled to obtain: 'By the end of the year 648, he had completed in all fifty-eight books, including the *Xiyuji* (undertaken at the emperor's express command).'[22]

Xuanzang believed that his survival was due to the protection of the Bodhisattva Guanyin who was to become a particular favourite of Chinese believers and the object of a special cult. The transformation of Buddhism in China from a strictly monastic origin to a mixed monastic and lay tradition enabled the religion to survive attacks on its idolatry and anti-family aspects. The monastic life made it theoretically impossible for a monk or nun to continue the Confucian tradition of family worship and care for the ancestral spirits, but documents from Dunhuang make it clear that many 'monks' and 'nuns' in the area still lived with family members and were very much involved in family responsibilities.

The sinicisation of Guanyin involved a sex change. In Indian Mahayana Buddhism, Bodhisattvas – beings who had achieved enlightenment but, instead of achieving personal nirvana, chose to stay in the world to lead others to enlightenment – were all male, insofar as they had any sex at all. The Bodhisattva Avalokitesvara, the one 'who hears the cries of the world', translated into Chinese as Guanshiyin or Guanyin (Compassionate listener), appears in early Chinese images as distinctly male, usually with a little narrow, curly moustache

Guanyin, or Avalokitesvara, in his fleshy and relaxed seated male guise and, right, a later Ming dynasty female version, known as the White-Robed Guanyin

and beard. By the Ming (1368–1644) Guanyin had become distinctly female, although the many ceramic figures of the deity reveal that he or she never had bound feet, characteristic of high-born Chinese ladies of the period. Whether these natural feet reflected the original maleness of the Bodhisattva or the different, Indian, origin of the icon is not clear. It was Guanyin's compassion that led to the sexual transformation in China because the quality was associated with women rather than men. The compassionate Guanyin gradually took over more 'womanly' tasks. She was invoked, for example, by the childless and the sick.

In the early period, from the Han to the Tang, as Faxian and Xuanzang's narratives show, Guanyin was also seen as a protector of travellers, a sort of St Christopher figure who would rescue travellers from thieves and murderers as well as natural disasters. Many travellers carried little books inscribed with the text of chapter 26 of the Lotus sutra which contains a series of invocations to Guanyin. Hundreds of such talismanic books have been found amongst the documents from Dunhuang.

These little paper books, made from folded paper sewn at the spine and small enough to slip into a pocket or purse, illustrate another aspect of the Dunhuang manuscripts and related finds from nearby Silk Road sites. The development of the book format and the invention of paper and printing are all aspects of Chinese history that have been revealed through these finds. The papers sealed up in the small cave, away from the light and protected from damp by the local climate, as well as other paper finds from desert sites, were perfectly preserved. Some paper fragments, thought to date back to about 200 BC, found in the desert by Sir Aurel Stein, have upset traditional Chinese historians because they appear to antedate the 'official' discovery of paper as recorded in the dynastic history. The *Hou Han shu* (*History of the Later Han Dynasty*) included a passage about the eunuch Cai Lun (d. AD 121) who reported to the emperor on the manufacture of paper in AD 105, describing it as being made from 'the bark of trees, remnants of hemp, rags of cloth and fishing nets'.[23] For conservative historians, imbued with 'respect for paper and writing', AD 105 had to stand as the date of the invention of paper: any earlier archaeological discoveries were not true paper, they were accidents or something more like felt.

Whatever the precise date, and allowing for a process of development and experimentation, the invention of paper was of enormous significance to China and, thanks to its transmission along the Silk Roads, to the world, providing a cheap medium that would facilitate the print revolution.

Silk Road sites, particularly the old Han beacon towers around the oasis of Dunhuang, also revealed earlier writing materials. The Chinese garrisons of the Han dynasty used the earlier standard format of strips of wood (bamboo was used in China proper where it grew widely, but it had to be replaced by wood in the desert). The wooden strips were inscribed with brush and ink from top to bottom and then tied together and rolled up for storage or transportation. Han wood-slips, found by Stein around the Dunhuang beacons, were mostly military in content, consisting of soldiers' sick-lists of the first century BC – 'Gao Zitang, private, no. 24 section, 7th day, 7th month, reported sick with headache and four limbs immobile . . . Jiang Jun, private, no. 2 section, 6th day, 4th month, reported sick . . . Wang Zhong, private, no. 31 section, 1st day, 4th month, reported sick, suffering from feverish cold . . . Feng Wuhu, private, Dangbi section . . . reported sick with internal illness, treated with 35 pills' – or military passports issued to travellers. There are also some wonderful accounts of the daily round in a military outpost on the edge of the Chinese empire by critical sergeant-major figures: 'Eight woodpiles undersized and not plastered; in two large woodpiles the stacking was not alternated; no matting for the collection of fodder . . . two water-storage jars missing . . . One large flag on the tower old and damaged . . . One dog absent; dogs present not kept in kennel; no pennants, smoke or flame flares.'[24]

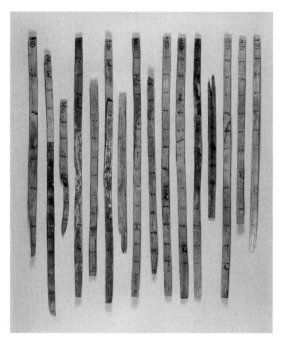

The earliest form of Chinese book, simply made of wooden slips. Below, a nineteenth-century palm-leaf pothi binding of a Sinhalese Buddhist tale within decorated boards. Bottom, two images of a 'whirlwind' binding. These bindings, one of the most unusual in the history of binding developments, are now very scarce. When the book is rolled for storage it is indistinguishable from a scroll, but when unfurled its pages curl up, suggestive of the circular movement of air in a whirlwind

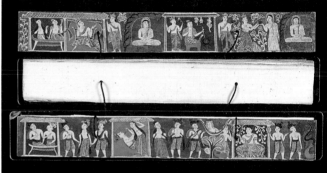

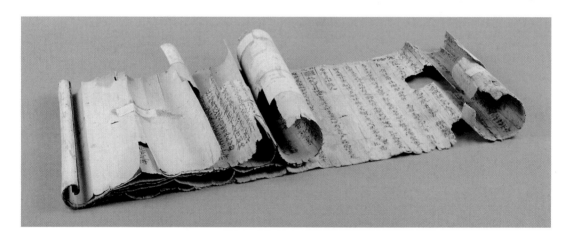

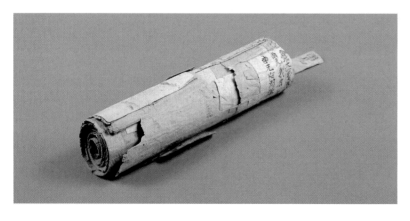

From these bundles of wooden strips, the paper scroll took its form. For Buddhist purposes, the scroll was adequate, as monks mumbled their way through the sacred texts: the term for a cat purring in Chinese is 'the cat is reading the sutras'. For reference books like rhyme dictionaries and copies of the *I-ching* (*Yi jing*) divinatory texts which needed to be consulted systematically, the undifferentiated scroll was inconvenient. Amongst the paper documents found at Dunhuang are examples of how the book evolved in China. The first improvement was called the 'whirlwind' binding, where pages were held together in a split bamboo cane attached to a long outer roll of paper. This could be rolled up for storage but when opened the separate pages flew open as if in a whirlwind. Later, using the thicker, probably local, paper introduced in the tenth and eleventh centuries when Dunhuang was cut off from metropolitan China and sources of fine mulberry paper, booklets were produced which were sewn or pasted at the spine, the true precursors of the thread-bound book of later traditional China.

Paper was valued, even when plentiful supplies were available. Many of the secular documents found at Dunhuang were written on scraps of paper, sometimes on the verso of discarded Buddhist texts. They included official documents like local census returns and local government ordinances, private contracts concerning the loan of a donkey or the sale of a slave-girl, wills, some written by nuns who owned a surprising amount of property considering that they were supposed to stick to the Buddhist list of authorised possessions, popular stories and model letters, to name but a few.[25]

Perhaps the most significant find amongst the thousands of treasures of several cultures in a range of languages and scripts was the woodblock-printed copy of the diamond sutra, dated to AD 868. This paper scroll, over twenty feet long, with a finely carved frontispiece, is the world's first printed 'book'. Financed by a man called Wang Jie, on behalf of his parents as an act of merit which would enable them to escape the Buddhist cycle of rebirths, many copies of this diamond sutra must have been printed and, perhaps, sent out to Buddhist

Four scenes of paper making, from the Tiangong kaiwu

Buddha preaching the Law. Frontispiece to the Diamond Sutra, from Cave 17 at Dunhuang, woodblock print, AD 868

temples all over China. It is not known where it was produced but there were other, possibly earlier, examples of woodblock-printing found in the cave at Dunhuang. The idea of repetition – repetition of prayers, repetition of images – was central to Buddhist practice as an act of merit. As the name implies, the temple-complex of the Caves of the Thousand Buddhas was filled with Buddha images. Quite a common form of wall decoration was the repetition of thousands of identical Buddha figures, often mass-produced by means of a pounce, the image punched with holes through which red chalk was blown so that identical outlines could be made on the walls to be coloured in by other painters. A number of sheets of paper with dozens of tiny stamped images of the Buddha or a Bodhisattva were found at Dunhuang, and the mass-production of these little woodblock stamps may have influenced the production of woodblock-printed books.

Closed up in the tiny cave, the documents of Dunhuang were hidden for a thousand years. With the fall of the Tang dynasty in China (AD 908), following the Buddhist persecutions of the ninth century which had reduced the power and wealth of the Buddhist monasteries, the great cave temple was abandoned and sand began to drift into the beautifully decorated caves. China was split into several parts before the Song emperor reunited the country in 1027. Though reunited, Song China was never as powerful as the Tang, and China lost its hold on its westernmost borders. The oasis towns of the Silk Roads were ruled by local leaders who saw the gradual arrival of Islam, which had been spreading eastwards since the eighth century.

- 8 -

Tanguts, Mongols, Nestorians and Marco Polo

AS THE POWER of the Tang declined in China proper, a series of independent states took power, particularly in the north and northeast and on China's borders. One of these, often referred to by their Mongol name of Tangut, was a tribe descended from the Tibetan Qiang, which, between 983 and 1227, was to seize and hold power in most of today's province of Gansu, within the great curve of the Yellow River, the area stretching from near Dunhuang eastwards to Lanzhou and into the Ordos desert. Defeated, though not entirely destroyed, by Genghis Khan, the Tangut empire is sometimes referred to as the last 'lost' empire of the Old World.

Known to the Chinese as the Xixia, the Tanguts themselves called their state Minia, 'the Great State of High and White'. Settled pastoralists who raised millet, buckwheat, hemp and cotton in irrigated fields, the Tangut also practised the traditional animal husbandry of the area, raising camels, goats, sheep and, above all, horses. This constant contact with animals may have affected their dress, for ordinary people wore loose-fitting gowns to the knees with trousers and boots, though officials wore long gowns and hats in the Chinese style. Tangut men adopted a peculiar hairstyle, tufa, where both the back and front of the head were shaved and a long fringe was grown over the forehead with two plaits on either side. Though their language was of Tibetan origin, the political institutions adopted by the Tangut were largely based upon those of China.

The first Tangut capital was at Ningxia, where the wonderful great assembly of stepped white pagodas can still be seen; by the twelfth century, Minia power had moved to Kharakhoto (the 'black' or 'dead' town), on the Mongolian border, where a ruined stupa just outside the great walls of the city yielded extraordinary archaeological treasures to the Russian explorer Pyotr Kuzmich Kozlov, a protégé of Przhevalsky, when he excavated the site in 1908. Hundreds of Buddhist images in terracotta, large and small, Buddhist paintings on silk depicting demons, monks, images of paradise, Bodhisattvas and meditation mandalas as well as piles of Buddhist woodblock-prints and manuscripts all testified to the significance of Buddhism to the Minia.

One of the most interesting things about the Tangut or Xixia or Minia is their script. At first glance it looks quite like Chinese but it is,

in fact, a more complex mixture of ideograms and phonograms and has not yet been completely deciphered. Some suggest that the writing system was deliberately created to obscure, that it was a form of secret, available only to the elite. Such interpretation of the script and reconstruction of the language as has taken place has been based upon the many translations of Chinese works (from Buddhist scriptures to legal codes). Some of the printed woodblock texts were beautifully illustrated with figures from the Buddhist pantheon. Individual items amongst the mass found by Kozlov (whose excavations at Kharakhoto were succeeded by those of Stein – see Chapter 13) include a long, painterly woodblock depicting an official in brocade gown with black velvet shoes and hat decorated with appliqué designs, who sits in front of an assemblage of objects including quantities of apparently Chinese coins threaded on a thong, and a coral tree (imported, perhaps through Tibet, from some distant sea). He is attended by a tame deer and a coarse-featured servant wearing the strange tufa hairstyle with a thick fringe. On a cloth-covered table is a branch of flowering peony in a highly decorated stem cup with tripod feet, and behind the official is a pair of pine-trees.

The end of the Tanguts is something of a mystery. Though it is clear that the state based at Kharakhoto was destroyed in 1227 in a campaign during which Genghis Khan himself died, close study of the artefacts recovered from the great stupa in Kharakhoto reveals some items that have to be dated to almost 150 years later. Dr Ksenia Kepping, the Tangut specialist at the Oriental Institute in St Petersburg, suggests that the stupa was filled twice: originally constructed as the burial place of a prominent Buddhist nun, it was re-opened around the time that the Yuan dynasty in China fell to the Ming (mid-fourteenth century), and the artefacts placed in the stupa during this second opening were, in some way, a last message from the Minia or Tanguts. The dates of these later artefacts present a historical puzzle. For some, the legend of Mongol destruction meant that Kharakhoto and its Minia or Tangut inhabitants were completely erased in 1227 and that Marco Polo's account of the flourishing city of Kharakhoto in the late thirteenth century is just another example of his unreliability. But the later dates of some of the great Tangut artefacts suggest that Tangut civilisation must have persisted in some form after the Mongol campaign. The imperial line may have died with Genghis Khan but Tangut civilisation continued for over a hundred years. Quite when the last real Tangut died is still uncertain but the enigma of this lost civilisation remains one of the puzzles of the Silk Road.

Thus, at the time when Islam was gaining popularity in the Silk Road oasis towns, a new power threatened Central Asia. In 1206 the

*Opposite: twelfth-century wood engraving of an official
and his servant, from Kharakhoto. Note the difference in
physiognomy between the impassive official and his servant*

various Mongol tribes met in the Mongol capital, Karakorum, to acknowledge the supremacy of a new Khan, Tumuchin, who adopted the name of Genghis (Chingiz, Qinggis), and soon set out at the head of his newly unified army to attack, first, in 1209, the Xixia kingdom to the west, then, in 1211, the Jin (rulers of northern China). In 1209 the Uighurs of Turfan acknowledged Mongol rule, Peking was captured in 1215, and in 1219 the Mongols attacked Samarkand, then moved on into Persia. In the 1230s they mounted attacks on Russia and Eastern Europe, famously reaching the gates of Vienna in 1242, and causing panic across Western Europe.

The campaigns were uninterrupted by the death of Genghis in 1227, by which time the Mongols ruled all of Northern Asia from the Caspian sea to Peking. By 1280 the empire was extended southwards to the edge of the Chinese empire, including Tibet, and westwards from northern India through the Persian gulf to Armenia. The expansion of the Mongol empire was to continue into the early fifteenth century under Timur (Tamerlane), who moved southwards, although it was not until the sixteenth century that one of his descendants (also descended from Genghis Khan) founded the Mughal empire in India.

Historians have revised the stories of the brutality of the Mongols. Looking at the plan of the Afghan city of Herat in the light of contemporary descriptions of 2,400,000 dead, it is clear that such a population was impossible given the area of the settlement;[1] and, if we are to believe Marco Polo and the Nestorian missionary, Rabban Sauma, even if the Xixia capital, Kharakhoto, was razed to the ground in 1227, it had been resurrected and re-inhabited fifty years later. But the actual death tolls and the exact amount of cruelty are almost irrelevant. Legends tell of the unbelievable cruelty of the Mongols in their conquests. The story of how they demanded 1,000 cats and 10,000

swallows before raising a siege, and then tied flammable material to their tails so that the animals fled home and set the town on fire, has been told about many warlike invaders; it is no doubt apocryphal (and would have been hard to achieve) but it represents how people felt about the Mongol threat.

Mongol control of the whole of Central Asia during the thirteenth and fourteenth centuries led to relatively favourable conditions for trade. Communication between Persia and China, for example, led to the development of blue and white porcelain, using cobalt imported from Persia (less impure than local Chinese sources), and many of the early blue and white ceramic forms were based on Persian silverware. But the Mongols certainly fought amongst themselves. 'The Golden Horde rulers and the Persian Ilkans were, to say the least, not friendly to each other and war was frequent. In short, it seems as if the Pax Mongolica is no more than one of those brilliant simplifications that can serve as chapter titles for world history books. There remains some doubt whether it was easier to get from, say, Venice or the Black Sea region or Persia to China under the Mongols than some centuries earlier.'[2]

The fact that the first direct Sino-Western contacts were made during the Mongol period may, therefore, have more to do with external factors, such as the desire to make alliances against the Arab threat to the Holy Land and the creation of the myth of Prester John, a supposedly Christian ruler living in the Far East (also regarded, mythical status or not, as a potential ally against the Moslems), than with any relative freedom to travel.

The sudden rise of Mongol supremacy, and its breakdown some two centuries later, is characteristic of the area. Mongol territory surrounding the old Mongol capital and the ancestral lands was later divided between Russia and China. Where once the Sogdians had ruled, where the Xixia kingdom flourished briefly, where the Uighurs controlled the Turfan area for a period, the Mongols also enjoyed their period of triumph. In China, their Yuan dynasty collapsed as a result of factional fighting, local uprisings and natural disasters; the Golden Horde was divided between the Ottoman Turks (1475) and Ivan the Terrible (1552, 1554), and the Crimea was finally annexed by Catherine the Great in 1783.3 In Samarkand the Timurid empire lasted until the fifteenth century and then, when it fell to the Uzbek Turks at the end of that century, Babur fled south to India and founded the Mughal empire.

At the height of Mongol power, and as Islam began to conquer the once Christian Holy Land, the Christian rulers of Europe sought to find new allies against Islamic expansion. The Islamic attacks on the Holy Land coincided with the spread of the Mongol empire with its devastating attacks on the Ukraine and Russia, Poland and Hungary. The fear of the Mongols was such that in 1241, instead of making its annual trip to East Anglia for herring, the Baltic fleet stayed at home to protect Baltic womanhood, and the herring catch rotted on the quays of Yarmouth. Fortunately for Western Europe, the death of Khan Ogodei meant that the Mongol armies returned home to Mongolia for the great conclave in which all the Mongol leaders selected his successor.

Encouraged by the Mongol retreat but mindful of Mongol power and legendary savagery, in 1246 Pope Innocent IV sent the first of several envoys to the Far East. The intention was to find out more about the Mongols and, if conditions and attitudes seemed appropriate, propose some kind of alliance in order to defend the Holy Land. The first envoy, John of Plano Carpine, was a disciple of St Francis of Assisi and was described by a friend as so fat that he had to ride on a sturdy ass rather than a horse. He trekked on his ass to the Khanate of the Golden Horde on the Volga, and then across the Altai mountains to the Mongol capital of Karakorum. Here he was accommodated outside the city in a tent city that had been erected for the succession conclave. Given the importance of the conclave, it is not surprising that John failed to achieve any diplomatic recognition. However, his description of the Mongols and their customs was an important source of information and widely copied.4

King Louis IX of France sent the next envoy to the Mongols, another Franciscan friar, William of Rubruck, who set out in 1248, carrying a collapsible (travelling) altar as a present for Guyug Khan. In their search for allies against the Islamic threat to Jerusalem, the Christian rulers of Europe were much encouraged by exaggerated rumours of

*The Nestorian stela,
from the Forest of
Stelae in Xi'an, 781*

members of the Mongol ruling house converting to Christianity (hence the portable altar). William of Rubruck was shocked to discover that there were, indeed, Christians at the Mongol court, but that they were schismatic Nestorians. The Nestorian schism was named after Nestorius (d. *c*.451), a Syrian ecclesiastic born in Antioch who was Patriarch of Constantinople until he clashed with Cyril, Patriarch of Alexandria. Cyril persuaded the Roman pope to condemn Nestorius (in his absence) at the Council of Ephesus in 431 and he was subsequently exiled by Emperor Theodosius II. Nestorius represented the Antiochene school of historical exegesis (of which the best exponent was said to be Theodore of Mopsuestia, 350–428), which opposed the allegorical and speculative school of Alexandria. Nestorius denied the validity of the title 'Bearer of God' to the Virgin Mary and also held that Jesus possessed a genuine human nature, connected with his equally genuine divine nature by means of free human will. Cyril of Alexandria opposed this, saying it made Jesus into two people.

Nestorian Christians had long been active on the Silk Roads. Their existence in Tang China is testified by the 'Nestorian monument', a stela still to be seen in the Forest of Stelae in Xi'an, and which was of overwhelming interest to nineteenth- and twentieth-century Christian missionaries to China. They were no longer concerned with the ancient schism but saw this stela as a means of historical validation for their missionary work. There are hundreds of rubbings of the inscription brought back by missionaries, now crumbling in attics together with mouldering copies of the Gospels translated into Chinese or phonetic dialect versions.

The Nestorian stela is dated 781 and is syncretic in its imagery, 'topped by a Maltese cross resting on a Taoist cloud with a Buddhist lotus flower beneath it'.5 The more serious aspect for the missionary was its three-fold inscription: 'Doctrinal, Historical, Eulogistic. The first part gives a brief outline of the teachings of the religion and of the ways and practices of its ministers; the second part tells of its first entrance into China, and of the patronage extended to it for the most part for nearly 150 years by various emperors; in the third part . . . the Christians express, in verse, their praise of God and their religion, and also of the emperors whose protection and favour they had enjoyed.

'From this inscription we learn that a priest, Olupun by name, made his way through difficulties and perils from the West, guided by the azure clouds to China, bringing with him the True Scriptures. He was favourably received by the emperor in the palace, in AD 635, where a portion of the scriptures was translated in the library of the palace, and approving of the new doctrine, with that eclecticism the Chinese are so noted for, the emperor gave special notice for its propagation, and a proclamation was issued a few years after with regard to it and ended with the words, "Let it have free course throughout the empire." '6*

A monastery for twenty-one priests was built and Nestorianism was said to have spread widely before the Buddhist empress Wu (625–705) banned it for twenty-five years, after which it was restored to some extent and persisted, in a small way, right up to the Mongol era, as William of Rubruck discovered in his exploration of the Mongol capital where, unlike John of Plano Carpine, stuck in his tent, he was allowed to wander freely. On this basis, William made a full description of Karakorum, its walls, temples, markets, separate quarters for Moslems and Chinese handicraft workers, and its surprisingly cosmopolitan inhabitants. These included fellow Europeans, captured by the Mongols in Eastern Europe and brought along the northern Silk Road to Karakorum. There was Basil, the nephew of an English bishop, a Frenchwoman from Lorraine who cooked William's lunch on Easter Sunday, and Guillaume Boucher, a Parisian silversmith. Boucher made silver ornaments for the Khan's women and altarpieces for the Nestorians (which never included depictions of the crucifixion). Boucher's greatest near-triumph was a massive silver alcohol-dispensing fountain with cherubs, silver trees and angels blowing trumpets. Unfortunately the complicated automatic internal mechanism never worked, so whenever fountains of kumiss were required, a small person had to crawl inside and work the bellows by hand.7

William of Rubruck had a trying time at Karakorum. His interpreter (Latin–Mongol, Mongol–Latin) was frequently so drunk that he was incapable of speech, and William was also highly suspicious of his Nestorian rivals. One Armenian priest administered rhubarb (a common medicine) when he was ill but William remained convinced he was trying to poison him.

Apart from information-gathering, William's mission was unsuccessful. Yet another Franciscan, John of Montecorvino (1247–1328), made the journey along the Silk Road as far as Peking where he arrived in 1291. He built the first proper Christian church, complete with bells, in Peking in 1299, and organised a choir of small boys to sing for the Khan. His letters home reveal the existence of a second church in 1305 and the less welcome 'Lombard leech and chirurgeon' Johannes Vitodoranus, who spread blasphemies about the Church and Rome around Peking in 1302.8

Though he claimed to be in Peking at the same time, Marco Polo left no mention of John of Montecorvino. By far the best-known traveller on the Silk Road, Marco Polo travelled by land from

---

* The emperor in question was Taizong (r. 626–49), not as famous for his interest in western exotica as Xuanzong (r. 712–56). Chinese rulers, with a few exceptions, were by no means famous for their liberality and inclusiveness. The author of this passage, Dyer Ball, writes as a wishful Christian.

Constantinople to Peking and then travelled all over China, Tibet and
the Burmese border for twenty years before returning home, arriving
back in Venice in 1295. The story of his trip is the inevitable prologue
to any children's book on China, but he is equally well known in
China itself where he is celebrated for having put China on the map
for the West, as if it had not been there before and as if John of Montecorvino and William of Rubruck had never existed.

The story goes that Maffeo and Niccolo Polo, Venetian traders who
had trading houses in Constantinople and at Sudak on the Black Sea,
found themselves in Constantinople in 1260 and decided to 'go further
afield'. They travelled east and found themselves compelled to continue in that direction owing to various inter-Mongol wars. They
ended up in Karakorum, the capital of the Mongol empire, where they
met Qubilai (Kublai) Khan (r. 1260–94). They discussed religion with
him and found themselves promising to return to Karakorum with
some oil from the lamp that burns in the Holy Sepulchre at Jerusalem,
a letter from the pope and a hundred Christian priests who would

120

debate with the (Buddhist) idolaters. These were somewhat unlikely demands as the Mongol rulers already possessed plenty of papal letters, one or two of which had even been answered (very negatively) but disbelief must be suspended. The Polos returned home (a single trip took at least a year) and acquired the Holy Oil on the way. There they found that the pope had died and his successor had not yet been appointed so they acquired a letter from the Papal Legate in Acre, forgot about the hundred debaters, and returned with Niccolo's son Marco, then aged about seventeen, instead.

Back in Mongolia, they were welcomed with feasts and Qubilai took a great liking to the young Marco. The Polos accompanied Qubilai to the Chinese capital, Peking, then called Dadu by the Chinese, and Marco was appointed as a sort of roving ambassador by the Khan, and sent off on missions all over the vast area of China which Qubilai was still in the process of finally subduing. The three Polos stayed in China for seventeen years before they begged the Khan to allow them to go home. He sent them back as part of the vast entourage that accompanied a young Mongol princess, destined as a bride for Arghun, ruler of the Ilkhanate of Persia. They finally arrived back in Venice, but Marco was subsequently taken prisoner in a naval battle between the Genoese and the Venetians, and held in Genoa. Whilst in captivity, he met a famous romance-writer, Rustichello of Pisa, whose Arthurian romances were supposed to have been the favourite reading matter of Edward I of England (who did not have much time for reading, nor many books, but was terribly interested in Arthur). Together, Marco Polo and Rustichello composed a book called the *Divisament dou Monde (Description of the World)* which described Marco's travels across Central Asia and China.

Marco Polo's book has been an invaluable source for travellers. Christopher Columbus took it with him on his famous voyage and managed to identify Cuba as Japan from the few sentences Marco Polo devoted to that country (which all experts agree he never saw). When Lord Macartney prepared for his embassy to China (1792–4), it was part of his background reading matter, and the fact that the Great Wall of China was nowhere mentioned was baffling to the English Ambassador when faced with that extraordinary feat of construction. When Aurel Stein crossed the deserts of Central Asia in the first decades of the twentieth century, he felt himself accompanied by the shade of Marco Polo and frequently quoted from him in his own written accounts of his explorations. When William Dalrymple wanted to explore the Silk Roads and the ruins of the ancient capital of Karakorum in the late 1980s, he took Marco Polo as his inspiration.[9] For Italo Calvino, Marco Polo was the ultimate storyteller, cheering Qubilai Khan, depressed by the evening shadows and 'the scent of

*A statue of camels
and driver outside the
Registan, Samarkand*

elephants after rain', with his stories of 'thin' cities, trading cities and hidden cities, improving upon the accounts of other travellers who listed distances, tons of salt and other boring things.[10]*

Most people read Marco Polo's account in a modern version. One of the pioneers of Polo studies was Colonel Sir Henry Yule (1820–89), who produced a wonderful, fat, three-volume study, *The Travels of Marco Polo*, with additions made after his death by the brilliant bibliographer Henri Cordier.

The Yule–Cordier version is interesting for it consists of one part translation of the Polo text to four parts notes. Yule left no term unturned in his pursuit of scientific truth and his work is particularly valuable since it was written at a time when methods and times of travel in China and Central Asia had not greatly changed since the thirteenth century. He based his translation into English mainly upon a French manuscript transcribed and published by the Société de Géographie in 1824. The original manuscript, now in the Bibliothèque nationale, was probably copied in about 1400 (some seventy years

* Ironically, a major complaint from today's readers of Marco Polo is that he is very boring and has a tendency to list distances and local produce.

after Marco Polo's death) and it is significant for being the only one of the early group that contains the prologue. It is in the prologue that the story of both the first trip of Niccolo and Maffeo Polo and the subsequent method of composition of the manuscript occur. Other early manuscripts of similar date, and the earliest printed versions made in the fifteenth and sixteenth centuries, lack the prologue and begin abruptly and mysteriously in Karakorum.

Yule was the first to tackle the difficulties faced by the serious reader of Marco Polo. Chapter LXX, 'Concerning the very noble city of Saianfu [Xiangyang] and how its capture was effected', tells how 'this city held out against the Great Khan for three years after the rest of Manzi [southern China] had surrendered. The Great Khan's troops made incessant attempts to take it, but they could not succeed because of the great and deep waters that were round about it, so that they could approach from one side only, which was the north. And I tell you they never would have taken it but for a circumstance that I am going to relate.

'You must know that when the Great Khan's host had lain for three years before the city without being able to take it, they were greatly chafed thereat. Then Messer Niccolo Polo and Messer Maffeo and Messer Marco said, "We could find you a way of forcing the city to surrender speedily", whereupon those of the army replied that they would be right glad to know how that should be . . . Then spoke up the two brothers and Messer Marco the son, and said, "Great Prince, we have with us amongst our followers men who are able to construct mangonels which shall cast such great stones that the garrison will never be able to stand them, but will surrender incontinently, as soon as the mangonels and trebuchets shall have shot into the town." ' And, of course, it worked.[11]

Yule follows the two pages of translation with nine pages of notes, single-spaced and in a much smaller type-face. 'I propose here to enter into some detailed explanation regarding the military engines that were in use in the Middle Ages.' There are diagrams, quotations from the *Romance of Richard Cœur de Lion*, and an awful lot of help from Emperor Napoleon III who had composed the *Études sur le passé et l'avenir de l'Artillerie*, 1851. We learn more than we will ever need to know about trebuchets before Yule touches on the real problem. 'According to the narrative as it stands in all the texts, the Polos *could not* [Yule's italics] have reached the court of Qubilai before the end of 1274, i.e. a year and a half after the fall of Saianfu, as represented in the Chinese histories.'[12]

It was not just the impossibility of the dates: Yule also encountered enormous problems with Polo's place names and distances. On the possibility of getting from Yongzhang to the Burmese capital in seventeen days he writes, 'I confess that the indications in this and the beginning of the following chapter are, to me, full of difficulty,' and between Burma and Laos he is forced to conclude, 'I do not believe . . . that Polo is now following a route which he had traced in person.'[13]

The place names are difficult, for the work first circulated in manuscript form and copyists, unfamiliar with the names and terms, made all sorts of errors. The language of the text is itself something of a puzzle and the variant content of different manuscripts, copied from 1400 to 1550, also presents complexities.

Many of the fundamental difficulties stem from the fact that there is no 'original' text, no copy of that supposed to have been composed by Polo and Rustichello. The earliest manuscripts (in Paris and in the Bodleian Library in Oxford) were written in medieval French. This is not necessarily a problem because Rustichello wrote in French since it was the language of many European courts, and particularly for Edward I, whose mother was French and who ruled quite a lot of France. It appears to have been translated into Italian not long after the first French manuscripts were copied in around 1400. Translation created further problems when, for example, 'bue', meaning mud, was translated into 'bulls', and 'feels', meaning 'followers', became sons, and so on.

One of the most extraordinary aspects of the manuscripts is that the names for places and things were almost entirely in Persian or Turkish. Qubilai Khan was rendered as 'facfur . . . Persian . . . a common designation of the Chinese emperor in Mussulman sources', and there are only three names apparently derived from Chinese.[14] Marco Polo's champions explain this by the fact that Persian was a kind of lingua franca east of Constantinople, and it is easy to imagine that any Italian in Mongol China would have required an interpreter who would almost certainly have been a Persian speaker. It still seems strange that so few Mongol or Chinese terms penetrated in all that time.

Despite his claim to have charmed the Great Khan and have been employed by him for seventeen years, there is no mention anywhere in the voluminous Chinese archives, nor in Mongol sources, of anyone who can be satisfactorily identified as Marco (or any other) Polo. The Mongols did employ a great number of 'foreigners' in their administration, possibly suspecting that the Chinese would undermine them. There were Persian siege-engineers (who might well have been at Xiangyang, unlike Marco), Indian doctors and a Turkish architect who laid out the new Chinese capital at Peking. These were, however, experts and, entertainment aside, it is difficult to imagine that the Great Khan, whose territories stretched from Karakorum to Canton, would have employed an Italian as a special ambassador and then have failed to have the fact noted in his official annals. Marco Polo's defenders say that perhaps he exaggerated his position and that he was not important enough to have been recorded. Moreover, the extraordinary claim that he once governed the important Yangtze delta city of Yangzhou has been accounted for as another copyist's error, copying *gouverna* instead of *sejourna*, meaning simply that he stayed there.

Interestingly, though it is impossible to tell whether they travelled by sea or took the Silk Road overland, there was, in fact, an Italian community in Yangzhou in the early fourteenth century. In 1951, a tombstone was discovered there. Gothic script carved into the marble described the deceased as Katarina, daughter of Domenico de Vilioni, who died in 1342. The tombstone, with a carved madonna and appropriate scenes of the martyrdom of St Catherine, sliced up by wheels fitted with knives, was carved by Chinese craftsmen. It suggests that Italian silk traders at that time took their families with them to China.[15]*

Despite the doubts attached to them, Marco Polo's accounts of the oases of the Silk Road remain an important early source. The text should be used, but used with care. When people read modern editions of Marco Polo's *Travels* they may not be aware that they are reading compendia, composed from up to forty different manuscript versions, written between 1400 and 1550. These compendia also incorporate material from the first 'critical' (actually hagiographic) version by Giovanni Battista Ramusio, printed in 1557, which includes much extra material, particularly relating to the legend of the Polos' return to Venice, clad in rags but with jewels sewn into the seams of their Tartar robes. As these multiple sources contain different material a richer picture is obtained, but the dating of observations becomes complex.

One of the richest Polo manuscripts, containing over two hundred useful passages that are not found in other versions, was discovered in Toledo in 1932 and is supposed to have been copied in the mid-fifteenth century.[16] No one has questioned the dating but the massive increase in the contents leads me to suspect that the copyist may have had access to more, different material on the areas covered and to have added this to the base text, to increase its interest and usefulness. Polo's defenders claim this as a 'lost' manuscript tradition but, with no original for comparison, who can say? Even if the material does not represent an eye-witness account made by Marco Polo, even if some represents later additions, it still remains useful evidence of European interest in, and information about, Central Asia and China somewhere between the late thirteenth and mid-fifteenth century.

The more reliable William of Rubruck failed to interest the Mongols

---

* It is perhaps churlish to wish that one of the Polos had died in China as a tombstone could have represented proof of the visit.

Latin-inscribed tombstone of Katarina Vilioni, from Yangzhou, 1342. The decorations, by a Chinese stone-carver, include, at top, a Madonna and Child, and below, scenes from the life of St Catherine

in alliance and the Christian attempt at contact via the Silk Roads ended with his mission. Subsequent medieval missionaries like Odoric of Pordenone (over whose account of his travels some doubt is now cast) arrived in Mongol-ruled China by sea, as did most of the sixteenth-century Jesuits.

The missionary traffic was not all from west to east. In 1287 a Nestorian cleric, Rabban Sauma, arrived in Genoa from Persia. He had started his journey in Peking some years before and had travelled along the southern Silk Road. Rabban Sauma was the son of a prominent Onggud family based in the Ordos, on the bend of the Yellow River north of the Great Wall. The Onggud were a Turkic people who had accepted Genghis Khan's rule. Though some were pastoral nomads, others had settled and become farmers, craftsmen and merchants, and many had converted to Nestorianism. When he was twenty, Rabban Sauma refused an arranged marriage and renounced alcohol and meat in preparation for the religious life into which he was formally accepted in 1248. In 1260, when he was living an isolated life in the Fang mountains, another young Nestorian, Markos, came to study with him. In about 1275 Markos persuaded Rabban Sauma to make a pilgrimage to the holy city of Jerusalem. They were not offered

much encouragement, for their fellow Nestorian clerics felt that, since God was 'within' a Nestorian monk, there was no need to travel.

The two monks were determined to go, and acquired their own camels and camel-handlers since they intended to make a different sort of journey from that commonly undertaken by the merchant caravans. Merchants travelled in groups of up to sixty and could not afford the luxury of stopping to visit Nestorian communities on the way. Markos and Rabban Sauma set off, staying in postal stations and garrisons along the Silk Road. The Central Asian postal station system had been much enlarged under the Mongols. Post stations organised the movement of official mail and tribute, offered hospitality to travelling dignitaries, served as military outposts with warning beacons to alert at times of threat, and also served as inns for ordinary travellers. From Markos's home town northeast of the Yellow river, they first travelled to Ningxia. For a couple of hundred years, until the arrival of the Mongols, this had been one of the capitals of the Xixia (Tangut) empire. Despite the fact that it was reported that it had been completely destroyed, razed to the ground by the Mongols, Rabban Sauma and Markos found a sizeable Nestorian community there fifty years later.

The citadel of Arg-é Bam in Iran. Its clay ramparts serve to deflect the harsh Iranian sunlight as well as affording protection from attack. Marco Polo may have passed such castles on his route through Iran, where he described being robbed by bandits

127

Rabban Sauma's account of his journey survived in part through a much-cut copy made in Syriac, which appears to have piously retained all references to religion and cut out most of the detail of the journey. The account of the Nestorians in Ningxia is interesting for the way it underlines the ability of Central Asian communities to survive disaster and recover within decades.

The details of their journey along the southern Silk Road are lost; all we know is that Rabban Sauma said they encountered 'great hardships' on this stretch of the route and that it was 'toilsome and frightening' until they reached the rich and fertile oasis of Khotan.[17] After resting there, they moved on to Kashgar, where the northern and southern Silk Roads meet. There, they discovered that the city had recently been destroyed in an intra-Mongol feud between Khaidu Khan, Qubilai's cousin, and Nomukhan, Qubilai's son whom he had sent out to Central Asia to wrest control back from Khaidu. The two monks met Khaidu at his camp at Talas in Khirghiz. Crossing the Oxus, they made their way southwest into another Mongol realm, the Ilkhanate of Persia. The Mongol ruler of the area, Arghun (whose Mongol bride was escorted by sea by the Polos) apparently planned to send a Christian envoy to the 'Western Christian world'. Rabban Sauma was recommended to him and carried Arghun's letters (whose contents are unknown) to the pope, the Byzantine emperor and the kings of France and England. From Persia Rabban Sauma was accompanied by two Italian interpreters, Persian speakers Ughetto and Thomas of Anfossi, from a Genoese banking family, frequent travellers to Persia.

Rabban Sauma's arrival in Italy was dramatic: Etna erupted on 18 June and he described how 'smoke ascended all the day long and in the night time fire showed itself on it'.[18] He then arrived in Naples in the middle of a sea battle. He made his way to Rome but, unfortunately, the pope had died and he could only visit cardinals who grilled him on his Nestorian beliefs. Diplomatically, Rabban Sauma asked to be shown around the old Basilica of St Peter with the chair of St Peter (later to be encased in gold by Bernini) and the saint's sarcophagus surrounded by a golden grille. He seems to have seen something like the Turin shroud and, looking at the throne where the popes enthroned the Holy Roman Emperors, ended with a gymnastically muddled idea of the procedure. He stated that the pope picked up the crown with his feet in order to place it on the emperor's head; possibly misunderstanding the ritual whereby the emperor bent to kiss the pope's feet. He also visited the Church of San Paolo fuori le Mura where the Apostle Paul was buried.

Rabban Sauma moved on to Paris where he continued his touristic activities, admiring the Crown of Thorns in the Sainte-Chapelle and

the royal tombs in Saint-Denis, before proceeding to Bordeaux where he met Edward I who happened to be visiting his domain in Gascony. Edward enthusiastically affirmed his intention to make a crusade to recapture Jerusalem and the Holy Land – 'we the kings of these cities bear upon our bodies the sign of the Cross, and we have no subject of thoughts except this matter' – although he was later too preoccupied with the subjugation of Wales and problems with the French to do so. Edward invited Rabban Sauma to celebrate the Eucharist at court and offered him a huge feast.[19]

Despite his contemporary success and reception in high places, the name and story of Rabban Sauma are barely known in Europe, his pioneering achievements being quite overshadowed by the Silk Road journey, in the other direction, of the dubious Marco Polo.

A traditional reed house of the Marsh Arabs, of the type which may have been seen by travellers along the Silk Route

129

A parterre of roses:
travellers to Ming China and Samarkand

THE FALL of the Mongols and the establishment of a new Chinese dynasty in China (the Ming, 1368–1644) did not result in much reassertion of Chinese power out along the Silk Roads. Dunhuang had been largely abandoned and such Chinese garrisons as were re-established in Central Asia were found within the Great Wall, to the east of Jiayuguan. As with trade, much of which was now by sea, Ming foreign relations are often characterised as dominated by the great exploratory sea voyages of the eunuch Admiral Zheng He (1371–1433) who directed huge fleets which made seven voyages, visiting thirty-seven countries from the Persian gulf to the Red Sea and the east African coast.[1]

'Tribute' envoys visited China from many peripheral states and the Persian historian Hafiz-I-Abru recorded the 1419 embassy in his 'universal history' *Aubdatu't-Tawarikh* (begun in 1423). Six envoys, accompanied by 510 men, set out from Herat, and travelled via Balkh, Samarkand and Tashkent. As they travelled along the northern Silk Road, they encountered snow in June, 'frozen snow to the thickness of two fingers'.[2] On 11 July 1420 they arrived at the busy oasis of Turfan, which was described in the same sort of reductive terms that Marco Polo used, though Hafiz-I-Abru's 'idolaters' were all Buddhists: 'The majority of the inhabitants of this town were unbelievers and worshipped idols. They had large idol temples of superb beauty inside which there were many idols, some of them being made newly and others old.' They proceeded to Kharakhoja (Gaochang) and en route were met by Chinese officials who 'took down the names of the envoys and the members of their suite'. They moved on to the oasis of Hami where Islam and Buddhism seemed to be in confrontation: 'In this town Amir Fakhru'd-Din had built a magnificent mosque, facing which they had constructed a Buddhist temple of a very large size, inside which there was set up a large idol ... Just in front of the big idol there stood a copper image of a child of ten years of age of great artistic beauty and excellence. On the walls of the building there were frescoes of expert workmanship and exquisite coloured paintings. At the gate of the temple there were statues of two of the demons which seemed ready to attack one another.'

The embassy proceeded across the Gobi desert, which was

described in terms often used by travellers well into the twentieth century – 'they could obtain water on every alternate day or every two days' – until they reached Jiayuguan, the fort at the end of the Great Wall. 'A number of Chinese officials had come out to bid welcome to the envoys under orders from the Emperor. It was a delectable meadow. On that very day, they had set up on the plain a high platform with canvas awnings, over which were placed tables and chairs. All sorts of viands consisting of geese, fowls, roasted meat, fresh and dry fruits had been served up in China dishes, and set up on tables and trays. After the repast, various kinds of intoxicants consisting of wines and liquors were served up and all became tipsy. Over and above the entertainment, every one was supplied with sheep, flour, barley, necessaries of journey [*sic*], wine and liquor according to his status.'3 This provisioning of the tribute envoys (as well as the subsequent presentation of gifts) recalls the expense the Han court encountered in trying to keep the Xiongnu from raiding some 1,500 years earlier, and anticipates the offering of sackloads of pepper and rice to the first British embassy in 1792. Foreign relations, conducted on this generous basis, were a drain on the economy.

Nine stages (stops at post-houses) beyond Jiayuguan, they were welcomed by the 'Chinese emperor's viceroy for those frontiers' and five or six thousand cavalrymen 'encamped in the form of a square, such as if it were drawn by means of compasses and rulers'. Another huge platform was built with 'a large tent . . . of the Chinese type . . . in the manner of a royal pavilion with its flaps turned up . . . The envoys were seated on the left and the Chinese officials on the right, for in their eyes the honour attaching to the left side is greater than that to the right. Thereafter in front of every one of the envoys and officials they placed two trays, in one of which there were different varieties of Chinese dried fruits, geese, fowls, poultry and roasted meat, while in the other there were cakes, fine bread and bouquets made of paper and silk of such excellence as to be incapable of description. In front of the rest of the party there was placed one tray apiece. By their side there was a high royal drum and beside this drum there were ranged up flagons, Chinese wines and large and small goblets of porcelain, silver and gold. To the left and right of this there stood a number of musicians with organs, fiddles, Chinese fifes and two types of flute . . . as well as Chinese bag-pipes, Pandean pipes, double-sided drums set upon tripods all of them playing in unison, while there were cymbals, castanets and small drums by their sides. There stood acrobats, who were handsome boys with their faces painted red and white in such a way that whoever happened to look at them took them for girls with caps on their heads and pearls in their ears. They performed feats that were peculiarly Chinese and the like of which does not exist in the world.'

The master of ceremonies proceeded to offer toasts to all in turn, accompanied by baskets of bouquets, and 'turned the whole assembly in a moment into a parterre of roses'. The acrobats performed, with convincing animal masks, as dishes circulated filled with 'filberts, jujubes, walnuts, pickled chestnuts, lemons, garlics and onions pickled in vinegar . . . sliced musk-melons and water-melons; all being disposed on plates made into various compartments and every one of them placed separately in each of them'.4 The picnic ended with a small boy dressed in a stork outfit, 'made of cotton and red silk with feathers stuck into it, of which the beak and legs were coloured red so that it exactly looked like a living stork but only bigger in size'. The boy 'covered himself up . . . so that he resembled the figure of that very stork. He danced to the tune of Chinese music, moving his head this way and that way to the amazement of the spectators.'

The majestic caravan proceeded towards China proper, staying each night at a Chinese post-house. 'Their animals and baggages were all taken into the registry office, whence they were made over into the charge of trustworthy servants. Thereafter whatever requirements the envoys had as regards horses, food, drink and bedding were all provided from the post-house. Every night as long as they were there every one of them was given a couch, a suit of silken sleeping dress, together with a servant to attend to their needs.' The Moslem envoys were horrified to note that in Suzhou (today's Jiuquan) in the Gansu corridor market, 'There were a good many domestic swine kept in their houses and in the butcher's shops mutton and pork were hung up for sale side by side!'5

With the exception of one feast that they had to decline as it was Ramadan, the envoys made their slow way into China proper, provided with silk pyjamas at every post-house and fed on honey, garlic, mutton and geese. In Peking they met the emperor, who presented each envoy with bags of silver and rolls of satin and 'seventy other stuffs consisting of under-vests, red silks, damask, velvets, together with five thousand bank-notes'. A rare and somewhat baffling description of Zhu Di, better known by his reign title Yongle, was included in the account of the embassy. 'The emperor was of middle height; his beard neither very large nor very small; nevertheless about two or three hundred hairs of his middle beard were long enough to form three or four curls on the chair when he was seated.'6 Unfortunately, during the embassy's stay in Peking the emperor's 'favourite wife' died and 'a conflagration started through the decree of God from the sky in the wake of a lightning striking the top of the palace that had been newly constructed by the emperor who repaired to the temple and prayed with great importunity saying: "The God of Heaven is angry with me, and therefore, hath burnt my palace; although I have done no evil act; I have neither offended my father, nor mother, nor have I acted tyrannically!" He fell ill owing to this anguish'; and the embassy soon returned home by the same route by which it had come.

It was easier for Moslems than for people of other faiths to travel the Silk Road in this period, for the local Islamic rulers were intolerant of unbelievers. A rare European missionary braved the dangers of discovery in 1603. Bento de Goes (1561/2–1607), a Jesuit missionary, had set out from Europe to convert India and the Far East. He travelled to India by sea, sailing with the Portuguese fleet as a soldier. Though the sea route had become the preferred choice for merchants and missionaries, Bento de Goes met a merchant in Lahore in 1598 who told him, on the strength of thirteen years' residence in China, that the land route was still possible. This news followed upon the recent relaxation of rules in China by which the local viceroy had granted permission to the Jesuits to buy land and settle in Zhaoqing, near Canton, in 1583.

Bento de Goes set out from India with a caravan of five hundred men and pack animals in February 1603 and, losing horses from the cold in the Pamirs, reached Yarkand in November. There, evading threats to his life as a non-Moslem, he gathered a new caravan of seventy-two men to move onwards to Peking. They took the northern Silk Road, through Aksu, Kucha, Turfan and Hami. On the way to Jiayuguan, Goes nearly died, falling off his horse at the back of the caravan. Fortunately, an Armenian named Isaac noticed that he was missing and went back to find him in the desert. When they reached Suzhou (Jiuquan), they met a Moslem caravan on its way from Peking, and learnt that fellow Jesuits had arrived in the Chinese capital. Goes made several attempts to communicate with them through the post system, and finally succeeded. From Peking, Matteo Ricci despatched a young Chinese priest, Zhong Mingli, to set out to meet Goes. Zhong Mingli arrived in Suzhou to find that Goes was dying, but at least he knew before he died that the land route was possible and that the Jesuits were beginning to establish themselves at the heart of the Chinese empire.[7]

Another European to experience the danger of travelling as a non-believer (saved by the quick wit of the leader of his caravan) was Anthony Jenkinson, the first English merchant to explore the western end of the Silk Road. Anthony Jenkinson, a City of London merchant, arrived in Bokhara in 1558 to investigate trading prospects. He described the local trade, which was dominated by textiles and clearly losing out to maritime competition. 'There is yeerly great resort of Merchants to this City of Boghar, which travaile in great Caravans from the Countries thereabout adjoining, as India, Persia, Balkh, Russia and in times past from Cathay . . . The Indians bring fine whites

Extraction of a Guinea worm from a man's leg, by the seventeenth-century Dutch engraver Jan Luyken. Such gruesome scenes were witnessed by Anthony Jenkinson a century earlier, and still take place, often in public ceremonies, in parts of Africa and the East today

which the Tartars doe roll about their heads, and all other kinds of whites which serve for apparell made from cotton wool and crasko [coarse linen], but gold silver and precious stones and spices they bring none. I enquirred and perceived that all such trade passeth to the Ocean sea, and the vaines where all such thins are gotten, are in the subjection of the Portingals. The Indians carie from Boghar again, wrought silks, redde hides [from Russia], slaves and horses . . . The Persians do bring thither crasko, woollen cloth, linnen cloth, divers kinds of wrought . . . silkes, Agomacks [Turcoman horses] . . . The Russes doe carrie into Boghar, redde hides, sheepskinnes, woollen cloth with divers sorts, wooden vessels, bridles, saddles . . . and doe carrie away from thence divers kinds of wares made of cotton wool, divers kinds of silks, crasko . . . From the countries of Cathay is brought thither in time of peace and when the way is open, musk, rhubarb, satin, damask, with divers other things.'[8]

The failure of the Chinese caravans was probably due to border troubles. The Mongol ruler Altan-qayan (1507–82) was established in the area just north of the Shanxi border and, until a peace treaty was arranged in 1571, repeatedly led border raids into China to 'replenish supplies' of food, silk and clothing.[9]

Though trade prospects were not very exciting to Anthony Jenkinson, he did describe what was to become one of the sights of Bokhara, an indispensable paragraph in any travel account, the extraction of the

Guinea worm. Describing the river running through Bokhara, he said: 'the water thereof is most unwholesome, for it breedeth sometimes in men that drink thereof . . . a worme of an ell long, which lieth commonly in the legge betwixt the flesh and the skin, and is plucked out about the ankle with great art and cunning, the Surgeons being much practised therein, and if shee break in plucking out, the partie dieth and every day shee cometh out about an inche, which is rolled up and so worketh till shee be all out.'[10]

Unconcerned by Anthony Jenkinson's assumption about the sex of the worm, Ella Christie went to watch the barbers at work in the Bokhara market place in the early 1920s and described the de-worming process in some detail. 'The worm is removed by being turned around a stick, while gentle massage is applied: a slow process, as only a few inches are extracted in one day, and if the worm is severed in the operation, the fragment left sets up blood-poisoning and the patient usually dies. In the case observed, the worm after removal was thrown into the tank! It is only necessary to add that the infection is normally due to foul drinking water . . . A protest on my part was quite ineffective, the

Building the mosque at Samarkand. From a Persian manuscript, c.1480

barber pointing out that other worms had already been flung into the tank.'[11]

The western Silk Road city that most struck visitors was Samarkand, the ancient Sogdian capital that had been transformed under the rule of Timur (1336–1405). Though contemporary with the Chinese Ming emperors who had thrown the Mongols out of China, and a Turk to boot, Timur dreamt of emulating Genghis Khan and was proud to claim descent from the Barlas clan of the Chagatay Khanate whose rule 'stretched over an ill-defined territory comprising the Ili valley and Transoxiana and, during some periods, parts of present-day Afghanistan'.[12]

Born near Samarkand, Timur suffered a deformity, evident to the Soviet archaeologist, Professor Mikhail Gerasimov, who opened his grave in 1941 (and discovered that, though lame, he was probably six feet tall). Owing to the deformity, he was known as Timur 'leng' (meaning 'lame') and it is this mixture of name and epithet that gave rise to the common Western form of his name, Tamerlane, which was further muddled by Christopher Marlowe in his drama *Tamburlaine the Great*, published in 1590. George Frideric Handel used the Italian form in the title of his opera, *Tamerlano*, written in 1724. Marlowe's sources for Tamburlaine, 'the scourge of God and the terror of the world',[13] were popular romances reflecting quite a considerable taste for orientalism in the sixteenth century. One of the earliest manuscripts of the Marco Polo text, a beautifully illustrated version in the Bodleian library, is bound together with a contemporary story about Alexander the Great (also famous for his eastwards progress) and a doggerel poem about 'Dindimus, King of the Brahmans'; a useful compendium of the romance of the East.[14]

Timur's dream of empire began when he led his army against Khorasan and Eastern Persia; then southwards to take Delhi in 1399, in a bloody campaign that left thousands dead. In 1400 he took Aleppo and Damascus; in 1401 Baghdad. Though known in the West mainly for the pyramids of skulls that symbolised the savagery of his military campaigns, he was a great patron of literature, presiding over 'a galaxy of talent in which the great Hafiz is merely the brightest of many stars'.[15] Diplomatic contacts were established with Charles VI of France and Henry III of Castile in an interesting repeat of Europe's response to the Mongol threat in the thirteenth century. Fear of Ottoman expansion led European rulers to seek alliance with this formidable ruler whose capture of the Ottoman sultan, Bayazid I, the Thunderbolt, effectively saved Hungary, for example, from Ottoman conquest.[16]

An early account of the beauties of Samarkand was given by Henry III's ambassador, Ruy Gonzalez de Clavijo, whose embassy lasted from

1403 to 1406. He found the city in a constant state of construction, for Timur was a great builder and sought perfection. 'The Mosque which Timur had caused to be built in memory of the mother of his wife . . . seemed to us the noblest of all those we visited in the city of Samarkand, but no sooner had it been completed than he began to find fault with its entrance gateway, which he now said was much too low and must forthwith be pulled down.'[17] Despite the fact that Timur was old and frail and, according to Clavijo, could barely keep his eyes open and hardly stand so that he had to be carried everywhere in a litter, he still determined to supervise the reconstruction, being carried to the building site every day and throwing coins and meat down to the workers digging the new foundations 'as though one should cast bones to dogs in a pit'.

Timur's campaigns sometimes seemed to have been carried out specifically to enrich and embellish Samarkand. Not only did he carry off treasures, but he also captured handicraft workers. From India, Persia and Syria came tile-makers, architects and craftsman-builders, gem-cutters, glass-makers and painters. The great city of Samarkand

Friday prayers in front of the Ulugh-beg madrasah, Samarkand, c.1908

137

*Opposite: The Sher
Dor madrasah (begun
1636) in Registan
Square, Samarkand.
Above: A detail of its
ceramic decoration*

was surrounded by a deep ditch and walls (built by Timur) of five
miles in circumference. The city centre was approached by roads from
the city gate and centred on a great domed market. Craftsmen were
grouped together in separate bazaars and the city, despite its constant
flurry of building work, was characterised by greenery. Each house
had a garden, watered by channels leading from the Zarafshan river
and shaded by great spreading plane trees, interspersed with tall white
poplars and fruit trees. Within the city, the many fountains and cis-
terns increased the coolness and comfort of inhabitants and visitors.

Beyond the walls, equally green and watered suburbs spread to
accommodate the growing population, and Timur himself oversaw the
construction of two major gardens, the New Garden and the Garden
of Heart's Delight, where he entertained ambassadors like Clavijo. The
latter's first meeting with Timur took place in 'a great orchard with a
palace therein', entered 'by a wide and very high gateway, most beautifully ornamented with tile-work in gold and blue'. As the embassy
proceeded beyond the gateway, he noticed 'six great elephants, each
bearing on its back a small castle of woodwork carrying two standards: and in these castles were their attendants who made the
elephants play tricks for our entertainment as we passed by.'[18]

Elephants were not well-known in Europe at the time so Clavijo
described them at some length. He saw elephants painted green and
red which could play tricks and elephant fights where wounded elephants grunted like pigs and the ground shook when they charged
abreast. For the benefit of those who had never seen one, he explained

138

that they were 'very black and their skins have no hair except indeed at the tail which is as hairy as is that of the camel . . . their bodies are clumsily built: they have no grace of form, and it is as though each were a great sack that had been stuffed out full . . . The elephant has no neck to speak of . . . and he cannot put his mouth to the ground for the purpose of eating.' The elephant's trunk, 'somewhat in shape like a sleeve . . . is perforated throughout and by means of it he drinks at his need, for he puts the end into the water sucking it up into his mouth, as may be said, through his nose . . . it is with his trunk the elephant purveys all his needs; and hence his trunk is never still but ever kept in motion, coiling and uncoiling like a snake.'[19]

Clavijo was not the only ambassador in Samarkand: others arrived from places that he was hard put to identify but he stood firm on protocol when placed below the ambassador from China who had arrived on the annual tribute mission (demanding tribute from Timur according to Chinese traditional practice). Though the Ming dynasty was firmly established and flourishing at the other end of the Silk Road, Timur reacted badly to the demand and an official 'publicly proclaimed that his Highness had sent him to inform this Chinaman that the ambassadors of the King of Spain, the good friend of Timur . . . must indeed take place above him who was the envoy of a robber and a bad man . . . and if only God were willing, he Timur would before long see to and dispose matters so that never again would any Chinaman dare to come with such an embassy as this man had brought.' Furthermore, Clavijo reported, the Moslem court referred to the great Huizong emperor of China as 'the Pig Emperor'.[20]

Timur entertained his guests in 'orchards' where lavish tented pavilions sheltered them from the sun. All were walled enclosures with the same sort of magnificent gateway of fine brickwork ornamented with gold and brilliant blue tiles. Within the walls were fruit trees for shade and raised pathways and square tanks with fountains, one with pretty red apples floating beneath the spray, and 'many tents' with 'pavilions of coloured tapestries for shade, and the silk hangings were of diverse patterns, some being quaintly embroidered and others plain in design'.

At the centre of the Bagh-I-chinar (Plane Tree garden) was a small cross-shaped building with a divan covered in silken cushions standing behind a silver and gilt screen. The walls were covered with silk hangings 'of a rose-coloured stuff, that was ornamented with spangles of silver plate gilt, each spangle set with an emerald or pearl or other precious stone. Above these wall-hangings were strips of silk dependant, and of the width each of a palm across, these coming down to join the hangings below . . . to the same were attached many coloured silk tassels, and in the draught that blew these waved about here and there after a very pleasant fashion to see.'²¹ Some of the tents set up in the garden were lined with squirrel fur or ermine, to keep out the summer sun, but also serving to keep the tent warm in winter. Everywhere the impression is one of oriental luxury at its height. There were tables of gold set with 'seven golden flasks, and two of them were ornamented outside with great pearls and emeralds and turquoises, set in the metal, while at the mouth there was a . . . ruby. Beside these seven flasks there were standing six cups of gold circular in shape, and one of them had set within the rim a very big round pearl of fine orient, while at the centre point of the cup was encrusted a balas ruby of beautiful colour that measured across two finger breadths.'²²

The surroundings were exquisite but trespassers were shot on sight and their corpses left strewing the borders, the drinking was heavy and competitive and the food ran the gamut from rough to delicate. Great masses of 'mutton, roast, boiled, and in stews, also horse-meat roasted' were piled in huge quantities on 'very large circular dishes of leather . . . and these had handles whereby the attendants could move them from place to place. Thus when Timur had called for any partic-ular dish, that leather dish would be dragged along the ground to him, for the attendants could not lift them.' Silver trenchers were filled with 'knots of the horse-tripe in balls the size of a fist, with a sheep's head all of a piece', served with 'thin cakes of their bread, which doubled fourfold they placed one on each of those charged trenchers'. After the roast meats came mutton stew and side dishes and the meals ended with 'melons and peaches and grapes', goblets of 'gold and silver that contained mare's milk sweetened with sugar' or 'other sweet-meats such as pancakes and sugared breads'.²³

Though the local people could hardly aspire to such luxury, they could enjoy the products that were traded through the local markets: prayer carpets from Bokhara, Khurasan satin, sables, ermines and fox-furs from Khorezmia, raisins, almonds, sesame, 'fish-teeth' (walrus-tusks?), swords, copper and iron from Ferghana, melons and hazelnuts.²⁴ Timur's fabulous constructions covered with gold and brilliant turquoise tiles made by handicraft workers from Isfahan, Baghdad, Shiraz, Damascus and India dominated the city for cen-turies. The colours struck Robert Byron: the turquoise dome of Timur's mausoleum, 'the ribs . . . scattered with black and white dia-monds'.²⁵ Ella Christie described the stunning contrast between the dark, narrow streets of the city and the great open square of the Registan: 'As one emerges from a narrow street and enters this vast space it seems at first sight almost to give one a sense of unreality, so totally unlike is it to anything one has ever seen or imagined. The del-icate proportions of slender minarets and fluted domes are combined with a wonderful strength in the general effect of those dazzlingly

beautiful coloured façades.' For Lord Curzon, 'The Reghistan was originally and is still, even in its ruins, the noblest public square in the world. I know nothing in the East approaching it in massive simplicity and grandeur, and nothing in Europe . . . What Samarkand must have been in its prime, when these great fabrics emerged from the mason's hands, intact and glittering with all the effulgence of the rainbow, their chambers crowded with students, their sanctuaries thronged with pilgrims, and their corporations endowed by kings, the imagination can still make some endeavour to depict.'[26]

The markets of Samarkand continued to offer some of the same sweetmeats and bustle seen by Clavijo: Ella Christie found 'trade brisk' and 'the morning avocation going on of barbers shaving heads beneath the mosque walls. Food is appetizingly set out on brass trays in the form of fried meat cakes and bowls of rice of the national pillau, while little braziers are kept alight by means of wisps of grass and twigs and serve to broil fragments of meat, called shashlik, on skewers.

'For the less affluent customers there was *omelette aux fines herbes*, which is made in a copper pan about one and a half feet in diameter. It is sold in slices . . . hard-boiled eggs were also sold, dyed red and blue . . .

'Sweets were very popular with old and young – even though mutton-fat does not sound a tempting foundation – under the form of pastes made of fruit, and candies of almonds and pistachio nuts in sugar coverings brightly coloured. The bakers, who are very clever at their trade, also make a cake of flour, honey and pistachio nuts . . .

'In spring, the stems of uncooked rhubarb are freely chewed along with spring onions; these last are sold in bundles, often by children, who delight in arranging them on their heads like caps, the bulbs forming a ball-like fringe.'[27]

Children wearing spring onions on their heads hardly form part of the image of Samarkand that was common in the poetic imagination. From the often anonymous medieval romances of Tamerlane and Alexander that had inspired Christopher Marlowe and John Keats's 'silken' Samarkand,[28] to the versions of Persian epics (of the sort encouraged by Timur) that were rife in the later nineteenth century, the image was one of oriental luxury and barbaric difference.

Matthew Arnold wrote of 'The Sick King in Bokhara' who was destined for 'a brickwork tomb, Hard by a close of apricots, Upon the road of Samarcand', and described the city and its surroundings:

> . . . the poor man
> Who loiters by the high-heaped booths,
> Below there, in the Registan,
>
> Says: 'Happy he, who lodges there!
> With silken raiment, store of rice,
> And for this drought, all kinds of fruits
> Grape-syrup, squares of coloured ice,
>
> 'With cherries served in drifts of snow.'
> In vain hath a king power to build
> Houses, arcades, enamelled mosques;
> And to make orchard-closes filled
>
> With curious fruit-trees brought from far;
> With cisterns for the winter rain,
> And in the desert, spacious inns
> In divers places . . .[29]

Some of Matthew Arnold's poetry was inspired by a combination of Persian poetry and travel books such as Alexander Burnes's *Travels into Bukhara*, published in 1834. Passages in Arnold's 'Sohrab and Rustum' (1853) echo Burnes, particularly the references to the

> black Tartar tents he passed, which stood
> Clustering like bee-hives on the low flat strand
> Of Oxus, where the summer-floods o'erflow
> When the sun melts the snows in high Pamere.[30]

Arnold's description of Sohrab's troops is similarly indebted to Burnes and, indeed, sounds like many accounts of the varied peoples encountered in the market-places of Samarkand and Bokhara, or the lists made in Kashgar by C. P. Skrine and his wife, though these are here gathered for war rather than shopping:

> The Tartars of the Oxus, the King's guard,
> First, with black sheep-skin caps and with long spears;
> Large men, large steeds; who from Bokhara come
> And Khiva, and ferment the milk of mares.
> Next, the more temperate Toorkmuns of the south,
> The Tukas, and the lances of Salore,
> And those from Attruck and the Caspian sands;
> Light men and on light steeds, who only drink
> The acrid milk of camels, and their wells.
> And then a swarm of wandering horse, who came
> From far, and a more doubtful service own'd;
> The Tartars of Ferghana, from the banks
> Of the Jaxartes, men with scanty beards
> And close-set skull-caps; and those wilder hordes
> Who roam o'er Kipchak and the northern waste,
> Kalmucks and unkempt Kuzzaks, tribes who stray
> Nearest the Pole, and wandering Khirgizzes,
> Who come on shaggy ponies from Pamere.[31]

Not long after the publication of 'Sohrab and Rustum', Edward Fitzgerald produced a very free version of the twelfth-century *Rubaiyat* of Omar Khayyam with its evocation of desert caravans, imperial campaigns and exotic flowers:

> Think, in this battered Caravanserai
> Whose Portals are alternate Night and Day,
>   How Sultan after Sultan with his Pomp
> Abode his destined Hour, and went his way . . .

I sometimes think that never blows so red
The Rose as where some buried Caesar bled;
   That every Hyacinth the Garden wears
Dropt in her Lap from some once lovely Head.[32]

Similar images and exotic geography were used by another stay-at-home orientaliser, Oscar Wilde, in his 'Ave Imperatrix' which features hints of the Great Game:

    The brazen-throated clarion blows
      Across the Pathan's reedy fen,
  And the high steeps of Indian snows
      Shake to the tread of armèd men.

  And many an Afghan chief, who lies
      Beneath his cool pomegranate-trees,
  Clutches his sword in fierce surmise
      When on the mountain-side he sees

Odalisque with a slave. Like Flecker's poem Ingres's painting reflects Western conceptions of the sumptuous hedonism of the East

The Silk Road

> The fleet-foot Marri scout, who comes
>   To tell how he hath heard afar
> The measured roll of English drums
>   Beat at the gates of Kandahar . . .
>
> The almond-groves of Samarcand,
>   Bokhara, where red lilies blow,
> And Oxus, by whose yellow sand
>   The grave white-turbanned merchants go:
>
> And on from thence to Ispahan,
>   The gilded garden of the sun,
> Whence the long dusty caravan
>   Brings cedar wood and vermilion.33

The most famous poetic reference to Samarkand was James Elroy Flecker's 'The Golden Journey to Samarkand':

> We travel not for trafficking alone:
>   By hotter winds our fiery hearts are fanned:
> For lust of knowing what should not be known
>   We make the Golden Journey to Samarkand.34

Incorporated into *Hassan*, a complicated verse-play with interjections by merchants, pilgrims, the Master of the Caravan and the Principal Jew, its lists of carpets, textiles, sweetmeats, spikenard, jewels and treasures epitomise the poetic vision of the Silk Road cities, and it has lent its name to many subsequent travel books. Flecker (1884–1915) had worked in the Consular Service in Constantinople, Smyrna and Beirut, so he had some experience of the Near East (which he did not much like) yet his work is still in the orientalising vein.35 If earlier readers had trembled at Timur's piles of skulls and Genghis Khan's hordes of bloodthirsty cavalry, the mood of terror was soon overlaid by sensations of gorging on sweetmeats, reclining on cushions covered in carpets and swathed in silk, with the constant ringing of camel bells filling the ears as the nose was overwhelmed by heavy floral fragrance.

- 10 -

The Great Game and the Silk Road

THE EXOTIC FRINGES of the British Empire to which Oscar Wilde referred saw increasing tension throughout the nineteenth and early twentieth centuries. Though the 'Great Game', played in a vast area at the western end of the Silk Roads, stretching from Afghanistan and Tibet north to Samarkand and Bokhara, is generally thought of as a nineteenth-century affair between Russia and Britain, Russian expansionism had been a preoccupation for the Chinese since the seventeenth century.

During the reign of the Kangxi emperor (1661–1722), the Russians had begun to advance on China's northern borders, colonising Siberia and moving down to the Amur river. In 1689, Russian and Chinese envoys met at Nerchinsk, to sign the first Sino-Western treaty of peace and, within a few years, Russian embassies began visiting Peking. It was not just the Russian threat that preoccupied Kangxi, for he was faced with further danger in Mongolia from the Eleuth king, Galdan (1644–97). Galdan's biography sets out some of the tribal complications of the Mongolian area: 'Bushktu Khan of the Sunggars (a tribe of the Eleuths) [Galdan] was a descendant in the twelfth generation of Essen who harassed the northern frontier in the fifteenth century. The Eleuths (or Oelots), known as the Kalmuks, were the Western Mongols – the Eastern Mongols occupying Outer Mongolia (Khalka) and Inner Mongolia. At the time of Galdan, the Eleuths embraced several nomadic tribes: the Khoshotes, ruled by descendants of a brother of Genghis Khan, the Turguts . . . and the Choros who in turn comprised three tribes: the Sunggars or Dzungars, the Derbets, and the Khoits. The Khoshotes, the Turguts, the Sunggars and the Derbets formed the four main tribes of Western Mongolia, and their alliance was called Uriad which by a change of sound was known in the Ming dynasty (1368–1644) as Wala. The Khoits were originally subject to the Derbets.'[1]

Further west, the Tarim basin was ruled by a family of khans. In the mid-seventeenth century the ruler of Yarkand sent an envoy to the Qing court in Peking. He reported that the 'rulers of Hami, Turfan and Yarkand are all brothers. Their father's name was Abdurrahim. He ruled in Yarkand. He died a long time ago. He had nine sons. The eldest is Abdullah Khan and he rules in Yarkand.' Other sons ruled in Kucha, Aksu and Khotan.[2]

Undeterred by tribal and family complexities, the Kangxi emperor

A group of Torguts, a Mongolian nomadic sect that travelled along the Volga into Russia

led several campaigns into Central Asia, first against Galdan, finally forcing him to commit suicide in 1697, 'thus stabilising the borders on the north and northwest for more than eighteen years'.3 Rebellions continued to break out on the borders until the Ili valley was conquered in 1757. Kangxi also led an army to subdue Tibet in 1720, closing off the southwestern borders. In the wake of his campaigns, he employed skilled Jesuit map-makers to survey and map his newly conquered domains.

The Kangxi emperor's grandson, the Qianlong emperor (1711–99) continued the campaigns. He boasted of conquering the Sunggars in two campaigns (1755, 1756–7), of 'pacifying' the Muhammedans of Turkestan (1758–9) and of twice conquering the Gurkhas (1790–2), and his campaigns were celebrated by the Jesuits at his court by massive engravings printed in Paris.4 The costs of the conquests of Ili and Turkestan were enormous but the result was that the Chinese empire was once again extended out into the Central Asian deserts, encompass-

148

ing the Silk Roads as it had in the Han and the Tang. The newly conquered areas were called the 'New Borders', Xinjiang or Sinkiang.5

Within these new borders, the conquered peoples were inevitably subject once more to Chinese government restrictions. Bento de Goes had described how caravans from Yarkand to China in the early seventeenth century in effect 'took on the role of a diplomatic mission', and were viewed in China as a tribute mission. Merchants bought places in the caravan but were restricted once they got to China. Each was allowed no more than '15 jin of tea, 50 sets of chinawares, 5 copper jugs, 15 bolts of . . . silk and satin of diverse colours . . . 30 bolts of blue striped cotton, 30 bolts of white linen . . . 300 sheets of paper for ritual purposes, 5 jin of paint . . . 30 jin each of sweetmeats, dried fruit and ginger, 30 jin of medicine, 30 jin of black prunes and 10 jin each of white and black alum. After departure from the capital . . . they can acquire oxen, sheep, ploughs, shovels and iron pots . . . but it is forbidden for them to purchase iron or military weapons.'6

In the mid-nineteenth century, the Qing dynasty, so strong under the Kangxi and Qianlong emperors, declined rapidly. As it did so, its hold on Xinjiang and the neighbouring province of Gansu weakened. Russia, expanding into Siberia, had also long been interested in the area to the south of its ever-enlarging borders, sending exploratory missions like those of Trushnikoff in 1713 and Yefremev in 1780.7 The British in India were slower to embark upon exploration. The mineral potential of the area (oil, natural gas, gold, silver, copper, iron-ore, zinc and coal) was enormous and, if it could be exploited, could have great potential influence upon the industrialising nations of Europe. But above all there was a political aspect to the exploration of Central Asia as Tsarist Russia and Imperial Britain, hampered and hindered by local rulers, sought to increase their own spheres of influence and contain those of their rivals.

Catherine the Great is said to have toyed with the idea of seizing British India and in 1807 Napoleon proposed to Tsar Alexander I of Russia 'that they should together invade India and wrest it from British domination'.8 Though this joint venture never materialised, during the first half of the nineteenth century the Russians moved southwards, taking the Moslem khanates of Bokhara, Khiva and Khokand, advancing apparently inexorably towards British India. In 1865, they took Tashkent; in 1868, Samarkand; and in 1873, Khiva. As Peter Hopkirk put it, 'At the beginning of the nineteenth century, more than 2,000 miles separated the British and Russian empires in Asia. By the end of it this had shrunk to a few hundred, and in parts of the Pamir region to less than twenty.'9

As Chinese control weakened, local leaders seized power and embarked upon uneasy relationships with the rival European powers.

In 1862, a Uighur leader Yakub Beg (1820–77), originally from Khokand, led an uprising and in 1865 founded an independent khanate based at Kashgar. Anxious to counter Russian expansion southwards across the western end of the Silk Road, he was given considerable British support.

The first of the oasis towns at the western end of the Silk Roads that attracted British interest was Yarkand. Only too well aware of Russian advances, the British administration in India was wary of sending British officers to the area, but in the 1860s the Survey of India in Dehra Dun, responsible for mapping India and measuring the height of mountains, began to send out Indians trained in surveying. As Captain Montgomerie of the Survey of India explained to the Royal Geographical Society, 'While I was in Ladakh . . . I noticed that the natives of India passed freely backwards and forwards between Ladakh and Yarkand, and it consequently occurred to me that it might be possible to make the exploration by their means.'[10] Known as 'moonshees', later 'pundits', the Indian surveyors were provided with tiny tin lanterns for reading sextants at night, and miniature copper jugs and oil lamps to enable them to calculate altitudes by boiling water. They carried standard travelling staffs adapted to include a thermometer, compasses concealed in prayer wheels, and some were given specially altered strands of beads, of the sort that Buddhists count between their fingers. Instead of the normal 108 prayer beads, the moonshees carried strings of 100, mostly of imitation coral, with each tenth bead larger in size, made from an udras seed. As they walked, they slipped the beads and every large bead represented a distance of a thousand paces or about half a mile.[11]

The moonshee Mohammed-I-Hameed joined a caravan which traversed 'the most elevated country in the world' from Ladakh to Yarkand in 1863. He stayed for six months, continuing his calculations and observations. Yarkand was a 'verdant' oasis with 'many fine poplars and elms', watered by the Yarkand river and flourishing in 'a climate more genial than that of Kashgar'. Swedish missionaries, the Raquettes, inhabited a house on a small lane off the bazaar, furnished with 'whatever seems needful for a simple European house. There were well-made tables and cupboards, framed pictures on the walls and a table laid out hospitably with all orthodox comforts.' The old town was 'far more picturesque and pleasing' than Kashgar, with 'the plentiful presence of fine shady trees and of tanks, which to the eye at least, were refreshing'. Sir Aurel Stein, who visited Yarkand several times, worried whether the water, stagnant in the tanks, might be 'largely responsible for that presence of goitre which old Marco Polo had noticed among "the inhabitants of Yarcan"'.[12] Francis Younghusband of the 1st King's Dragoon Guards at Meerut, visiting Yarkand in 1890, in the footsteps of his tea-planter uncle, Robert Shaw, who had been there in 1868, enjoyed 'a sumptuous feast in a fruit garden . . . Few people know better the way to enjoy life and make themselves comfortable than these merchants. We first of all sat about under the shade of the trees, while huge bunches of grapes and delicious melons and peaches were freshly plucked and brought to us to eat. Then dinner was announced and, after water for washing the hands had been passed around, we set to at dish after dish of "pillaos" and stews, all beautifully cooked, and we ended up with a pudding made of whipped egg and sugar and some other ingredients, which it would be hard to beat anywhere. All the time the merchants were chaffing away amongst themselves, and were as "gay" and talkative as Frenchmen. You could scarcely wish for more genial hosts. On the way home we had races, each man trying to make out that his horse was better than the others.'13

Mohammed-I-Hameed had little opportunity to enjoy such gatherings. Warned that he had been betrayed, he left Yarkand in a hurry and died on his way back home. His death was investigated by the first British surveyor to explore the region, Civil-Assistant William Johnson, who managed to recover all his notes and papers. Johnson was, to his surprise, invited to visit Khotan by the Khan himself, who had heard of his earlier tentative forays. He stayed as the Khan's guest in a Chinese fort and learnt in his daily meetings with the Khan that there was a plan to keep him as a hostage to force the British government in India to send troops to keep back the Russians, who were 'daily approaching towards Yarkand and Khotan'.14 Despite his personal significance in the Great Game, during his enforced stay in Khotan Johnson was able to gather more information on the sand-buried cities of the Taklamakan desert that had been mentioned in Mohammed-I-Hameed's notes on the area.

Khotan was a serious centre of trade, for millennia (until Burmese sources were discovered in the nineteenth century) the major source of jade to be worked in China, and a silk-producing area. When the Chinese Buddhist pilgrim Xuanzang passed through Khotan in about 645 on his way back to China from India, he noted the dark and light jade in the market and admired the locally produced silks. The tradition was that silk was introduced to the Khotan oasis in AD 440 when a Chinese princess arrived, carrying silk cocoons hidden in her piled-up hair. Local silks were woven in the distinctive ikat weave, with wave-like stripes produced by tie-dyeing the warp threads so that the pattern is in the warp. Marco Polo is also said to have passed through Khotan but, with his usual unerring ability to miss the point, failed to notice either silk or jade, singling out only 'cotton . . . wheat, flax, hemp and wine'.15 He also reported that the people had vineyards and gardens, lived by commerce and manufactures, and that there were no soldiers.

Carpet weaver, Khotan

Soldiers, 'picturesque figures with swords and halberds representing a selection from the garrison', were much in evidence when Aurel Stein visited Khotan some six hundred years later, bringing gifts of 'fine yellow Liberty brocade which always pleases Chinese taste'.

Stein was put up in a 'garden-palace', the Nar-bagh, a 'green wilderness refreshing to the eyes' despite the thick layers of dust on every leaf and twig. He stayed there several times, in the central pavilion, surrounded by 'shady Aiwans'. These were 'a prominent feature in well-to-do people's houses throughout the southern oases'. They were tall central halls, with clerestory openings of decorative wooden lattice on all sides beneath the high roof. Raised platforms along the walls, and the floors themselves, were covered with thick Khotan carpets with 'gay cotton prints hung as dados round the walls'.[16]

The foremost oasis for the British in the period of the Great Game was Kashgar. Set at the western end of the old trade routes, where the southern and northern Silk Roads met, it formed a crossroads and an entrepôt. From Kashgar, one branch of the Silk Road ran further westwards over the High Pamir to Khokand, Samarkand, Bokhara and Merv, another ran through Balkh in Northern Afghanistan to Merv, and yet another ran southwards through the Karakorams to Leh and Srinagar and down into India.

A Chinese garrison had been posted to Kashgar in AD 78, to guard the western frontier, but it was soon overrun by the Western Turks. The Chinese re-established control in the early Tang but were soon challenged by the Arabs. In 747, a Chinese army was sent out across the Hindu Kush to repel the 'invaders' but it was eventually defeated at the battle of the Talas river, northeast of Tashkent, in 751. The defeat left Central Asia open to the Arabs and Islam, and is also supposed to mark a major event in the history of European civilisation with the transfer of paper-making technology to the Arabs and thence to Spain, Italy and the rest of Europe. According to legend, Chinese paper-makers were amongst the soldiers captured in battle and taken off to Samarkand to make paper there. However, the excavation of numerous paper documents dating from the Han dynasty onwards at sites all along the Silk Roads, suggests that the transfer of the technology may have been a longer, more gradual process.

Kashgar became a Moslem centre and did not come under Chinese control again until the eighteenth century. Before that, it had been visited by the ubiquitous Marco Polo who was not much taken by it. 'Kashgar's inhabitants live by trade and handicrafts; they have beautiful gardens and vineyards, and fine estates and grow a great deal of cotton. From this country many merchants go forth about the world on trading journeys. The natives are a wretched, niggardly set of people; they eat and drink in a miserable fashion. There are in this country many Nestorian Christians, who have churches of their own. The people of the country have a peculiar language.' The reference to Nestorianism is mysterious and historians are puzzled by his claim that Kashgar was subject to Mongol rule.[17]

Chinese control of Kashgar in the eighteenth and nineteenth centuries was precarious at best, though it retained a romantic connection with Kashgar through the 'fragrant concubine' who smelled wonderful. She was said to have been the daughter of a local Moslem of great saintliness, Abakh Hoja (though she is sometimes claimed as the concubine of the Khan of Yarkand), captured in 1758 and taken to Peking. The Qianlong emperor was greatly taken with her, building her a tower so that she could look at her fellow Moslems in the Muhammedan quarter southwest of his Winter Palace, and a Turkish bath. Despite these constructions, she pined for the desert and either committed suicide or was murdered by the Emperor's mother, as she was said to have repudiated the emperor and always to have carried a knife to reinforce her refusal. Two paintings by the Jesuit painter Giuseppe Castiglione in the Palace Museum collections, depicting a woman in a Western suit of armour, are often described as portraits of the fragrant concubine. Kashgar legend maintains that she was buried in Abakh Hoja's tomb on the outskirts of Kashgar, a fine rather

153

Gaudi-esque construction of unmatching green and yellow tiles; and there was once a wooden board there with an inscription by the Qian-long emperor.[18]

In 1865, Yakub Beg proclaimed himself Khan of East Turkestan with his capital at Kashgar. He controlled the oases of Khotan and Yarkand, Aksu and Kucha, the whole of the Tarim basin from the Pamirs to Lop Nor, and was courted by both Russians and British, pre-ferring the latter since he had fought against the Russian invasion of his home-town Khokand in the early 1860s. The Hungarian traveller Arminius Vámbéry described Yakub Beg's foreign policy: 'All that the Sovereign of the Six Cities understood by diplomatic relations with England was, in the first place, money and arms; in the second place, money and arms; and in the third place, money and arms.'[19] One of the Russian envoys sent to Yakub Beg was General Nikolai Mikhailovich Przhevalsky (see Chapter 11) who had a rather similar view of the importance of arms in diplomacy and Russia's place in Central Asia: 'Our military conquests in Asia bring glory not only to Russia; they are also victories for the good of mankind. Carbine bul-lets and rifled cannon bear those elements of civilization which would otherwise be very long in coming to the petrified realms of the Inner

Asian khans,' and he wrote in a letter to his brother, 'Yakub Beg is the same shit as all feckless Asiatics. The Kashgarian Empire isn't worth a kopek.'[20]

Whatever the worth of the Kashgarian empire, it stood between Russian and British expansion and control of Central Asia, and Kashgar became a vital 'listening post' in the Great Game, with a Russian Consulate opened in 1882 (in what is now the Seman Hotel), ostensibly to promote trade, and a British 'listening post' established in 1890 and raised to consular status in 1909. The gap between the establishment of the Russian and British consulates was unfortunate. In 1877, when Yakub Beg died, Ney Elias, a merchant turned surveyor and diplomat, began to press for British representation, particularly since the Russian consul, Petrovsky, exerted every effort to make life difficult for Indian traders in the area, as well as seizing the political initiative, but Ney Elias's views were ignored in the Foreign Office.[21]

The first British consul in Kashgar was Sir George Macartney (1866–1938), son of Sir Halliday Macartney who had fought against the Taiping rebels in 1863 alongside 'Chinese' Gordon and, after their defeat, married a daughter of one of the Taiping 'kings'. George Macartney spoke fluent Chinese though he always seemed embarrassed about his parentage. In 1898 he brought his new wife to Kashgar, and it was largely her influence that transformed the oasis for British explorers and travellers into what Peter Fleming was later to call 'Kashgar-les-Bains'. Those who travelled out into Central Asia from India, like Sir Aurel Stein, always stayed at the consulate, Chini Bagh (Chinese Garden), a long bungalow above a terraced garden where Lady Macartney struggled to grow English flowers, 'only the hardiest kind', and where her gardener, fed up with staining his clothes when he picked mulberries for her pies, decided to climb the mulberry tree naked. 'I had to tell him he must wear his oldest things and spoil them and I would give him a new shirt and trousers to make up.'[22] She described the 'old Muhammedan' city of Kashgar with its narrow streets and dark shops and the same wealth of grapes, peaches and apricots seen in Turfan; but there was also a 'new, Chinese' city, 'smaller and newer-looking'.

Very far from home and sources of supply, Lady Macartney had to put up with home-made furniture (neither the consul nor his great friend, a Dutch Roman Catholic priest, were skilled at DIY), a cook who dropped the Christmas pudding and a piano that got very wet somewhere in Russia and had to be reconstructed by a Swedish missionary. Her husband had to attempt to maintain diplomatic relations with the Russian consul Petrovsky, an unreliable character who once gave Macartney a pane of glass for Chini Bagh and then demanded its return.

The cast of characters in such a remote outpost was very small and remarkably stable. In 1890 Francis Younghusband had travelled across the mountain passes to Kashgar with George Macartney when Macartney was despatched to open the British 'listening post' (later Consulate). Younghusband met the local Dutch priest (who in more recent works is always described as 'defrocked') Père Hendricks, who came round for a chat every day. Though 'many of his methods of conversion' surprised Younghusband, the future founder of the World Congress of Faiths was impressed with Hendricks's knowledge, 'ready to talk in any language, from Mongol to English, and upon any subject, from the geological structures of the Himalayas to his various conflicts with the Russian authorities'. His extreme poverty, perhaps the result of being cut off from his order, meant that he 'lived on bread and vegetables only', until the arrival of Younghusband who fed him twice daily, and with meat. Great Game diplomacy was enhanced by a Christmas meal complete with exploding plum-pudding. 'We were able . . . with the Russian consul, his secretary, his son, the Cossack Officer of the escort and Père Hendricks, to have a good-sized dinner-party on Christmas Day. Beech had a wonderful tinned plum-pudding, which went off with an explosion when it was opened at the table, and I had another, which a kind friend in India had sent up, and which arrived on Christmas Eve, so we were able to show our Russian friends what "le plum-pudding anglais", which they had heard so much about but never seen, was really like.'[23]

Younghusband described Petrovsky, the Russian consul who tantalised Macartney with a pane of glass, as 'an interesting feature of my stay in Kashgar'. He was immensely well-read 'on subjects connected with India and Central Asia' and on England. 'M. Petrovsky had read the report of the Sweating Committee, our Factory Legislation Reports, accounts in our newspapers of the strikes which continually occur. All this had produced on his mind the impression that we were in a bad way. Forty thousand men held all the riches, and the rest of the thirty-six millions were just ground down to the last penny. This was his idea of the state of things in England; and he compared it with the condition of Russia. In Russia there was no great gulf between rich and poor. Strikes, which he looked upon as mild revolutions, were unknown, and all lived together in peaceful contentment under the Czar.' Younghusband found him 'more sound' on India. Despite criticising the British in India for holding themselves 'too much aloof' from the Indians, Petrovsky despised the Chinese amongst whom he lived and did not know a word of the language (see Chapter 12).[24]

Despite their many exchanges of views, Petrovsky finally revealed the same petty unpleasantness he frequently displayed to Macartney, and refused to say goodbye to Younghusband. 'His dignity had been

hurt because I took Davidson to call upon him in the afternoon. He refused to receive us and afterwards informed Macartney that first calls ought always to be made in the middle of the day. I did my best to appease him by explaining by letter that we had only intended to do him a civility; that it was our custom to call in the afternoon; and that, at Peking, I had myself called upon his own official superior, the Russian minister, in the afternoon, and been called on in return by him. But M. Petrovsky replied that he was only concerned with Kashgar, and that at Kashgar the custom was to call in the middle of the day.'[25]

Whilst crossing the Pamirs, Younghusband had several encounters with Russian troops. In 1889, on an expedition to establish friendly relations with the Mir of Hunza, he met Colonel Grombtchevski, who was doing the same for the Russian side. Younghusband described Grombtchevski as 'a thorough gentleman' and Grombtchevski was to report to the Imperial Russian Geographical Society that Younghusband 'was a young man who had made his name with a brave journey from Peking to Kashmir across the whole of China . . . Our encounter was most friendly.'[26] Conversing in French, however, Grombtchevski assured Younghusband that 'half a million Russian troops were ready to march south' and was answered with 'a rousing cheer' when he asked his Cossacks if they would like to invade India. Younghusband

Foreign residents in the garden of the British consul at Kashgar, c.1908: Sir George Macartney (left) and his wife; David Fraser; the Swedish missionaries Lars Erik and Sigrid Högberg, John and Ellen Törnquist and Adolf Bohlin; Paul Pelliot with two members of his expedition, the doctor Louis Vaillant and the photographer Charles Nouette

157

Sir Francis Younghusband, June 1895

was sceptical of the Russians' ability to maintain supplies to such an army crossing deserts and mountains and, upon learning that Grombtchevski and his Cossacks intended to enter British territory in Ladakh, advised them on the best route. In fact, he meanly sent them on what he described to a friend as a route 'of absolutely no importance, leading from nowhere to nowhere, and passing over very elevated plateaux and mountains without grass or fuel, and to cross which in winter will cause him extreme hardships and loss to his party' (a detail which he omitted from his published memoirs).[27]

Younghusband used his extraordinary knowledge of the area on his return to India from Kashgar. At Bazai-Gumbaz in the Oxus valley, he encountered a Cossack party, including Colonel Yanov (who had been on Grombtchevski's expedition), a doctor and a surveyor 'named Benderski, who had been in Kabul with the Russian mission of 1878, and had also surveyed the Pamirs with Ivanoff's expedition of 1883'. The Russians ('doubled up in very small tents') were amazed at Younghusband's 'field-officer's Kabul tent, about eight feet in length, breadth and height, and with a bath-room and double fly. I had, too, a bed, table and chair . . . it is much better to take a whole pony-load and make oneself comfortable, than to take half a load and be miserable.' The Russians' luggage priorities were apparently different because they offered Younghusband 'a dinner, which for its excellence astonished me quite as much as my camp arrangements had astonished the

158

Opposite: A caravan crossing a difficult glacial pass, the famous ice steps of the Muzart pass, c.1908

Russians. Russians always seem able to produce soups and stews of a good, wholesome, satisfying nature, such as native servants from India never seem able to imitate. The Russians had vegetables, too – a luxury to me – and sauces and relishes, and, besides vodka, two different kinds of wine and brandy.'[28]

Despite this conviviality, three nights later Colonel Yanov informed Younghusband that he had been ordered by 'his government' to escort him from Russian territory back to Chinese territory. Outraged that this order had been received at Lake Victoria, on the Great Pamir, Younghusband 'told him I did not consider I was on Russian territory at all, and that in any case, I was returning to India'. Pausing to report the 'whole matter to my Government' (resulting in a protest by the British Ambassador in St Petersburg and a Russian apology), Younghusband, joined by Lieutenant Davison, who had been 'treated in a much more cavalier manner by the Russians' and marched into Chinese Turkestan for which he had no passport or permit, revealed how a gentleman played the Great Game. 'Colonel Yanov had barred all the known passes to me, so our only resource was to discover an unknown pass – always an easy matter in those parts.' Hampered by heavy snow, they found a glacier and followed it upwards, 'knowing that it must necessarily lead to the pass. We had, of course, to proceed very slowly and carefully, for fear of crevasses hidden by the snow.

160

But, like the elephant, which will not cross a shaky bridge, the yak knows by instinct the parts that will not bear, and, snorting and sniffing along, he finds his way unerringly up a glacier.' The summit soon appeared, with a knife-like wind which blew up the narrow pass that led down towards the Karumbar river and, eventually, Gilgit.[29]

Whilst borders and areas of influence in the Pamirs were pushed this way and that by Russia and Britain, at the far western end of the Silk Roads the Russians were pushing forward. A few brave English pioneers made their way into the Khanates. William Moorcroft of the East India Company visited Bokhara in 1825, hoping to find a new market for Company goods. He was disappointed to discover that the Russians had preceded him economically as well as politically and the famous bazaar was full of cheap, shoddy Russian wares. Moorcroft died on his way back to India but was followed in 1832 by Lieutenant Alexander 'Bokhara' Burnes, also of the East India Company, who was very impressed with the 'lofty and arched bazaars of brick . . . ponderous and massy buildings . . . mosques and minarets', and the twenty caravanserais for merchants from different countries. In the evening he sat in the great Registan, 'a spacious area in the city, near the palace, which opens upon it. On two other sides there are massive buildings, colleges of the learned, and on the fourth side is a fountain, shaded by lofty trees. A stranger has only to seat himself on a bench of the *Registan*, to know the Uzbeks and the people of Bokhara. He may here converse with the natives of Persia, Turkey, Russia, Tartary, China, India and Cabool. He will meet with Toorkmans, Calmuks and Cossacks from the surrounding deserts . . .'[30]

Part of Bokhara's attraction for many of these visitors, if they were Moslems, was the shrine of the founder of the Nakshbandiyya (a Sufi order) which served to create a mercantile network, stretching across the whole Silk Road area and giving Bokhara such a predominant position from the fifteenth century that merchants from anywhere in Central Asia became known as Bokharans. Thus, a merchant from Turfan might be described as a 'Bokharan from Turfan' and the whole Tarim basin was sometimes called 'Little Bokhara' as late as the nineteenth century, much to the irritation of pedantic German geographers.[31]

Unaware of the significance of pilgrimage for trade, Western visitors to Bokhara were most struck, and horrified, by the slave trade that flourished there and in Khiva. In the sixteenth century Anthony Jenkinson described it as an odious traffic, and in the nineteenth century, it was so much part of local life that Arminius Vámbéry claimed that Turkmens 'would not hesitate to sell into slavery the Prophet himself, did he fall into their hands'.[32] Horror of slavery and a desire to stamp it out was the main pretext used by the Russians in their advance on

Interior of the Harem of Tash Kauli, at Khiva. Slaves, along with silk stuffs and spices, were traded along the Silk Route and Khiva was an important centre for the slave trade

the Khanates. It was difficult for the British to disagree but, in an attempt to forestall the Russian advance, Lieutenant-Colonel Charles Stoddart was sent from India in 1838 to try to persuade the emir of Bokhara to abandon the trade. His mission was unsuccessful and he was shut up in a foul, rat-infested underground prison. Captain Arthur Conolly of the Indian Cavalry, who had ridden to his rescue, was also thrown into prison and both were beheaded in 1842. The Reverend Joseph Wolff who, in 1844, politely requested their bones for Christian burial, was told 'that his own bones would need to be sent home if he was not careful'.33 It was said that Dr Wolff was infected with a Guinea-worm in Bokhara but, instead of the barbers in the market place, he had his worm extracted in London 'eastern-fashion' by Sir Benjamin Brodie, surgeon to George IV, William IV and Queen Victoria.34

Another Silk Road city that achieved a reputation for medieval savagery was Khiva. Provoked by Russian advances into the area that were bringing Russian influence uncomfortably close to British India, Captain James Abbott was despatched from Afghanistan in 1839 to assure the khan of Khiva of Britain's wish for a friendly relationship. He was detained for several weeks as a 'guest' of the khan during the freezing winter of 1840 when his towel froze in minutes into a block of ice. He had some retrospectively amusing interviews with the khan who found it hard to imagine a country ruled by a woman. "Do you always choose women as your kings?" enquired the khan incredulously. And what about ministers and officers, did they have to be women too?'35

When the Russians took Samarkand, and decreed that no foreigners were allowed into 'Russian Central Asia', Captain Frederick Burnaby of the Household Cavalry determined to follow Abbott to Khiva. He set off in 1875 and was able to reassure an old mullah who enquired fondly after Abbott ('He was such a nice gentleman') that Abbott had not been killed by the Russians as the mullah supposed, but had returned to England safely. Though not on official business, Burnaby had an opportunity to convey British attitudes to Russian expansion when visited by the khan's treasurer. The latter remarked of the Russians, ' "They are pushing onward . . . You will have the opportunity of shaking hands with your friends [on the Indian border] before long. Four years ago we were quite as far from Russia as you are at the present time; and you have not many white men in India." "Quite sufficient to give Russia a good beating," ' Burnaby responded.36

Burnaby enjoyed the Khivan version of a Turkish bath: 'After steaming for about half an hour', he was led to 'a large reservoir filled with water and floating ice'. Furthermore, he provided entertainment for the local people: 'My manner of eating with a knife and fork much astonished some of the visitors. One of them, coming up, tried to imitate the proceeding, the consequence being that he ran the fork into his cheek. This greatly amused the rest of the party.' Like Abbott before him, he suffered greatly from the cold, narrowly avoiding frostbite and finding it impossible to maintain his correspondence, for 'the ink, which was frozen into a solid lump, has smashed the bottle'.

Burnaby's published account of his ride to Khiva was a great popular success, partly because of the detail he offered of the difference of every aspect of life there, but also because of his rather flippant tone. He described the Kirghiz manner of 'bidding for a wife': ' "She has sheep's eyes, and is lovely," says her mother. "Yes," replied the female relative, the wife-seeker's advocate. "She has sheep's eyes, but is not moon-faced and has no hips whatsoever! Let us say 200 roubles." ' He relayed stories of the emir of Bokhara, 'not a very enlightened ruler,

and it was said of him that on one occasion he sent to a Russian
officer, who had been seen looking at the moon through a telescope
and enquired what it was he could see there. "Mountains and extinct
volcanoes" was the answer. "Dear me!" said the Ameer, "how very
curious. Pray who is the Khan in the moon? I should like to make his
acquaintance." '37

The national preoccupation with the Great Game and the publication of Burnaby's *Ride to Khiva* led to a fashionable interest in the
area. In a letter of 1879 to his friend Robert Louis Stevenson, from
whom he had not heard for some time (Stevenson was in California),
the critic and man of letters, Edmund Gosse, wrote, 'Lang is consumed
with curiosity to know where you are. He fancies you have gone to
Khiva; but I have dropped a hint that it is really Merv. We all think
you are somewhere in Central Asia.'38

~ 11 ~

Asia held them captive in her cold embrace:
explorers on the Silk Road

SURVEYING and exploration of Silk Road terrain were often used as the acceptable face of the Great Game. As the Survey of India sent out its pundits to measure and map the great mountain ranges of India's northern borders, with an eye on routes through the passes, trade prospects and possible annexations or 'spheres of influence', Russia sent similar expeditions. There were also semi-independent explorers like Sven Hedin and Sir Aurel Stein, whose lengthy expeditions involved a complex combination of mapping, collecting and information-gathering. Many of the great names of Silk Road exploration in the nineteenth and early twentieth centuries, Przhevalsky, Hedin, Stein and Ney Elias, were very distinct characters, determined, immensely brave, highly intelligent and extremely anti-social. The very length of their expeditions, the distance they set between themselves and the drawing-rooms of Oxford, St Petersburg and Oslo, may have contributed to their isolation, but it seems clear that they chose to isolate themselves in the deserts and mountains of Central Asia. None of them married. Some have suggested that Przhevalsky was homosexual, and he was certainly a contradictory character: 'a man of ruthless determination and of shy tenderness, an apostle of European superiority who loathed European society, an explorer of China who despised the Chinese, a big-game hunter on an epic scale who mourned the death of his dogs, a major-general who disliked the army . . .'[1]

Hedin offered a rather evasive explanation for his single state: 'I have been in love many times, but Asia remained my bride. She has held me captive in her cold embrace, and out of jealousy would never let me love any other. And I have been faithful to her, that is certain.'[2] Aurel Stein maintained an enormous, engaged correspondence with family and friends, writing letters every night from frozen tents in the deserts, but seems to have preferred to maintain his social and emotional life at this epistolary remove. When Ney Elias died in 1897, Professor E. H. Parker wrote to *The Times* recalling a conversation they had had in Tianjin in 1872, when Elias was still working for an import–export company in Shanghai and Parker was a language student in the Chinese Consular Service:

'We sat up talking until two in the morning . . . in the course of our conversation he said: "I have definitely cut myself off from a business

Sven Hedin in Kashgar,
1893–6

career. I hate business and have no aptitude for it. But I feel I have the capacity to do something worth doing and if I cannot get a big job in the engineering line I am thinking of striking across Mongolia and hunting up the mysterious city of Karakorum. I would give anything to be able to face company as you do. I am not a bit timid and have complete confidence in myself: but I am cursed with the most extraordinary constitutional shyness and the moment I walk into a room I feel as though my tongue were glued to my mouth. I have tried to conquer it in every way, but it is perfectly hopeless. I shall never be able to do anything in the social line, but I am not going to give in, I will do something." '3

The earliest of these great explorers to travel through the wilder regions of the Silk Roads was Nikolai Przhevalsky (1839–88). His first expedition (1870–3) was financed by the Russian War Department, the Imperial Geographical Society and the St Petersburg Botanical Gardens. His ambition was to map the Ordos plateau, explore Southern Mongolia and, ambitiously, locate the source of the Yellow River and get to Lhasa. Though he was unsuccessful in the last two aims, he was able to inform the War Department about Yakub Beg's uprising and the Empire of Western Turkestan based in Kashgar: for the Imperial Geographical Society he mapped and surveyed 7,000 miles, and he overwhelmed the Academy of Sciences in St Petersburg with '5,000 plant specimens, 1,000 birds, 130 skins of large and small mammals, 70 specimens of reptiles, and in excess of 3,000 insects'.[4]

Przhevalsky's second expedition (1876–8) was more political, for he was to proceed to Kashgar and negotiate with Yakub Beg. On this trip, unimpressed by Yakub Beg (who died in 1877), he found Lop Nor (which was to be more extensively investigated by Sven Hedin and Aurel Stein) and proceeded towards Lhasa with 70 lbs of Turkish delight as a bribe. As on his previous attempt, his supplies ran out and he himself became ill and had to turn back before reaching Lhasa. Determined to reach the Tibetan capital, he returned on his third expedition (1879).

Tibet, with its borders with China and India, long part of Silk Road trade (tea-bricks and silks from China exchanged for gold and precious stones) offered tantalising prospects to explorers and players in the Great Game. Its altitude, protected by mountains, made it difficult of access but it was largely the Tibetans' determination to keep foreigners out that frustrated early efforts to reach it. Conscious of the pressure from expansionist Russia and Britain, determined to protect their religion and culture (rumours flew that Przhevalsky had come to kidnap the Dalai Lama) and their gold fields which were only partially exploited owing to the Tibetans' belief that 'nuggets contained life and were the parents of gold dust',[5] the Tibetan militia turned Przhevalsky back from the frontier. Furious, Przhevalsky recorded in his diary that, in order to make life harder for any British rivals, he showed the Tibetans maps and surveys that had been made secretly at great personal risk several years earlier by Survey of India pundits and published by the Royal Geographical Society in London.[6]

Przhevalsky made a further, final attempt to reach Lhasa on his fourth expedition (1883–5). Once again, he failed. On this last expedition, he took with him a young distillery clerk, Pyotr Kozlov

Nikolai Przhevalsky

(1863–1935), who was to succeed him as Russia's foremost explorer of Central Asia, collecting masses of documents from Dunhuang and, above all, the ancient Tangut capital of Kharakhoto in 1909 and 1923.

Though he failed to reach Lhasa, Przhevalsky's discoveries, particularly of animal and botanical specimens, many of which bear his name, were of considerable importance. He found new rhododendrons, delphiniums, gentians, a new maidenhair fern, three new honeysuckles, a new poppy, the red *Rosa przewalskii*, a rare hedge-sparrow that he named for Kozlov, *Prunella koslowi*, and, on his third expedition, the last wild horse sub-species, Przhevalsky's Horse.7 This small yellowish animal, with a 'short and erect' or punk mane, was discovered in western Mongolia but now survives only in zoos. In the 1880s a circus proprietor, Carl Hagenbeck, paid for the explorer William Greiger to go out to collect the small horses for him. They were not easy to catch but Greiger developed a system of chasing the herds till the foals could no longer keep up, whereupon they were collected and introduced to suckling mares back at camp. The mortality rate was high:

setting off for home with fifty-two foals, Greiger only managed to deliver twenty-eight animals to the Hamburg circus.[8]

Not far behind Przhevalsky was Sven Hedin (1865–1952) who began by surveying and map-making and gradually came to include the collection of antiquities in his explorations. A small man, trained in geology, physics and zoology at the University of Stockholm, and in physical geography at Berlin University by the great Baron von Richthoven (who had given the Silk Roads their name), he was, perhaps, the most physically reckless of all, coming very near death at times and, though he survived to old age, leaving a trail of dead men, ponies and camels behind him. To be hired by Hedin on one of his trips meant almost certain death for man or beast. His autobiography, which dealt only with his explorations, not any other aspect of his life, was entitled *My Life as an Explorer* (1926) and is a 'Boy's Own' series of death-defying exploits. He began on a confident note: 'Happy is the boy who discovers the bent of his life's work during childhood. That, indeed, was my good fortune. At the early age of twelve my goal was fairly clear. My closest friends were Fenimore Cooper and Jules Verne, Livingstone and Stanley, Franklin, Payer and Nordenskiold, particularly the long line of heroes and martyrs of Arctic exploration. Nordenskiold was then on his daring journey to Spitsbergen, Novaya Zemlya and the mouth of the Yenisei river. I was just fifteen when he returned to my native city – Stockholm – having accomplished the North-East Passage.'[9]

On one of his early journeys to Persia, Hedin had been asked by 'a famous professor of medicine and anthropology' to bring back the skulls of some Zoroastrians from the Tower of Silence where the dead were laid out to be dried by the sun. Cranial measurement was one of the main activities of nineteenth-century anthropologists but collecting these skulls was an unpleasant task, told with scandalous relish by Hedin. 'Accordingly, in the middle of June, when summer was at its height, and the thermometer registered 106 in the shade, I set out with Dr Hybennet for the Tower of Silence, the funeral-place of the fire-worshippers, southeast of Teheran. We chose the early hours for our raid . . .

'We took with us a kurchin, or soft saddle-bag, in the two pockets of which we put straw, paper and two water-melons, each the size of a man's head.'

When they arrived at Hashemabad, Hedin scaled a ladder and hauled Dr Hybennet on to the coping of the tower. 'A rank, sickening smell of decaying corpses met us . . . There were sixty-one open shallow graves. In about ten of them lay skeletons and corpses in various stages of putrefaction. Whitened and weatherbeaten bones lay piled alongside the wall.

169

Tower of Silence near Teheran, photographed by Hedin in the 1890s

'After some deliberation I selected the corpses of three adult men. The freshest corpse had been there only a few days; yet its soft parts, the muscles and entrails, had already been torn away and eaten by birds of prey. The eyes had been picked out but the rest of the face remained, dried up and as hard as parchment. I detached the dead man's skull and emptied it of its contents. I did similarly with the second head. The third had been lying in the sun so long that its brains were dried up.

'We had taken the saddle-bag and the crock of water with us over the wall, pretending that we were going to have lunch there. I used the water to wash my hands. Then I emptied the bag, wrapped the skulls in the paper, after first filling them with straw, and then put them in the bag in place of the water-melons. The bag thus retained its shape and did nothing to arouse the driver's suspicion except the offensive smell . . .

'We buried the skulls in the ground, left them there for a month, and

170

afterwards boiled them in milk, until they were as clean and white as ivory.

'The need for all this secrecy is obvious. What would the superstitious Persians and Parsees have thought of us had they learnt that we infidels were going about stealing skulls from their funeral places? Besides, Hybennet was physician-in-ordinary to the Shah and, specifically, his dentist. People might have supposed that we intended to remove the teeth from the jaws of the skulls for subsequent use in the Shah's gracious mouth. There might have been disturbances and riots.'[10]

He explored the old Khanates: Merv with oxblood-coloured rugs, Bactrian camels, 'the famous Turkoman horses with clumsy heads and slender necks', and Bokhara, 'the Sogdiana of the Greeks, the Transoxiana of the Romans', described in a mysterious couplet quoted by Hedin,

> If that Bold One of Shiraz gain our hearts,
> For his dark mole, I will give Samarkand and Bokhara.

Hedin discoursed on Bokhara's history, sacked by Genghis Khan and taken by Tamerlane, and recounted the more recent horror, early in the Great Game, when Colonel Stoddart and Captain Conolly had been seized in 1842, thrown into the 'famous vermin pit' and beheaded. By the time Hedin visited it, the population was very mixed, as it had probably been centuries earlier when it was a major entrepôt near the end of the Silk Roads. There were 'Tajiks, of Iranian stock . . . the Uzbeks and Jaggatai Turks of the Mongolian race; and the Sarts, a mixed race . . . Persians, Afghans, Kirghiz, Turks, Tatars, Caucasians and Jews'.[11]

On his first crossing of the Pamirs in 1894, which he made, against advice, in winter, he 'became afflicted with a violent rheumatic inflammation of the eyes . . . The expedition was broken up and, blindfolded, I proceeded with my little caravan past Kara-kul and Bulun-kul and further along the wild narrow valley of the Gez-daria, notorious as the resort of robbers and escaped thieves.'

Still blindfolded, he crossed the river, which 'hurled itself between mighty boulders, foaming and roaring. The men waded through the water in order to support the horses, which might have drowned but for this assistance.'[12]

He survived to reach Kashgar (his second visit) where, running across Great Game enmities, he re-acquainted himself with 'my old friend Petrovsky', the Russian consul, 'the hospitable Mr Macartney and the witty Father Hendricks', who had helped the British representative Macartney to construct his household furniture out of old boxes.

In 1895, Hedin proposed to travel from Merket on the Yarkand river, just east of Kashgar, across the southwestern corner of the Taklamakan desert to the Khotan river, down to the oases of the southern Silk Road, taking with him four men, eight camels, two guard-dogs and a mobile larder of sheep, hens and a cockerel. 'I hoped to cross the desert in less than a month, and move towards the cool heights of northern Tibet during the warm summer months. We therefore took fur coats, blankets and winter clothes. Our arsenal consisted of three rifles, six revolvers and two heavy ammunition boxes. I had three cameras, together with a thousand glass and celluloid plates, the usual astronomical and meteorological instruments, and finally some scientific instruments and a Bible.'

The journey started off quite pleasantly, though the camels misbehaved, and they travelled past sweet-water pools, through groves of poplars and vast reed-fields where Hedin dozed off to sleep in his tent as he listened to 'the sound of the splashing water as the men poured it into the tanks' ready for the next stage. One dog disappeared: Hedin later considered the dog had been wise to stay by the lake as the camel-train moved off into the sands where 'not a trace of vegetable or animal life was to be seen, not a wind-driven leaf, not a moth'.

In the barren sands, Hedin soon discovered that the water-tanks had not been fully filled. Within days, deprived of any water at all, two camels were dead. A few days later, two more camels died, Hedin sparing his readers none of the details. 'The "Old Man" had lain down, his legs and head stretched out on the sand, while "Big Blackie" had stood erect, with trembling legs, unable to take another step . . . The blood flowing in their veins grew thicker and thicker. The "Old Man" had probably died first. Then "Big Blackie" was alone. Finally he, too, died, in the majestic stillness of the desert; and in due time the shifting sand-hillocks would bury the remains of the two martyrs.'

A violent sandstorm halted the caravan; another camel fell down a ridge and was abandoned, together with his load, for by now Hedin was desperately jettisoning ammunition, fur coats and empty water-tanks to reduce the load on the surviving camels.

On May Day, 'a spring-time feast of joy and light at home in Sweden', Hedin was reduced to drinking Primus fuel (which was turned down by the remaining dog) and by next morning, the first of his men 'had already begun his death-struggle'. The others drained the blood of the rooster and then the sheep, 'which had followed us as faithfully as a dog without complaining', and then turned to camel's urine which gave them stomach cramps and made them vomit.

Leaving the two moribund men behind, the survivors – 'only the hens remained cheerful' – struggled on for a while, until another of the men collapsed and the camels lay down. At this point, Hedin abandoned hope, but still in a terribly organised way: 'seeing that the game was up, I decided to forfeit everything except my life. I even sacrificed diaries and records of observations, and took along only what I always carried in my pockets, namely, a compass, watch, two chronometers, a box of matches, handkerchief, pocket-knife, pencil, a piece of folded paper, and by the merest chance, cigarettes.' He stroked the surviving dog, 'and left it to him to decide whether he would stay or go with us. He stayed, and I never saw the faithful dog again.'

He walked on with one servant, Kasim, who soon collapsed, particularly when they discovered that they had, like Pooh and Piglet, been following their own tracks, hoping that they might have been those of previous travellers who knew where they were going. Leaving Kasim to die amongst a group of poplars, Hedin struggled on, 'as though led by an invisible hand'. He finally came to the dried bed of the Khotan river. But a waterbird led him to a pool, a rare survivor of the freshet floods of the early summer.

Hedin returned to Kashgar in June: two of his men had survived, and one camel, amazingly enough the one carrying his diary, maps, money and two rifles. And, despite the horror of the trip and its considerable waste of men and animals, he set off again in December 1895, with one of the survivors (jobs must have been scarce in Kashgar). This time, he was not just surveying and map-making, but also actively looking for treasures and lost cities. In Khotan and Yarkand he acquired terracotta figurines, Buddha images, Christian relics, coins and manuscripts, and he explored some of the ruins near the Keriya river.

On his return to Europe in 1896, he describes in his autobiography how he was fêted: in Berlin by the Baron von Richthofen; in London, where he stayed with 'Dr Livingstone, I presume' Henry Stanley, and met the Prince of Wales and Sir Clements Markham of the Royal Geographical Society who awarded him a Founder's Medal and made him an honorary member; and in Paris, where he met Félix Faure, President of the Republic, and Roland Bonaparte and Milne Edwards of the French Geographical Society. In Sweden, the king himself linked Hedin's name with that of the great explorer Nansen: 'At the risk of his life and with indomitable energy, Nansen has searched for land among the ice-fields of the Arctic Ocean. Sven Hedin, a son of Sweden, has searched for water – the water that does not flow very freely in the sandy deserts and steppes of interior Asia. A king's duties are often heavy but his privileges are often precious. I am exercising one of these privileges when, in the name of the Swedish nation, I address myself to the political and social representatives of that people assembled here and call on them to join with me as spokesman of the

sentiments cherished by the Swedish people, when I cry aloud the
name of Sven Hedin.'[13]

In 1899, sustained by the support of King Oscar and Emmanuel
Nobel, Hedin set off once more from Kashgar to the Yarkand river in
order to cross the Taklamakan by boat until the river froze. After three
months of drifting with the current, occasionally hoisting a sail to
improve progress, to the open-mouthed amazement of passing caravans, he made a twenty-day trek across the desert, carrying water in
the form of ice-blocks, to the oasis of Cherchen on the southern Silk
Road. From there, he headed northeast to the Lop desert at the eastern end of the Taklamakan.[14] Discovering the ruins of houses, he
picked up a few coins and pieces of carved wood before heading back
(once again with the intention of getting to Tibet). In a complicated
series of events – a man left a spade behind and, when he went to fetch
it, reported on more and better woodcarvings – and amid disasters of
the normal Hedin sort in Tibet – loss of one man, ten horses and three

camels and one man left footless through frost-bite – he returned to the site in the Lop desert and collected documents on wood and paper, in Kharosthi and Chinese, which eventually revealed that the site was that of Loulan, lost to sight and knowledge for hundreds of years.

Hedin's description of the site – 'Houses, towers, walls, gardens, roads . . . the habitat of Death and Silence' – and the finds – 'horizontal friezes with seated Buddhas, and vertical wooden posts with standing Buddhas . . . lotus and other flower ornaments . . . rags, fish-bones [illustrating the very different way of life before the desertification of the Lop lake], a few grains of wheat and rice' – was enhanced by his pencil sketches. He was a good amateur artist, publishing a number of volumes of drawings of places and people in Central Asia and Tibet which were informative and occasionally elegant.

In 1901 Hedin made his first attempt to reach Lhasa. Knowing how unlikely it was that the Tibetans would allow him to pass, he followed the example of the earlier Survey of India pundits and disguised himself as a Buriat Buddhist pilgrim. He was discovered and turned back, five days' journey short of his objective, which he afterwards described (sight unseen) as not worth the effort, anyway.[15]

He made a second attempt to reach Tibet in 1906, eschewing Lhasa in favour of a 'systematic scientific exploration of southern Tibet'.[16] But this was after the British had finally broken through Tibetan resistance with a military expedition led by Francis Younghusband, riding into Lhasa in 1904. Younghusband's expedition, which proceeded despite contradictory telegrams flying backwards and forwards between London, Delhi and Tibet, had been despatched by Lord Curzon, the viceroy of India, as a result of rumours of an agreement between Russia and China over Tibet. Though the Tibetans resisted Younghusband's advance, the conflict was hopelessly one-sided, for the Tibetans were poorly armed and no match for the British machine-guns 'Bubble and Squeak' which, at Guru, killed 628 Tibetans and left 222 wounded, with only 12 wounded soldiers on the British side.[17] Growing increasingly ambivalent about the expedition, Lord Curzon summarised three conflicting schools of thought, just before Younghusband entered Lhasa, as:

1. The extreme – Younghusband
2. The less extreme like myself who think that the treaty ought to be concluded, that it ought to provide for an agent somewhere, that we ought not to leave Tibet and possibly Lhasa until it is concluded, and who want to exercise some sort of influence in Tibet in the future.
3. Those who think that any treaty, even if we can conclude it, will be a farce . . . they want the expedition to be merely retributive.[18]

The treaty that was signed between Tibet and Britain on 7 September 1904 provided for recognition of the frontier of Sikkim, open trade routes between India and Tibet and the razing of forts along the way, and the establishment of a British Agent in Gyantse with the right to visit Lhasa as he felt necessary. It also stipulated that Tibet should have no 'dealings of any kind with any foreign power without Britain's consent'.[19] The freedom of the British Agent to visit Lhasa, and the occupation of the Chumbi valley for seventy-five years, ostensibly to protect Indian traders, were both additions of 'the extreme – Younghusband'.

Lord Curzon admired Sven Hedin and encouraged him in his preparations for his second expedition to Tibet, even ordering that pundits be specially trained in Dehra Dun to assist him in his survey. After Curzon resigned in 1905, his successor, Lord Minto, also supported Hedin, believing that his survey would be useful to the British, but the new Secretary of State for India, Lord Morley, refused to allow Hedin into Tibet. Hedin wrote, 'My God, how I hated Morley . . . The English were worse than the Tibetans.'[20]

Already anti-English, Sven Hedin was in Sweden when the First World War broke out and found himself with 'an irrepressible desire to observe war at close quarters under fire. Studying modern war on the battlefield is a valuable experience.' Fresh from his rather destructive expeditions, he expressed the pious view that he might therefore learn to 'abhor war as such' and the irresponsibility of national leaders. He chose to admire the German armies in action. 'No-one but the Kaiser could grant permission for a foreigner to visit the German fronts' and permission was granted. Hedin spent time with Ludendorff, Hindenburg and von Bülow, and on the Italian front, and was widely criticised and satirised for his pro-German stance.[21]

In 1937, Hedin arrived in China once more, to reconnoitre a link for a Lufthansa route from Berlin to Urumqi and thence to Peking. He brought with him aviation experts, meteorologists, archaeologists and palaeontologists for a thorough scientific survey. In Peking, the expedition was met with hostility and informed that foreigners were not needed to explore China. Rumours spread that the air-route was only planned so that Silk Road treasures could be conveniently airfreighted out of China. Hedin argued for six months and finally had to agree to take ten Chinese scientists with him, re-name the trip the Sino-Swedish Expedition and refrain from taking anything out of the country. His expedition did manage to take some textile finds and manuscripts back to Sweden but they worked under very difficult conditions, having to arm themselves with rifles and revolvers because of local unrest. And true to Hedin's usual form, eight members of the expedition died from various causes.

Hedin's employment by Lufthansa was not surprising. He had never been a neutral Swede. Having supported Germany in the First World War, he was fêted by the Nazis in the Second World War (when he does appear to have been trying to do something for Finland).

In 1935, he accepted an invitation to make a lecture tour in Germany. When he was visiting Goering, his host 'suddenly pulled out his watch and exclaimed, "Donnerwetter, it is five to six and at six o'clock you have to be with Hitler!" ' Hedin described Hitler as affable: 'He received me at the Reich Chancellery as though we had been old friends. He was tall and manly, a powerful and harmonious figure who held his head high, walked erect and moved with assurance and control.'

Hitler asked the seventy-year-old Hedin for ' "the key to your secret . . . Tell me what you do to keep so healthy and alert at your age?" "It is all very simple. I have spent a large part of my life among the high mountains of Asia and in their pure fresh air, and in the limitless deserts, where no microbes find their way. I have lived for years in tents both winter and summer, and I have ridden thousands of miles, which is the finest exercise you can have. If I ever felt tired I have

Sven Hedin with two Mongolian postmen on an expedition to the region, c.1934

rested for a day and I have never – except for a matter of life or death – over-exerted myself. In Asia I never drank alcohol, and under civilised conditions only with the utmost moderation. I used to tire very quickly of tinned foods and preferred to live on the native fare and whatever the country had to offer. In the lowlands I preferred milk, eggs and rice, in Tibet I always took adequate supplies of flour and rice with me and had freshly-baked bread every morning. My rifleman kept the caravan supplied with game: antelopes, gazelle and birds, especially wild geese, wild ducks and partridge. But my staple diet in Tibet was always the thick yellow sour milk, and also the delicious sweet milk of the yak cows." Hitler: "Yes, yogurt and sour milk is the best of all foods, healthy and good to eat. Anyone who has made yogurt his staple diet for twenty years will be as strong as a bear and live longer than other people." '

Hitler the vegetarian asked Hedin about the organisation of his expeditions and his map-making but 'returned once more to the subject of diet, which evidently interested him particularly. He asked, "But a people that lives at such a terrific height and in such a hard, cold climate must surely eat a great deal of meat and fat?"

' "Yes, the rich nomads who own large flocks of sheep eat a great deal of meat: but they mix their diet with milk in various forms, and grain which they get from the Himalayan people in exchange for salt. In Central Tibet there are small tribes of huntsmen who hunt wild yak and trap antelopes. They live almost exclusively on meat. Even the horses are fed meat in districts where there is no grazing for them."

' "Are these tribes not liable to certain diseases brought on by their constant meat diet?"

' "No, these huntsmen are strong and hardy and can stand up with ease to both the cold and the snowstorms. Of course I too ate meat in Tibet, though I preferred sour yak's milk and bread. Here in Berlin I have a special predilection for *die fleischlosen Tage* [meatless days]."

'He laughed at this remark. But by now I was beginning to fear that the reason he was digging his teeth so firmly into the Tibetan diet was to keep me off the subject of Finland.'[22]

Hedin's open friendship with Nazi leaders, maintained despite his part-Jewish ancestry,[23] and his anti-British outbursts which dated back half a century, meant that he was stripped of the honours that had been piled upon him for his pioneering survey and map-making work: he lost a knighthood, honorary doctorates from Oxford and Cambridge universities and two gold medals awarded by the Royal Geographical Society in London. He died in 1952. His maps and surveys were still valued, for he had filled in much of the blank areas of Central Asia and formed a solid scientific contribution to the understanding of the lands and cultures crossed by the Silk Roads.

- 12 -

Trophies and tiger entrails: hunting and theorising on the Silk Road

THE SCIENTIFIC ACHIEVEMENTS of expeditions like those of Przhevalsky and Hedin did not inform their pronouncements on the nature of the people who inhabited the areas they mapped. Though Przhevalsky wrote longingly of the wide open spaces where he found 'an exceptional bliss' and a sense of freedom,[1] he wrote scathingly of the people he saw. 'The Chinaman here is a Jew plus a Muscovite pickpocket, both squared,' he wrote, and boasted how rifle-fire 'has a spell-binding effect on the half-savage natives'.[2] Ralph Cobbold, 'late 60th Rifles', who wrote *Innermost Asia: travel and sport in the Pamirs*, described the Kashgarians in 1900 in terms of the local weather: 'From May till September it is intensely hot, while in the winter months the temperature sinks to zero, these extremes being due to the country's position in the midst of a great continent, and far removed from the tempering influence of the sea. Curiously enough the people do not share these extremes in their characteristics. They are by nature listless, indifferent and imperturbable; they can satisfy their wants too easily for it to be worth their while to labour. All that is necessary is to divert the water from one of the channels so as to cause it to flow over a tract of the barren sand, and fruitfulness will come. The mountain ranges shield Kashgar from the keen competition of outside traders, and the great plain is inhabited by races as apathetic as themselves. And so the Kashgarians continue to enjoy a careless existence, indifferent to passing events, and watching revolutions as idle spectators of what is going on in their midst.'[3]

The nature of politics in Central Asia as the Qing empire began to crumble and a variety of local leaders fought for supremacy was enough to confuse anyone into indifference, but, as Cobbold noted, the Russian consul took a forthright approach to the Chinese, then in nominal control of the area. 'Of the Chinese Petrovsky has the greatest contempt. He characterises them as being effete and corrupt, and claims that it is impossible to permit such a nation to continue as a ruling power much longer; he instanced the fact that the Taotai [Chinese Circuit Intendant] was entirely in his hands, and had to do exactly as he wished him. In the event of the mandarin proving recalcitrant, he had it in his power to make it unpleasant for him. He told me that on one occasion the Taotai had remained obdurate on a small point

180

which it was deemed essential he should abandon; and as the China-man refused to listen to reason, he had arranged with another mandarin, who was a mutual friend, to bring the great man to take a Russian vapour bath at the Consulate. While enjoying his ablutions, he was to be seized and artistically whipped by four stalwart Cossacks. "Fortunately," added the consul-general, "the Taotai became convinced by the force of the argument and gave way, so that extreme measures became on this occasion unnecessary." '4

Not long after Cobbold's book appeared, Ellsworth Huntington, an American geographer who had met Aurel Stein in Peshawar and who had been surveying in the desert beyond Kashgar as Stein set off on his second expedition, published the results of his surveys and the theory of history that had evolved from them in *The Pulse of Asia: a journey in Central Asia illustrating the geographic basis of history*.

Huntington had joined Raphael Pumpelly's expedition to Russian Turkestan in 1903–4 and travelled with Robert Barrett on an expedition to Chinese Turkestan in 1905. On that second expedition he described the hardships of crossing the Karakorum pass: 'In twenty-one miles I counted four hundred and seventy-four dead horses, not to mention numerous dismembered skeletons, thirty-two bales of merchandise and one human corpse. His fellows had no time or strength to bury him: they simply wound him in cloth and laid him on the ground with his face toward Mecca.'

Next Huntington examined the ruins of the old oasis towns along the southern Silk Road, journeying to what he called, ignoring both Przhevalsky and Hedin, 'the unexplored desert of Lop'. He nearly lost his camel as they rode across a salt plain which, 'as we progressed, assumed a fresher, white appearance and began to look slightly damp. I was riding the biggest of the camels, whose load of wood and ice had now been partly used. Suddenly I found myself turning a somersault backwards off the animal. His hind legs had broken through the saline crust and had plunged a yard deep into soft, oozy muck. As he struggled ponderously to extricate himself, his front legs also sank in; and oily water came bubbling up in muddy pools about the prostrate creature's belly. Two other camels fell into the mire at the same time. In the haste in which we began to tear off their loads I forgot to investigate whether my neck was broken. Relieved of their loads, the two smaller camels extricated themselves. My big, heavy animal, however, was so completely mired that we had to put ropes around his legs and pull his feet out onto felts which we had spread on the soft mud to keep him from sinking in again. It was a grim jest on the part of nature to lead us into an unfrozen watery salt-bog in zero weather, in a region so cold and dry that we were carrying ten or twelve days' supplies of ice for drinking water.'5

*Hunting scene from a
Persian manuscript,
1560*

Where the ground was harder, Huntington's camels' feet suffered.
'The smallest, a truly pretty little animal, had lately developed huge
and evidently painful blisters on its soft, padded feet. To prevent its
becoming useless, the men cut off the upper portion of a pair of high,
native boots, such as we all wore, and cleverly converted the lower
part into camel shoes. The poor animal screamed like an angry, fright-
ened child when the men tied its legs together and rolled it over on its
side; but it seemed decidedly grateful when, on rising, it found that its

feet were no longer so painful. We were nearly overcome with laugh-ter, for the little camel shook its ungainly feet as a cat does hers when a small boy ties papers to them; and then walked off with its hind legs a yard apart.'[6] Boots must have been more comfortable than leather sewn directly on to their pads, which other camels had to suffer. The softness of camels' feet and their proneness to suppurating saddle sores if badly loaded made them sometimes less than practical.

Despite the massive areas of salt-flat, rivers fed by melting snow still allowed the construction of tiny hamlets of mud and reed houses and attempts at settled agriculture at Tikkenlik and fishing in what remained of Lop Nor. The main impression was of the shrinking of what had once been a vast inland sea. 'Plants show signs of drying up: the tamarisks usually stand on mounds; the poplars are dead or dying except in the moistest places; and beds of dead reeds cover scores of square miles . . . Thirteen of the seventeen rivers have on their lower courses the ruins of towns dating from the Buddhist era, a thousand or more years ago. In almost every case the ancient towns were larger than their successors, this being notably true of Niya . . . Endere, Cherchen . . . and Miran. The older towns are situated so far out in the desert, or upon rivers so small and saline, that it would be impos-sible to locate towns of equal size in the same places . . .'[7] It was changes in the course of the Tarim river that seem to have affected the size of the lake which once supported large communities based upon farming, hunting and fishing, such as that at Loulan, abandoned some-time after AD 300.

Huntington concluded that the climate of Central Asia 'has been subject to notable changes' and developed the theory that 'not only the habits, but to a large extent the character, of the people of Central Asia appear to have been moulded by physiographic environment.' This led him to the view that 'changes in climate must have caused corresponding changes, not only in the distribution of man, but in his occupation, habits, and even character.' This was his 'Geographic Basis of History' with its rather dangerous sweeping statements. 'We have seen that the plateaus and deserts of Central Asia entail upon the Khirghiz the nomadic life, and this accentuates certain characteristics, such as hardihood, hospitality, laziness, morality and family affection. The oases of the basin floors, on the other hand, cause the Chantos [a term applied to cover the inhabitants of the western oases such as Yarkand and Kashgar] to practise intensive agriculture; and the shel-tered, easy life, thus made possible, seems to induce weakness of will, cowardice, immorality, and the weakening of those ties between par-ents and children which lead to careful training of the growing generation.'[8]

Plunging deeper into the problem, Huntington asked, 'Why has

Persia, which once shared many of the virtues of ancient Rome, now become one of the most degenerate of nations?' He described Persians as liars, though 'one of the ancient Greek historians declared that Persians were remarkable for telling the truth. The habit of telling the truth can be acquired only by long practice, by a continual exercise of the will in opposition to suggestions of fear, greed or the other feelings. So, after all, perhaps it is a "matter of climate". And the obvious corollary is that during the last two thousand years a change in the climate of Persia may have contributed materially to a change in the character of the people.'[9]

Huntington's 'scientific evidence' that climate change affected human beings came from an American study 'of the influence of various meteorological conditions upon the conduct of school-children, upon the occurrence of crime and upon mistakes made by bank clerks'. Clear, cool weather, according to the survey, has a beneficial effect, dampness slows people down, and dry weather 'stimulates the vital processes', but 'when the dryness becomes extreme, people's nervous equilibrium is upset. The power to control emotional impulses of all kinds seems to be weakened' so 'we should expect to find that people in extremely hot, dry countries like Persia and Chinese Turkestan, where parching winds abound, are nervous, emotional and uncontrolled. As a matter of fact they are not so nervous as might be expected; but they are certainly highly emotional and very lacking in self-control.'[10]

On less dangerous ground, Huntington was a sensitive observer of natural features, defending the beauty of the desert on a calm September day and listing the wild flowers he found in the Tian Shan. But everything he saw was used for his thesis: 'It may be worthwhile to print here a list of the plants . . . which grow wild among the lower slopes of the mountains northeast of the Lop basin, but are cultivated in Europe and America. They comprise the apple, apricot, plum and olive (not the commercial species); the asparagus, onion and rhubarb; the candytuft, chrysanthemum, crocus, heliotrope, peony, phlox and tulip; the large blue and purple varieties of columbine; the pansy and lady's delight, both purple and yellow; and the red, white and yellow varieties of the poppy and the rose . . . The list is of interest in view of the much controverted theory that Central Asia was the original home of the chief races in Europe. So far as it goes, it supports the theory; for it suggests that the original migrants from Central Asia carried with them plants which there grow wild and which have since been cultivated in the new lands where the wanderers finally settled . . .'[11]

Plant-hunters did make some discoveries on the Silk Roads, as Przhevalsky's finds demonstrate, and the Himalayan foothills and areas adjacent to the Chinese province of Yunnan were the richest

A Mongolian with the horned skull of an
argali *sheep*

source of new species, but one of the great attractions of the mountains along and through which the Silk Roads ran was the game, the Pamirs pullulating with 'markhor, ibex, oorial and red bear'. At Gilgit, 'the furthest point of the Indian Empire where regular troops were stationed . . . in winter they have the finest stalking in the world, whilst woodcock and duck keep them in practice with the shot-gun' and, when not shooting and stalking, 'there is gold, football with the natives, lawn tennis . . .'

In his memoir of shooting, Ralph Cobbold noted that 'the feature mainly responsible which has of late years been manifested in the Pamir region is the variety of wild animals which everywhere abound, most notable among which is the *Ovis poli*, a wild sheep of great size, which is found in most parts of the Pamir region. The peculiarity of these beasts is their horns, which at times attain extraordinary dimensions, one head now in the possession of Lord Roberts has horns measuring 75 inches from base to tip, with a base circumference of 16 inches, though this is an unusual specimen.'[12] Named after Marco Polo, the sheep photographed by Cobbold (after he had shot them) have extraordinary horns that curl down over the ears and then, in older specimens, continue to curl outwards in an S-shape.

They had also attracted the notice of the impresario Carl Hagenbeck, who had financed the expedition in the 1880s to collect a herd of Przhevalsky's Horse for his circus. A couple of years later he arranged an expedition to collect *Ovis poli*. He spent £5,000 on the expedition and sixty animals were caught but every single one died of diarrhoea on the way to Europe, so it was not only guns that they had to fear.[13]

Ralph Cobbold's first sighting of *Ovis poli* came after a long stalk 'over loose ground, involving many a slip, and the constant sound of rolling stones'. The noise appeared to have alerted his prey but suddenly, 'Mirza Bey seized my arm and exclaimed in Turki, "Look, Sahib, there they are." And sure enough, there they were, their spreading horns being all that was visible over some rocks, behind which they were resting, some 400 yards below us . . . the descent was steep and noisy, and I feared every moment that the sound of the slithering stones we dislodged would alarm our game. Half-way down, we halted and took off our boots, so as to go more quietly, and then I noticed that the wind which had been blowing downhill had suddenly shifted and was now coming up the nullah, and I realised that the *poli* would be sure to get wind of the Kirghiz, whom we had left in charge of our things below. The notion had barely flashed through my mind when my anticipation was realised, for I saw the two great sheep coming up the nullah at a lumbering gallop straight towards us: they were evidently so intent on getting away from the man behind that they neglected their usual caution as to what might be in front. Seeing that they must pass within fifty yards of where we stood, I sat down and covered the whitest of the two, which I knew should be the largest; on they came pell-mell until almost abreast of us they halted out of breath. My hands were quivering with excitement as I pulled, half expecting to miss from sheer eagerness, but the ram fell dead and the second beast, pulling himself up, suddenly turned and made off across the ravine. Another shot, this time a miss, but the 200-yard sight was instantly slid up, and a third shot claimed him, thus justifying the reputation of my little Mannlicher, which is in every respect a perfect weapon. My shikari's delight forthwith got the better of him; he became delirious with joy at the sight of so much good meat in front of him, and he seized my hands and kissed them and my feet . . . Between us we cut off their heads and quartered the carcases . . . I was gratified to find they were even finer specimens than I had supposed.

[The trophy horns of] the larger one measured 64 inches and the smaller 56 inches in length.'¹⁴

'After a week's shooting the game began to get scarce,' reported Cobbold who had cut a swathe through 'ibex, the common fox, the wolf, brown bear, the golden marmot, the Tibetan hare, the ibis, gull, owl, kite and many birds of the plover and lark tribe'. In his view, 'The Pamirs may be regarded as a species of sportsman's paradise, and few travellers who have visited the region have failed to return with a collection of trophies.'¹⁵

When he met the Taotai of Kashgar, Cobbold's hunting exploits were of interest for the medicinal and culinary potential of various animal parts. The Taotai 'begged me to bring on my return journey some of the entrails of a tiger, to be used for medicinal purposes, notably to wind round pregnant women to assist them in childbirth, and some bear's feet, which he considered the choicest of all table delicacies.' Cobbold had intended to proceed from Kashgar to the Tian Shan range on the northern Silk Road because 'M. Gourdet informed me that he had shot many *Ovis poli* or *Ovis karelini*, as they are called in the Tianshan, where he told me they are extremely numerous; their horns, although more massive, are not so long as those found in the Pamirs. Ibex are also met with in most of the steeper nullahs. Besides these, two kinds of bears are to be met with. One, a large brown brute peculiar to those mountains, is distinguishable by the long white claws on its forefeet, a peculiarity which induced Severtseff to name it *Ursus leuconyx*. Snow leopards are also plentiful. All these animals may be shot within a few days of Vierny, which is an excellent starting point for the sportsman, being within a few days' drive of Tashkent, a terminus of the Trans-Asiatic Railway. I was very anxious to get a shot at a Tianshan wapiti . . .'¹⁶ but, fortunately for the wapiti and other wildlife, changes of regime in Russian Turkestan and the consequent difficulties of obtaining passports forced him back to the Pamirs, where he took a photograph which he captioned '*Ovis poli* alive – never before photographed' (presumably because most people were too busy taking a pot-shot). Hobbling onwards because 'the terrible road along the Bartang valley had worn the soles of my boots until the bare skin of my feet became exposed', Cobbold made his way back to India.

By the early 1930s, when R. C. F. Schomberg explored the Karakorams, *Ovis poli* had become rare: 'These fine sheep are nearly extinct in the Chinese Pamirs owing to relentless slaughter.' The only ones he saw were dead: 'There were some horns of *Ovis poli* in one or two places on both sides of the pass. The Tajiks declared that those animals had died of disease but it was an evident lie, as there were no bones. In the winter, these sheep are driven by snow and cold into the lower valleys and are killed by the nomads' – who did not value the trophy horns.[17]

Schomberg was interested in the caravan trails through the mountains, which led down to 'the different marts of the country. Caravans to Khotan diverge to the East, those to Yarkand and Kashgar to the West . . . All routes north of the Karakorum keep together as far as Aktagh, at the head of the Yarkand River. Here the Khotan route turns away East to the Suget Pass and the caravans for Kashgar and Yarkand follow the Yarkand River for some way . . . In former times, however . . . the caravans to and from Central Asia were by no means restricted to the Karakorum Pass. I believe that so long as was possible, the present route was avoided. It has always been a merciless track, going for days down stony nullahs devoid of fuel and grass, with little or no shelter, and without help in case of catastrophe. From what I saw of the Mustagh valley, there was certainly a frequented route . . . For the carefully made and well-graded road which we found was intended for pack animals.'[18]

Schomberg's aim in his two journeys to the Karakoram was to explore the three sources of the Yarkand river, but he encountered a difficulty in describing the area, which was 'the lack of names for the mountains . . . In the *Geographical Journal* . . . that distinguished mountaineer, Dr T. G. Longstaff, emphasises the prejudice of the Royal Geographical Society against giving personal names to peaks. It would be impertinent of me to criticise the merits of the attitude. I may be permitted to point out, however, that unless something is done, foreign travellers will give names to these unnamed peaks and these will be incorporated into foreign maps, finally finding a place in our own. Unless therefore steps are taken, and that quickly, travellers in the mapped but unnamed valleys of the British Empire will find themselves crossing the Hitler Pass, descending the Goering Glacier, and admiring Mount Mussolini – and quite rightly too . . . To an amateur and outsider like myself, it is difficult to understand why it is improper to give the names of famous travellers like Younghusband, Stein or Mason to the scenes of their discoveries.'[19]

The old Great Game was over by then but Schomberg returned again to his theme of the dangers of creeping geographical nazification due to the lack of imagination at the control centres. 'Both the Survey of India and the Royal Geographical Society taboo giving names to unknown peaks, and advocate labelling snow mountains by a letter and a number, as cattle are marked at a show or objects in a cloakroom. It is often the privilege of science to be dreary, insipid and confusing, but why burden the memory of the public and disfigure their atlases with a string of meaningless letters and numbers? The mere amateur fails to understand why it is improper to commemorate

great alpinists or explorers to unnamed mountains. Pope Pius XI, Mr Douglas Freshfield, Lord Conway, Sir Aurel Stein, and Mr Arthur Hinks, the genial Secretary of the Royal Geographical Society, might well be commemorated. Why should Mount Smith be wrong and K999 right?'[20]

The problem of nomenclature remains, with a mixture of names in the region. Everest was named after the second Superintendent of the Great Trigonometrical Survey in Calcutta, Sir George Everest (1790–1866) although it is increasingly referred to by a version of the Tibetan name, Chumolongma; there is Kachenjunga, and K2 appears to have escaped unscathed, which would have annoyed Schomberg.

That Schomberg found the western end of the Silk Road denuded of animal life owed far more to the efforts of the many adventurous sportsmen armed with enormously efficient guns and in search of trophies than to the few local travellers looking for food. In fact, one earlier traveller managed to miss one of the Silk Road's greatest prizes through his passion for shooting. Baron Carl Gustav Mannerheim (1867–1951) was a Finn who, between 1906 and 1908, carried out a Central Asian expedition under the auspices of the Russian General Staff and the Finno-Ugrian Society and the Antell Fund. Where the boundaries between fact-finding and collecting were sometimes rather

Wild flowers growing in the Tian Shan mountains, Xinjiang province

189

hazy, in Mannerheim's case he had two distinct tasks. For the Russians he was to undertake a military intelligence-gathering mission, whilst for the Finnish learned society he was to 'copy inscriptions, purchase ancient manuscripts, archaeological and ethnographical artefacts, make anthropometric measurements, photograph racial types and collect ethnographical and linguistic material about the little-known peoples of North China'.[21] Setting off from Russian Turkestan, he traversed Xinjiang, taking the northern Silk Road, and then went down the Gansu corridor into Shanxi and Shaanxi provinces of northwest China. He purchased coins and artefacts in Khotan, photographed rock inscriptions and drawings in Torgut and Kirghiz areas, but, though he visited sites such as Yarkhoto, Idiqut Shakri and Chiktym, he was appalled at the archaeological havoc already wrought and refrained from adding to it. He purchased quite a number of documents in Uighur, Chinese and Middle Persian, probably in the Turfan area. According to his diary entry for 20 November 1907, 'I had intended to visit a miao [temple] called Qianfodong [the Caves of the Thousand Buddhas near Dunhuang], lying in the mountains to the S . . . However, the pheasants and djeirans [gazelle] were too tempting. After losing much time in shooting, we reached the mouth of the gorge but the sun was already low so we had no alternative than to drop all idea of the "thousand gods" and try to find our way back to the serai before nightfall.'

He was probably unaware that, less than six months earlier, Aurel Stein had acquired twenty-nine cases full of priceless silk banner paintings, early printed documents and manuscripts from the Caves of the Thousand Buddhas. As his biographer concluded sadly, 'Thus a great scientific treasure was exchanged for roast pheasant and gazelle.'[22]

Despite this early failure, Mannerheim went on to be Commander-in-Chief of the Finnish army and served as president from 1944 to 1946.

- 13 -

Securing specimens: Aurel Stein

BARON MANNERHEIM had been entrusted with military investigation, ethnographic and anthropological research and with the accumulation of documents and artefacts known to be found in the ancient deserted oasis towns of the old Silk Roads. As he neared Dunhuang and the Caves of the Thousand Buddhas in late 1907, Sir Aurel Stein's twenty-nine cases, packed with manuscripts and paintings from the Caves, were making their slow way westwards from Dunhuang to Kashgar, where Consul George Macartney and his staff would ensure their safe despatch to India and then on to London and the basement of the British Museum. Mannerheim missed the opportunity to collect from amongst the many thousands of early manuscripts that Stein had left behind in the sealed-up temple library concealed amongst the abandoned shrines.

Stein made perhaps the greatest of the archaeological finds of the Silk Road sites when he gained entrance to the Caves of the Thousand Buddhas. He had little idea of what he would find but rumours of the treasures to be had in the deserts had long been circulating amongst the explorers of the Silk Roads.

In 1876, Przhevalsky found the ruins of sand-buried sites in the Lop Nor on his travels, and in 1879, a Russian botanist called Albert Regel found the ruins of the ancient Uighur city of Kharakhoja/Gaochang Qoco near Turfan and reported that there were Buddhist figures there. A Hungarian geological expedition saw the exterior of the painted caves at the oasis near Dunhuang and all such sightings added to the stories of buried empires, buried cities and, naturally, buried treasure in the sands of Central Asia. The soldier and explorer Sir Francis Younghusband (who had made his own expedition to the Pamirs in 1887) encapsulated these rumours when he advised a young Pathan on how to make money and get to England: 'I told him that if he would search about among the old ruined cities of this country and those buried by the sand, he might find old ornaments and books for which large sums of money would be given him in England.'[1]

Considerable encouragement to such book-collectors was given from India quite early on. For many of those who went out to serve in the government of India, their chief preoccupation was to avoid any real encounter with Asian culture, but rather to preserve the British way of life complete with marmalade and acceptable substitutes for porridge, under difficult and overheated circumstances. But for some,

India was a revelation and understanding the history and culture of the place became a passion. From the late eighteenth century onwards, philology, epigraphy and palaeography were popular pursuits for gentlemen. The pursuit of rare philological treasures could involve danger. As the Rosetta Stone, captured from Napoleon in Egypt in 1799, was being deciphered in London, a British diplomat, Sir Henry Rawlinson, was dangling from ropes on a 1,200-metre cliff (approximately 4,000 feet) at Behistun, copying down the cuneiform inscription of Darius (in Old Persian, Elamite and Babylonian) which had been carved into the cliff 150 metres (approximately 500 feet) above the ground.

India provided a wealth of opportunities to explore unfamiliar languages and scripts. James Prinsep, Assistant Assay Master in the Calcutta Mint, worked for five years to decipher the Brahmi and Kharosthi scripts and Sir William Jones (1746–94), a judge on the Calcutta Circuit and founder of the Asiatic Society of Bengal, 'the first Englishman to know Sanskrit', said of that language that it was 'more perfect than the Greek, more copious than the Latin, and more exquisitely refined than either'. The entry in Buckland's *Dictionary of Indian Biography* (1906) noted the deleterious effects of these part-time intellectual exertions over and above the call of duty: Sir William 'overtaxed himself', and Prinsep died in 1840, 'from softening of the brain caused by overwork'.

It was not only intellectual curiosity that stimulated the search for ancient manuscripts in Central Asia, beyond the confines of British India. Such had been the movement of peoples and the rise and fall of states from the Kushans in the Pamirs to Loulan in the Lop lake, that languages, and above all scripts, were sometimes used from one end of the Silk Road to the other. Kharosthi script was used in Afghanistan and Loulan, Persian was used to write Hebrew, and Brahmi was used widely by Buddhist scribes. Thus the scripts used in documents found in Central Asia were closely related to Indian culture, and Buddhism, which spread from its Indian homeland, was a linking factor in the content of many manuscripts.

What made Central Asia so extra interesting was the survival of ancient documents: whether written on palm-leaves, wood or, later, paper, documents abandoned in long-forgotten settlements survived infinitely better in the dry desert lands than in India, subject annually to monsoon humidity. Dr Augustus Frederic Rudolf Hoernle (1841–1918), Secretary to the Asiatic Society of Bengal, combined Great Game politics with 'epigraphical exploration' in a report on his 'Collection of Antiquities from Central Asia'. 'It was the discovery of the Bower and Weber manuscripts that first drew my attention to Eastern Turkestan as a promising field for epigraphical exploration. My hopes regarding the archaeological possibilities of that country were confirmed by what I heard about the success of the Russians, whose Political Agents were said to actively collect manuscripts and other antiquities for St Petersburg. Accordingly on the 1st June, 1893, I wrote to . . . the Home Secretary of the Government of India, suggesting that the Government might send instructions to their Political Agents in different parts of Central Asia, to make enquiries and secure such specimens as they may be able to obtain.'[2]

Hoernle's 'collection' had been developed through gifts from explorers who found antiquities and documents for sale in the markets of Silk Road towns like Yarkand and Kashgar. His desire to develop and expand the collection was to provide an impetus to the expeditions of one of the greatest explorer-archaeologists and collectors of Silk Road antiquities, Sir Marc Aurel Stein.

Stein was born in Hungary in 1862, the youngest child (after a gap of nineteen years) of a close Jewish family but baptised a Christian. His father's business had collapsed but the family was supported by Uncle Ignaz and by Ernst, Aurel's brother, who ensured that his much younger sibling had a sound education. He studied Sanskrit and philology at the University of Vienna, and spent a term in Leipzig attending classes given by Georg Buhler (1837–98), who had taught oriental languages in the University of Bombay and made a survey of Sanskrit manuscripts in private collections for the Indian government. Stein then went to Tübingen to study with Rudolf von Roth, a prominent Sanskrit specialist and an authority on the religions of the east. After being awarded his doctorate in 1883, Stein went to England where he used the collections of oriental books and coins in the Ashmolean Museum, Bodleian Library, India Office Library and British Museum and spent some time at a mysterious Oriental College in Woking run by another native of Budapest, William Gottfried Leitner. It was said that when in the college, the students were not allowed to speak anything except Sanskrit. Recalled to Hungary for military service, Stein learnt surveying and map-making at the Ludovica Academy. His academic interests and map-making skills were to make his career and reputation but his first job was administrative, as Registrar of Punjab University and Principal of Oriental College in Lahore.

In his first long vacation in 1888, Stein set out to follow in the footsteps of Georg Buhler by searching for a manuscript of the *Rajatarangini* (*Chronicle of the Kings of Kashmir*) by the twelfth-century writer Kalhana. His careful arrangements for this first small collecting trip were to characterise his later expeditions: he obtained letters of recommendation from the highest authorities, in this case the Secretary of State for the Punjab, his Vice-Chancellor and the British Resident in Kashmir. He did not succeed in seeing his manuscript on his first visit to Kashmir but his characteristic persistence and diplomatic skill triumphed in the end and he spent most of his spare time over the next ten years working on a translation of the chronicle.3 The translation was published in 1900, but he never lost interest in the text and its contents and was preparing a new edition at the time of his death in 1943.

In Lahore, Stein met Rudyard Kipling's father, John Lockwood Kipling, who was curator of the Central Museum where the collection of Graeco-Buddhist art from Gandhara struck Stein most forcibly. Rudyard Kipling described his father's museum: 'In the entrance hall stood the larger figures of the Greco-Buddhist sculptures done, savants know how long since, by forgotten workmen whose hands were feeling, and not unskilfully, for the mysteriously transmitted Grecian touch. There were hundreds of pieces, friezes of figures in relief, fragments of statues and slabs crowded with figures that had encrusted the brick walls of Buddhist stupas and viharas of the North Country and now, dug up and labelled, made the pride of the Museum.'4 Lockwood Kipling's main job was as Principal of the Mayo School of Art and in 1890 he introduced Stein to his new vice-principal, Fred Andrews, who was to become not only one of Stein's closest friends, but a vital part of the small team that Stein eventually built up to work on his discoveries. Andrews accompanied Stein on a trip to record a Jain temple in Murti, which Stein had identified as one described by the great seventh-century Chinese Buddhist pilgrim Xuanzang in his *Xiyuji* (*Record of the Western Regions*). Andrews taught Stein how to take photographs on site, another important element in Stein's expeditionary skills.

Stein eventually moved into the Andrews family house in Lahore (sharing accommodation was common practice amongst expatriates in the East although it was more common to find bachelors 'messing' together) where they were joined in their 'chummery' in 1897 by another bachelor, Percy Allen (Professor of History, Government College, Lahore) who also became a lifelong friend of Stein's. Another couple who eventually moved into Mayo House were the Arnolds: Thomas (a lecturer in philosophy at the Anglo-Oriental College) and May, who were also to become essential supports to Stein. And in 1895 Stein camped for the summer on an alpine meadow at Mohand Marg in Kashmir. For the rest of his life he remained in close contact with the Andrewses, Arnolds and Allens and spent much of his spare time in Kashmir, especially at Mohand Marg.

Stein's first expedition to Central Asia (1900–1) was made to try to map some of the ancient sites along the western end of the southern Silk Road from which manuscripts were beginning to make their way to India, purchased in the bazaars of Khotan and Kashgar by British diplomats for their philological compatriots back in India who were hungry for texts. Hoernle's appeal to the government to instruct its agents to collect ancient texts had produced a flow of manuscripts, many of which arrived courtesy of a Khotanese treasure-seeker called Islam Akhun. Hoernle was also quick to support Stein (though his determination that 'the idea of that expedition was first conceived by myself'5 was irritating) and Stein himself obtained official support from none other than the viceroy, Lord Curzon, who was preoccupied by Russian influence in the area.

Fred Andrews, who was in England at the time, arranged for samples of tinned food to be sent out and chased up a medical chest from Burroughs Wellcome whilst Thomas Arnold was entrusted with the task of checking the final proofs of the translation of the *Rajatarangini* during Stein's absence. Stein took saddlery, a green Willesden canvas bath, a wool-lined tent with rot-proof ground-sheet, meat lozenges, chocolate, jam, camel blankets, books (including Curzon's *The Pamirs and the Source of the Oxus*), two cooks, a surveyor and a small black and white terrier called Dash.6

The caravan of donkeys and horses crossed the Pamirs and made its way to Kashgar. Stein stayed with the Macartneys at Chini Bagh where, surrounded by 'all the comforts of an English home', he developed the photographs he had taken en route, made final corrections to his proofs, which had been sent by post, and supervised the preparations which included hiring twelve horses, eight camels and four more men.

Stein made forays out into the desert, mapping and surveying, connecting Khotan with the Great Trigonometrical Survey in Calcutta, and hired thirty extra men and a dozen donkeys for his first major excavation at Dandan-Uiliq, out in the Taklamakan desert, northeast of Khotan. The site had been visited by Sven Hedin five years earlier; now Stein spent two weeks collecting fragments of frescoes, stucco figures, *pothi* manuscripts in Brahmi script, paintings on wood depicting the rat king who had saved Khotan from the Huns by chewing through their bridles, and documents in Chinese (later dated to 782). He excavated, in all, fourteen buildings, collapsed and abandoned in the sand.

At Niya, further to the east, a similarly abandoned settlement yielded wooden tablets with Kharosthi inscriptions. These were, in effect, letters, matched pieces of wood, with the inscriptions on the inside, tied together and sealed with mud seals, some stamped with classical heads, one with a fine Pallas Athene figure. One bore two seals, one in Chinese, from the political officer in distant Lop, the other a Western classical head. There were carved wooden fragments of furniture, an ancient mousetrap and, buried under an extremely old rubbish dump which still smelled ('I had to inhale its odours, still pungent after so many centuries, and to swallow in liberal doses antique

microbes luckily now dead'), more tablets in Prakrit, written in Kharosthi script. Work was not Stein's only preoccupation at Niya: his interpreter and the camel man fought until he separated them with his walking stick. The interpreter then tried to strangle himself and Stein had to keep an eye on all of them.

Further east, along the southern Silk Road in Endere, Stein excavated a ruined temple which revealed very early Tibetan Buddhist texts written on paper, and Tibetan graffiti, confirming the invasion of the eighth century which drove the Chinese from the area. Though he found nothing of interest at Karadong, a runner, sent by Macartney from Kashgar, informed him of the death of Queen Victoria.

His excavations had been carried out in winter, in conditions of the utmost cold. He heated his tent with a Stormont-Murphy Arctic Stove but still found his moustache frozen in the mornings until he resorted to wrapping himself in a fur-lined coat and breathing through the sleeve. Dash slept in his bed, wearing a Kashmiri coat of his own. Despite the cold (Hedin had found that the ink froze in his pen), Stein sat up every night making maps, recording all his finds in minute detail, writing a detailed diary and very long letters to his friends. The volumes of Stein's correspondence, his many diaries and his hundreds of volumes of photographs demonstrate his extraordinary attention to detail and his determination that his finds should be known in all their aspects, from photographs in situ, through careful catalogue entries and publication in his massive expedition reports. His devotion to his circle of friends was constant. He barely saw his family after his move to India but the Andrewses, Allens and Arnolds formed a 'magic circle' for him.

As the desert heated up in April and sandstorms blew daily, Stein undertook his last task, a visit to Islam Akhun in Khotan. In all his excavations in the desert he had found nothing remotely resembling the manuscripts and woodblocks that had reached Hoernle via Islam Akhun, who claimed to have found them in desert sites. Hoernle had announced in 1899 that he was on the track of a hitherto unknown script found in these documents, but Stein was already beginning to doubt it. In Khotan, Islam Akhun was summoned from a nearby village where he was practising as a medicine man, armed with 'some pages from a French novel and fragments of a Persian text' (whether these were to be taken internally or consulted as oracles was unclear).7 Though he had started off with the intention of helping European philologists by supplying home-made manuscripts, loosely based on the Brahmi script that he had seen on real old manuscripts, such had been the demand that mass-production appeared the only answer. Islam Akhun described his manuscript factory, where sheets of local paper were dyed yellow or brown, block-printed and smoked over fires until they looked old enough. Some were bound together with fragments of bronze, stabbed through and pinned by circular, coin-like fragments.

Stein informed Hoernle of Islam Akhun's activities in July 1901 at Hoernle's house in Oxford. Hoping that the passage of time might erase the memory of his 'newly discovered' language and script in Islam Akhun's earlier forgeries, Hoernle published the second part of his 'Collection of Antiquities from Central Asia' without referring to his earlier insistence on the genuineness of these manuscripts in unknown script, merely noting, 'Dr Stein has obtained definite proof that all "blockprints" and all the manuscripts in "unknown characters" procured from Khotan since 1895 are modern fabrications of Islam Akhun and a few others working with him.'8

When all his finds had been sent back to England from Kashgar, Stein was allotted a room in the British Museum where they could be recorded and photographed by Fred Andrews, who was employed as a temporary assistant by the British Museum for the purpose. Where photography was insufficient, as, for example, in recording the faint traces of impressions in the mud seals of the Kharosthi 'envelopes' from Niya, Fred Andrews made detailed drawings. His vignette of the

Pallas Athene figure seen in the mud-seal impression found at Niya was to be used on the title page of most of Stein's books. Stein published two books about this first expedition, a popular work, *Sand-buried Ruins of Khotan* (1903) and the full, detailed, archaeological report, *Ancient Khotan* (1908).

Stein's second expedition (1906–8) was perhaps his greatest triumph for it was then that he reached the cave temple complex of the Thousand Buddhas near Dunhuang and acquired tens of thousands of precious paper documents and paintings from Cave 17. He had not originally planned to visit Dunhuang: his plan was to revisit the sites along the southern Silk Road and then to excavate Loulan and Miran in the Lop desert, east of the Taklamakan, and cross the Taklamakan from north to south. On this second expedition, he was supported by the British Museum and the government of India and his finds were to be distributed between the two. The expedition was undertaken against the background of other, competitive expeditions led by the German linguist Albert von Le Coq, Paul Pelliot from France, and the American geographer Ellsworth Huntington, who was surveying in the deserts.

Stein travelled across Afghanistan, accompanied by an incompetent cook and a new fox terrier, Dash II, who replaced the first Dash who had pined and died in Kashmir whilst Stein was in England. Dash II would jump on to the pommel of Stein's saddle as they crossed the difficult mountain passes, and survived in the desert on cups of tea. Through the good offices of Macartney in Kashgar Stein also acquired a Chinese secretary, Jiang Siye, as he had felt the lack of a Chinese linguist on his first expedition when faced with Chinese documents. After excavating at Khadalik and Niya, he made his way to Charkhlik to prepare for the crossing of the Lop desert to Loulan. The crossing took seven days, with stops to sew ox-hides on to the camels' pads which had been damaged by the rough ground. Spending five days in Loulan, Stein picked up more wooden documents inscribed in Kharosthi script, demonstrating the connections between the Lop desert and far-off Bactria, Sogdian documents and Sven Hedin's tape-measure. His party then moved on to Miran. There he found evidence of the presence of Western Turks and Tibetans, as well as stunning Graeco-Buddhist heads and frescoes.

Moving on to Dunhuang, Stein's first interest was to investigate the ancient beacon towers, the *limes*, which marked the end of the Chinese presence in the desert two thousand years before. There he found the woodslips which documented the daily round of the military encampments of the Han dynasty.

Stein first set out to survey the Caves of the Thousand Buddhas on 16 March 1907. He found the caves deserted, for Wang Yuanlu, the

The limes, *the ancient beacon towers near Dunhuang, photographed by Stein*

Daoist priest and self-appointed guardian of the caves, was away on a begging tour of the nearby oases, trying to raise money to restore the Buddhist figures. Stein occupied himself by excavating the beacon towers until Wang returned, Stein going out to meet him on 21 May. By then the poplars and elms, fed by the small stream that ran along the bottom of the cliff, were in leaf, offering 'gratifying shade'. Stein moved his men into empty caves, reserving one as a dark-room, and pitched his tent in the shade of the trees. Stein was rather shocked by Wang Yuanlu's restoration work, 'the painful contrast these statues presented to the tasteful and remarkably well-preserved fresco decoration on the walls and ceiling', yet he admired 'the queer little figure by my side' for his personal frugality, 'spending next to nothing on his person or private interests'.[9]

Late one night, after long negotiations with Wang, Jiang crept into Stein's tent 'with a bundle of Chinese rolls', and a couple of days later Wang opened the cave for Stein. 'Heaped up in layers, but without any order, there appeared in the dim light of the priest's little lamp a solid mass of manuscript bundles rising to the height of nearly ten feet and

199

filling, as subsequent measurement showed, close on 500 cubic feet.'[10] As the little priest brought out bundles of manuscripts, there were Chinese canonical Buddhist texts and Tibetan texts, texts in Sanskrit, Brahmi, Sogdian, Uighur, Runic Turkic, block-prints and ex-votos in silk and brocade. There were all sorts of different formats: scrolls, booklets and prayer sheets. There were book-wrappers and 'cushion-covers'.

Stein photographed as many of the caves as he could reach and was struck by the Graeco-Buddhist influence but also by the Chinese landscape style found in some of the wall-paintings. As his camels grazed in the mountains, Stein worked, photographing and writing and sending Jiang off to reassure local officials that all was well. Then, with his refreshed camels and donkeys loaded with bundles of manuscripts and paintings, for which he had paid 500 rupees, he left Dunhuang.

He then set off, via Anxi, to survey the westernmost end of the Nan Shan, the mountain range south of Dunhuang, 'true alpine sensations! . . . Edelweiss, gentians and a host of alpine flowers which, alas! I had never learned to name, covered the slopes . . . Wild rhubarb, for which the Nan-shan was famous in Marco Polo's day, spread its huge fleshy leaves everywhere.'[11] Dash II had to be carried across icy mountain streams and he spent much time chasing marmots. They then moved towards Hami on the northern Silk Road, where they encountered Cecil Clementi, Assistant Colonial Secretary of Hong Kong: 'Of course it did not take us long to discover that we had common friends both in Oxford and India.'[12] Hearing that von Le Coq and Grünwedel had been excavating at Turfan, Stein made his way there, finding the Turfan bazaars full of 'Europe goods' and the houses decorated with kerosene lamps, chintz-covered ceilings, occasional glass windows, so that he felt himself 'on the very edge of what I call "Demi-Europe"'.[13]

At Mingoi (Kumtura) in the foothills of the Tian Shan range, west of Turfan, Stein found masses of stucco heads and figures, again showing the distinctive forms of the Graeco-Buddhist tradition. Kucha, however, had been effectively 'cleared with a thoroughness and method deserving of all praise by the French mission under Professor Pelliot'.[14] Thus, at the end of January 1908, Stein struck southwards across the 'Sea of Sand' that was the Taklamakan. The expedition carried water in the form of blocks of ice and directions were all compass-directed because there were no landmarks at all, save endless ridges of dunes. They passed clumps of dead trees marking the old bed of the dried-up Keriya river and, after sixteen anxious days watching the ice-block water supply dwindle and the pack animals grow weak, they finally found the Keriya river flowing under a sheet of ice. Stein celebrated by getting out his canvas bath so that he could 'indulge in

View of the ruined site of Ara-tam, the country seat of Wang of Hami, photographed by Stein, c.1908

a tub'.[15] They had arrived near Karadong, northwest of the familiar site of Niya on the southern Silk Road.

Closer to Khotan, he excavated frescoes at Domoko and then turned northwards again, towards Aksu and thence to Yarkand. In Yarkand he stayed with Mr and Mrs Raquette of the Swedish Medical Mission. It was Mr Raquette who diagnosed incurable glaucoma in Stein's photographic assistant Naik Ram Singh. He was sent back to India, his eyesight too far damaged for treatment and his mind, apparently, going. Stein fought hard to get him a pension from the government of India but 'he did not live long to benefit by it; for before the end of 1909 gentle death had relieved him from all further pain, physical and mental.' However, his wife and son continued to receive it as a compassionate allowance.

After despatching his archaeological treasures from Khotan, in fifty camel-loads, Stein undertook further surveying work in the Kunlun range which ran along beside the southern Silk Road and separated the Taklamakan and Tibet. There his pony, Badakhshi, which had carried him 'ever since I entered Turkestan', died after a morning's illness. This was unusual for Stein who rarely lost a man or a beast (in complete

contrast to Sven Hedin) and he regretted not being able to take the pony back to Kashmir so that he could taste 'what real grass and Alpine flowers were like'.[16]

This last part of the expedition became more dangerous owing to the extreme cold: donkeys had to be shot to put them out of their misery and Stein made the mistake of riding a yak down the rocky path beside a glacier. His boots were soaked by snow and when he hobbled to his tent he discovered that his feet were severely frost-bitten. The next morning (23 September), 'I found myself suffering from severe pains in my feet, and quite unable to move . . . My mountaineering manual, in which the subject [of frost-bite] was discussed at some length, plainly indicated that in such cases gangrene would set in, and recommended that "the aid of an experienced surgeon should be sought at once". The advice was excellent but scarcely reassuring.'[17] He found it too uncomfortable to ride on a yak and his Kirghiz bearers refused to help carry him on an improvised litter, so he had to be strapped to the padded saddle of a camel. Crossing the Kunlun range and the Karakorams in much pain, Stein finally reached Leh and the Revd S. Schmitt of the Moravian Mission, where he had all the toes of his right foot amputated.

Stein sailed back to England at the end of 1908, this time taking Dash II with him. The terrier endured his four months of quarantine and was 'joyfully restored to his master under Mr P. Allen's hospitable roof at Oxford'.[18] As with his first expedition, Stein was concerned that the materials should be recorded in his own publications. The 'popular' version of the second expedition, *Ruins of Desert Cathay*, was published as early as 1912, but the full five-volume version, *Serindia*, did not appear until 1921. In his full accounts Stein included inventories of all the artefacts collected, photographs and maps, and appendices by specialists on certain aspects of the collections. As soon as he touched base, he invariably began bombarding the relevant specialists all over Europe, sometimes sending precious artefacts to them so that they could produce descriptions for his full reports.

His determination to make his finds known amounted to a scholarly obsession. While Fred Andrews photographed, Miss Lorimer, 'the Recording Angel', recorded and kept track of items sent out and chased up dilatory scholars for their descriptions.[19] All the artefacts and documents were examined and described in London before being divided (on account of their financial contributions) between the British Museum and the government of India, which meant that the items destined for India had to make a return journey. In the case of the second expedition materials, the First World War intervened and they all remained in London for the duration, which enabled Laurence Binyon, the poet and curator in charge of Oriental Antiquities, to

Opposite: A lion. Detail of a silk painting of
Manjusri from Dunhuang, ninth century

Monumental Buddha heads uncovered by Sir Aurel Stein in the sand near Loulan. Below, painted stucco figures of monsters from Tomb iii.2, Astana, photographed by Stein

make a few judicious swaps in favour of the British Museum.[20]

Paul Pelliot of the Collège de France, clearly keen to see Stein's materials and compare them with those that he had managed to collect a mere year after Stein from Cave 17, volunteered to produce a catalogue of some of the Chinese manuscripts but, though many were posted off to him, he never produced one.[21] Pelliot's teacher, Édouard Chavannes, undertook the catalogue of the woodslips from the Dunhuang beacon sites (1913) and, after a few false starts (the original cataloguer Rafael Petrucci died during the First World War), the paintings and banners were catalogued by Arthur Waley (1931) who disapproved. He wrote, 'Imagine how we should feel if a Chinese archaeologist were to come to England, discover a cache of medieval manuscripts at a ruined monastery, bribe the custodian to part with them and carry them off to Peking.'[22] It was not until 1956 that Lionel Giles's catalogue of about half the total of Chinese manuscripts and documents appeared (described by Giles as between ten and twenty miles of closely written text[23]), with a subsequent catalogue of the remains of the secular manuscripts produced by Professor Rong Xinjiang of Peking University in 1989.

Stein made two more expeditions to Central Asia. In 1913–16 he returned to the area, calling again at Dunhuang where he acquired some five hundred extra scrolls. These are slightly contentious because, after Pelliot's visit in 1908, the Chinese government had ordered that all the remaining manuscripts be taken to Peking. Stein did not see where they came from, as he had done with his previous acquisitions, and he supposed that Wang Yuanlu had kept a considerable cache for himself in order to continue financing his restoration work. The question of whether some of them are faked has also been raised and investigations continue. Stein revisited other sites in the Turfan area, including the burial ground at Astana where the sand-dried mummies were accompanied by little dried dumplings and cakes over a thousand years old, and he made his first visit to Kharakhoto, up the Etsin-Gol river, east of the Gobi desert, the site of an ancient fort which had been excavated by the Russian archaeologist Pyotr Kozlov in 1908.

In 1930 Stein set off on his fourth expedition to Chinese Central Asia. He was financed by Harvard, keen to follow up on Langdon Warner's expeditions of 1924 and 1925 (see Chapter 14). The fact that Langdon Warner's 1925 expedition had been a complete failure, for angry Chinese watched his every move, reflected a dramatic change in China. Ever since the humiliation of the Versailles conference at the end of the First World War, when Germany's colonial 'possessions' in China were handed over to Japan, Chinese nationalism had been growing. As more and more young Chinese were trained

Jiao river, Turfan

in universities in Europe and America (often supported by scholarships created from the indemnity paid by China after the Boxer uprising of 1900), they became more aware of the drain of Chinese works of art to museums and collections abroad. Within China, problems in the Treaty Ports provoked frequent anti-foreign riots and Stein was careful to try to avoid confrontation. From the beginning of his negotiations with Harvard, Stein made it clear that his fall-back position in case of trouble was to return all his finds to the Chinese authorities and only insist on retaining photographs. This approach was cynical: Stein had had enough experience of getting round local authorities in the distant oases, and of corruption, to assume that he could probably get away with his finds.

With these rather different conditions, Stein also approached China in a different way. He had previously slipped in via Kashgar and obtained his permissions locally. Kashgar was a logical point of entry from India but it was also easier to intimidate or evade local officials on the very edge of China. This time, Stein decided to ask for permission through the highest British representative in China, the British Minister at Nanjing. Stein was granted a passport and he returned to Kashmir where he received news from Kashgar that the Provincial

Governor in Urumqi, on the other side of the Taklamakan, had been ordered to deny him entry to China. He pressed on to Kashgar (where Dash V suddenly died) and there the new consul, Captain George Sherriff, began negotiations on his behalf. He was granted permission but forced to take along a Chinese who he was convinced was just a spy, and he was closely watched in Khotan. At Domoko he received a message saying that he was not allowed to dig; at Niya his staff were terrorised; at Cherchen he was informed that his passport had been withdrawn and he returned to Kashgar. He did have a few artefacts, surreptitiously collected at Niya, and at the consulate in Kashgar they were all carefully photographed. The artefacts themselves were retained by the authorities in Kashgar, supposedly to be sent to Peking, and they have since disappeared completely.[24] Even the photographs disappeared for several decades, but when the India Office Library (which held all the documents in Tibetan, Khotanese and Sanskrit of his first three expeditions) was made part of the British Library in 1976, a box of photographs was turned over to the Chinese section which Professor Wang Jiqing of Lanzhou University recognised as the lost record of the artefacts of the fourth expedition.

Stein never returned to China. He continued to explore and excavate, but on the other side of the Pamirs, in Persia and Afghanistan. He died in 1943 in Kabul, leaving a newly acquired Dash (the seventh). Of all the explorers he was the most thorough, and his massive series of expedition reports, *Ancient Khotan*, *Serindia* and *Innermost Asia* (on the third expedition, published in 1928) still remain a primary source, as do his photographs and maps.

- 14 -

An end to excavation:
Pelliot, von Le Coq and Warner

LESS THAN A YEAR after Stein had left Dunhuang with his crates of manuscripts, the French scholar, Paul Pelliot (1878–1945), whose excavations at Kucha Stein had admired on his way home, arrived at the caves and made a selection of material for French collections.

Although he only made one expedition in the area, Paul Pelliot was perhaps the most brilliant scholar of all those who explored and collected on the Silk Roads in the early part of the twentieth century. Appointed to what was to become the École française d'Extrême-Orient in Hanoi in 1899, he was almost immediately sent off to Peking where the Boxer rebellion was beginning to threaten. He stayed to participate in the defence of Peking's Legation Quarter (13 June–14 August 1900) and his diary of the period reveals the excitement of a young man caught up in battle: not for him the 'study of modern war' but an exciting and dangerous series of skirmishes. He captured a Boxer flag and cheekily claimed to have had tea with some Boxers. A photograph of the young Pelliot with his trophy still survives (see p. 212) and he was awarded the Légion d'Honneur.[1]

In 1901 he was sent by the École française back to China to collect books and he acquired a copy of the massive eighteenth-century illustrated encyclopaedia *Tushu jicheng*, most of a Ming edition of the Daoist canon, *Daozang*, and the Tibetan *Kanjur* and *Tanjur*, all of which are now in the Bibliothèque nationale. In 1906 he set off on his first 'scientific mission' in Central Asia, with Dr Louis Vaillant, 'géographe-astronome', and Charles Nouette, 'naturaliste-photographe'. They started in Tashkent and then went on to Kashgar where Pelliot undertook a 'linguistic enquiry'. In the Tarim basin he collected statuettes and polychrome sculptures in the Graeco-Buddhist style from Tumchuq, and manuscripts from Kucha where they arrived on 2 January 1907. Nearby, in a burnt-out monastery, he found manuscripts and wooden documents inscribed in Sanskrit and Kuchean. It was in Urumqi, then the capital of Xinjiang, that they heard of Stein's finds at Dunhuang. There, too, Pelliot met, for the second time, a minor member of the Manchu ruling house who had been exiled to Urumqi for his part in the Boxer uprising. Whilst the exile remarked sadly that he had to stay whilst Pelliot could move on freely, Pelliot 'forbore from

Opposite: Buddhist cave temples at Toyuk, discovered by von Le Coq

Pelliot in one of the library caves at Dunhuang,
photographed by his assistant Charles Nouette

reminding [him] that, some seven years earlier, there had been a day
"when he had forced us to stay when we would have asked nothing better than to leave".'[2]

Pelliot arrived at the Caves of the Thousand Buddhas near Dunhuang in February 1908. Like Stein before him, he had to wait for
Wang to grant him access to the library cave in particular, and it was
not until 3 March that he was shown the cave, piled high with rolled-
up paper manuscripts. Pelliot spent three weeks in the cave, only able
to work because of the space created by Stein's removal of thousands
of manuscripts and hundreds of paintings. The photograph of him in
his cubby-hole shows a candle perilously perched on bundles of paper
manuscripts as he worked through up to 20,000 scrolls: in his own
words, a philologist travelling at the speed of a racing car.

Whilst Stein had had to rely upon his Chinese assistant, who was
rather at sea with Buddhist texts and quite unable to deal with non-
Chinese scripts, Pelliot was the first scholar to see the cave library.
Though his main knowledge was of China and Chinese culture, he was
the first person to be able to appreciate fully the range of documents
held in the cave. He selected texts in Chinese, Tibetan, Khotanese,
Sogdian and Uighur, and paid particular attention to unusual types:
Manichean texts, for example. Dr Vaillant recalled how one evening
'he showed us a Nestorian Gospel of St John; on another a description,

210

dating from the year 800, of the curious little lake . . . situated in the high dunes south of Tun-huang; another time it was the monastery accounts.'3 Whilst Pelliot raced through the scrolls, his photographer recorded everything he could, which was fortunate because, several years later, when White Russian soldiers were interned in the caves, they caused considerable damage both wilful and careless, and Nouette's photographs remain the only record of the damaged wall-paintings.

In May 1908 Pelliot headed back to Peking where, as a sinologist of reputation, he could not resist taking a few precious scrolls to show to Chinese scholars in Peking (once he knew that the bulk of his collection was safely stowed on a ship heading for France). His action saved most of the rest of the collection for China as Peking immediately sent a telegram to Dunhuang instructing the local sub-prefect to close the cave. It was not, however, welcomed by later foreign explorers, including Stein on his third expedition.

Pelliot was welcomed back to Paris in 1909 by government and scholars but it was not long before the French sinological world was divided in a bitter argument in which Pelliot was attacked as a gullible dupe. The origins of the argument, pursued by another sinologist, Fernand Farjenel, probably lay in jealousy that this young scholar was receiving such flattering attention from the highest in the land. Farjenel pursued several attacks at once: he attacked the École française at Hanoi in the columns of an anti-colonialist journal and cast doubts on the language skills of Pelliot's mentor in Hanoi, Édouard Chavannes, but above all he accused Pelliot of frittering away French government funds on the acquisition of forgeries. Stein must have cleared the cave, said Farjenel, and Pelliot had been presented with a heap of forgeries of the type that Islam Akhun had been making in Khotan. Stein himself was greatly concerned about Farjenel's attack, as his letters of the period demonstrate, and he agreed to allow Pelliot to have the first sight of the collection of Dunhuang manuscripts he had made himself, with a view to the production of a limited catalogue. Pelliot had made the proposal rather on the basis of his work in the caves, projecting a catalogue of some two thousand manuscripts in a remarkably short time, but with the distractions of work and academic warfare in Paris, Stein had to abandon hope that Pelliot would ever produce anything.

Pelliot remains an enigmatic figure, an 'undisputed master', with a memory that was so prodigious as to seem incredible to many. He effectively closed the cave to others after he left and he was equally difficult about access to his own collection which had been placed in the Bibliothèque nationale. He insisted that the documents be kept in a locked room to which only he held the key, an action which

naturally infuriated the librarians and which set up a combative relationship between the Bibliothèque nationale and the Collège de France (where he was appointed Professor of the History and Archaeology of Central Asia in 1911). The printed catalogues of the Pelliot collection are still appearing, and some of the prefaces reveal a continuing tension between curators and cataloguers, established nearly a century ago by Pelliot himself. He died in 1945 and there are strangely few obituaries: nothing, for example, in *T'oung Pao*, to which he had contributed for over thirty years[4] and of which he was joint editor at the time of his death. The summary by the anonymous author of the catalogue of a centenary exhibition at the Bibliothèque nationale suggests a frightening figure: 'His rigorous precision, his habit of going back to the sources, his merciless scientific rigour and his prodigious memory made him an undisputed master but one who was sometimes dreaded.'[5]

There was only one Pelliot expedition but between 1902 and 1914 four German expeditions to Chinese Turkestan were led by members of the Museum für Völkerkunde (Ethnological Museum) in Berlin. The first was led by the head of the Indian section, Professor Albert Grünwedel, accompanied by an art historian called Georg Huth who

unfortunately died soon after his return. They also took along the
Museum handyman, Theodor Bartus, a resourceful ex-sailor. The
interest of the German academics had been aroused by meetings with
Russian explorers, particularly Dimitri Klementz and his wife, who
had photographed the ruins near Turfan and brought back manuscripts and fragments of wall-paintings to the Academy of Sciences in
St Petersburg. In late 1899 Russian archaeologists stopped in Berlin on
their way to the International Congress of Orientalists in Rome, and
they showed Grünwedel the fragments of wall-paintings, documents
and block-prints that they were going to show at the Congress.

Grünwedel reported, 'Russian merchants [largely responsible for
the Europeanisation of the Turfan bazaar noticed by Stein] having
reported to the Academy on unusually interesting relics of ancient
times, Mr Radlov commissioned the sinologist Professor Hirth, resident in Munich, to compile comprehensive material from Chinese
sources on Buddhist cities in Central Asia, and dispatched Mr Klementz therewith to Central Asia. Equipped with this literature, the
said gentleman and his self-sacrificing spouse found a whole series of
cave temples from the Buddhist era, the entrances to which had been
blocked up by sand drifts, but which were accessible through small
openings made by the present inhabitants. All these cave temples are
full of wall-paintings (frescoes), the preservation of which is now
greatly endangered by the fact that the Muhammedan population of
the neighbouring villages has got into the habit of breaking off pieces
thereof to fertilise their fields. Thanks to the foresight of the Imperial
Academy, about 50 lb of such detached fragments have already been
brought to St Petersburg, and a painter has been sent to make copies
on the spot.'[6] Grünwedel described the pieces he had seen as 'types of
frescoes characteristic of ancient Indian, ancient Iranian, and Buddhist
Chinese styles . . . There is no doubt that we are confronted with a
Central Asian sister school of the Buddhist painting of ancient India.'

At the same Congress, the Germans saw examples of the Indian
Government collection (described by Hoernle). The Turfan file in the
Berlin Museum states: 'The greatest significance among the discoveries attaches to the manuscripts, most of which are in totally unknown
tongues and scripts [perhaps a few Islam Akhun products had slipped
in], presenting Orientalists overnight with a number of fascinating
problems of the greatest import, the solution of which would constitute a great leap forward in the study of Central Asian scripts,
languages and history.

'Of great importance also are the sculptures and paintings, as they
illustrate extremely interesting associations with the art of China,
India, and Persia, and indeed with that of Greece, Rome and the Near
East, of incalculable scientific significance.'[7]

Grünwedel was offered nothing but moral support by the Berlin Academy of Sciences and obtained about twenty-five per cent of his funding from the Museum, the rest being made up of contributions from a wealthy art-lover, an industrialist and the Berlin Committee for the Advancement of Ethnology. In 1901 Stein called by and offered advice. In late November 1902 the German expedition reached Turfan, on the northern Silk Road, and worked until April 1903 on several oasis sites, most notably Kharakhoja/Gaochang/Khocho/Qoco. Grünwedel wrote, 'This is without doubt a forgotten Asian city of extraordinary interest. The size of it alone is remarkable: the inner, holy city, consisting only of temples and palaces, measures 7,400 feet at the widest point of the still standing walls. Hundreds of tiered temples and grandiose vaulted edifices cover an extensive area of land, where the present-day inhabitants lay their irrigation canals.' Unfortunately, 'The city serves as a quarry for materials to build the modern houses, as a gold mine for those who dig for treasures, as a place of amusement where one can smash frescoes and statues of the Buddha to the glory of Allah – not to mention the practical benefit of being able to use the fragments to fertilise the sugarcane, cotton and sorghum fields among the ruins.'

Grünwedel was surprised to find that this was not only a Buddhist city but yielded manuscripts in Sanskrit, Uighur, Mongolian, Ancient Turkish, Chinese and Tibetan, as well as Manichean and Nestorian relics, characteristic of the melting-pot oases of the ancient Silk Roads. They collected forty-four crates of materials – clay and wooden figures, wall-paintings, block-prints and manuscripts – and shipped them to Berlin via St Petersburg.

The arrival of the finds changed the situation. A Committee for the Exploration of Central Asia had been set up and money was much easier to find to support the second expedition. The Kaiser added a grant from his discretionary fund, and a third expedition was being planned even before the second got underway.

Huth died soon after his return and Grünwedel's health was poor, so a volunteer at the Museum was chosen to lead the second expedition. Albert von Le Coq (1860–1930) was the son of a wine merchant and, having studied commerce in London and America, joined his father's firm, but when he was forty he changed careers and started to study oriental languages in Berlin. As a mature student he worked as a volunteer in the Museum, joining the Indian department in 1902. He was jolly and outgoing, unlike the quiet and sometimes difficult Grünwedel.

Von Le Coq and Bartus arrived in Turfan in 1904. Von Le Coq was struck, like Grünwedel, by the damage already done and the continuing depredations of the local inhabitants. 'Our expeditions reached

Khocho too late – if they had arrived sooner, more of these remarkable paintings could have been saved. We could also have salvaged more of the Manichaean literature, important for the history of religion and language alike. One of the peasants told me that, five years before the first expedition arrived, he had found five wagon-loads of the manuscripts so valuable to us, those with the "small characters", i.e. the Manichaean script, in a temple which was being demolished to make way for a field. Many of them, he related, were illustrated with pictures in coloured ink and gold paint. But he had been fearful . . . of the sinister nature of the writings . . . and without more ado had thrown the entire library into the river!'[8]

The use of frescoes as fertiliser, the obliteration by Moslems of figure paintings, and von Le Coq's opinion that 'The Chinese officials who govern the land couldn't care less about these ravages; they are all Confucians and despise Buddhism as a religion of the "lower classes" ' all seemed to provide justification for the removal to safety of documents and artefacts.

In 1905, von Le Coq moved to Bezeklik. Here he found that the caves carved into the soft cliff were largely untouched, so that Bartus was able to remove numerous murals for the Museum. It is ironic that they now mainly survive in photographs reproduced in von Le Coq's book, *Chotscho* (1913), because the originals were severely damaged by the bombing of Berlin in the Second World War.

As the summer progressed, von Le Coq retreated northwards to the higher region of Hami but he and Bartus were soon recalled to Kashgar to meet Grünwedel and his assistant, Pohrt. Having lost his luggage in Russian Turkestan, Grünwedel was delayed, but von Le Coq and Bartus were entertained by the legendarily hospitable Macartneys at the British consulate. When Grünwedel arrived, the third German expedition (1905–7) began. This time they began exploring some of the sites on the northern Silk Road: Kumtura (Mingoi) with its more 'Western' frescoes than those they had seen to the northeast in Turfan and Kyzil. They decided not to number the caves but to name them after their contents: the Cave of the Sixteen Swordbearers, the Cave of the Seafarers, and the Cave of the Red Dome. After enduring three earthquakes, they moved eastwards towards Karashahr, where von Le Coq fell ill, and returned to Kashgar and thence to India over the Karakorams.

The others continued work in Khocho and Komul until 1907 when they returned home via Urumqi and Semipalatinsk. Such was the quantity of material collected thus far that it was six years before the fourth and final German expedition was mounted. In the meantime, Russian expeditions led by Kozlov and Sergei Oldenburg visited the northern Silk Road between 1907 and 1911. In 1913, having signed declarations that they travelled at their own risk (for the collapse of the Qing dynasty in 1911 had made Xinjiang unstable), Bartus and von Le Coq set off to explore Kucha, Simsim (fifteen miles northeast) and Kumtura, all on the northern Silk Road. They became increasingly aware of the instability in the area: Sir George Macartney telegraphed them in September 1913, warning that there were disturbances in Kashgar, and someone appears to have tried to murder Bartus in the night. It was quite a triumph to get their finds safely back to Berlin in 1914.

Silk Road archaeological work by foreigners was virtually halted by the expeditions of Langdon Warner. Born in 1881 to an impeccably Yankee family, he is commemorated in the Horyuji temple near Nara in Japan, where a stone pagoda stands over an inscription dedicated to 'the American scholar who had saved Kyoto and Nara from bombing in World War Two'. Though he did do a great deal to preserve the Japanese cultural heritage, the description is not strictly accurate, but it reflects his position in the 'Japanese hagiography', which is counter-balanced by the place he occupies in 'Chinese demonology'. He joined Raphael Pumpelly's geographical and archaeological expedition to Russian Turkestan (along with Ellsworth Huntington) in 1904, seeing Samarkand and Bokhara, and then made a solo trip to the (still independent) Khanate of Khiva, which he was the first American to see. In 1908 he studied with the sculpture restorer at the Todaiji temple in Kyoto, and in 1913 he was appointed head of the proposed American School of Archaeology at Peking (an offshoot of the Smithsonian). Before taking up his post, he visited Pelliot and Chavannes in Paris, travelled to St Petersburg, where he saw the paintings from Kharakhoto brought back by Kozlov, and went on to Berlin to see the frescoes from the Turfan area collected by von Le Coq.

In 1915 he was asked to start an Oriental department at the new Cleveland Museum, and in 1917 he was appointed Director of the Pennsylvania Museum (now the Philadelphia Museum of Art) after serving in Siberia as Liaison Officer between the US government and displaced Czech soldiers (deserting conscripts and released prisoners of war).

In 1923–4 Langdon Warner and Howard Jayne set off on a Fogg Museum expedition to collect artefacts from Kharakhoto, Dunhuang and any other sites to which they could gain access. Warner described his expedition and its vicissitudes in a joking tone which he only abandoned in the face of beauty. Arranging transport from Xi'an, he received a letter from the local postmaster: 'Good morning Sirs. One wagon for Sianfu charge $70.00, three mule carts to same charge $105.00 at $35 each. It is their cheapest price. If you please, you will pay some earnest money $10 or $20 in advance. The half price must be prepaid when you start. And beg to inform you that it is sure to set out tomorrow morning. Further, have you your national flag? Each cart must be stick upon with one flag of yours. If not do so, the soldier will get those carts for arm articles, Yours truly, Chow Hsing Yueh.'[9] After serious disputes about the number of stars – 'neither of us could get beyond forty-two, and even then each suspected the other of counting Idaho twice' – failure to produce patterns for the five-pointed stars – 'I was sure that (if I could only remember how, in nursery days, they folded the paper) I could with a snip of the scissors produce an accurate five-pointed star. The result was cocked hats and a whole fleet of sailing ships and a series of those small dolls that dance hand in hand down the counterpane when you have a sore throat' – the tailor sent his boy to inform them that there was only room for six stars.

The next ordeal was a night on a brick bed in a Chinese inn where Warner was woken 'by an odd whirring sound . . . and . . . a huge luminous mound which emitted a whirr and a pulsing white light', which was Howard Jayne in his supposedly bug-proof sheet, 'convulsively working the lever on his little motor-driven flashlight and searching for his tormentors'.[10] Just outside Xi'an, Warner acquired two of the great stone-carved portraits of the horses of the Tang Taizong emperor (r. 626–49). 'About his [Taizong's] tomb six huge stone horses were set up, the portraits of his chargers killed under him in battle. They have been pulley-hauled from their place now. Four of them were brought into town, where we saw them rather meanly set up against the garden wall in the little museum, but happily safe from our American dollars. The other two, somewhat split and battered, are the pride of the University Museum in Philadelphia.' They appear to have been split (quite neatly into four parts) to facilitate transportation. The loss of the two carvings remains a matter of serious anger in China where photographs of the Philadelphia panels are displayed beside the remaining four in the fine new Shanxi Provincial Museum in Xi'an.[11]

Like so many travellers before and after him, Warner waxed lyrical over the fare offered by missionaries, in this case at the Scandinavian Alliance Mission (Shanxi and Gansu were very much Scandinavian mission areas). 'Real milk to drink! Twelve cups of tea! Raisin bread! Fresh or salt butter to our hands and a mammoth frosted cake new browned from the oven! Perhaps after I began to realise ruefully that I could hold no more, it was the amber-coloured apple jelly which made the strongest impression.'[12]

Warner was thrilled to arrive at Kharakhoto, which he recognised from Stein's photographs, but dismayed to find that Stein and Kozlov had taken all the frescoes. Nevertheless, his description of Kharakhoto is lyrical: 'The place itself is lovely beyond all my imagination of it. The plain around is flat pebbles for a mile or so before the dunes begin. The walls are huge, big-bastioned and thick, and instead of the loess grey that all China is made from and of which one gets heartily sick, the grey clay is distinctly glowing with pink. Sunsets and sunrises literally gild those walls, and the moon sets the shadows of the but-tresses and bastions inky black against a huge silver stretch above one's head. At night the wolves howl till our caravan dog gets nearly crazy, and the tent flaps crackling and frozen, and the camels belch and bubble nearby. Of course it is cold and the wind-borne sand and dust play hob with your eyes and face but, except for shaving and bathing, we aren't uncomfortable.'[13]

As they trekked towards Jiayuguan – 'the Ultima Thule of the Chinese where the Great Wall of China ends in a tiny walled town set against the foothills' – the weather was fantastically cold, for it was November. Warner walked – 'I dared not climb aboard a camel as Jayne had done' – and avoided the subsequent disaster. Kept immobile on the camel, Jayne's feet became badly frostbitten. 'For three hours and a half, Wang and I scrubbed with snow till the feeling came back with a vengeance and he quietly fainted. Still we scrubbed feverishly, hardening our hearts . . . The last half hour of rubbing was done with grease in the hope that some of the skin might be saved and the sub-sequent swelling be less painful. We put his soles against the bare skin inside our shirts.' The next morning, 'Jayne's feet were an enormous mass of blisters and were swollen to the knees. Worse still, he had a high fever.' Warner bandaged his feet with four boiled handkerchiefs as 'outside the tent a half gale howled around us, driving the dry snow in drifts against the scarred grey walls of the deserted fort'.[14] Jayne survived but Warner went on to Dunhuang alone.

He spent ten days just looking at the wall-paintings: 'The Holy men of fourteen centuries ago had left their gods in splendour on those walls. Tens of thousands of them, walking in slow procession, seated calm on flowering lotus blossoms, with hands raised to bless mankind, or wrapt in meditation or deeper still sunk in thoughtless Nirvana.'[15]

The White Russian deserters who had fled across the mountains and deserts in 1921 and had been interned in the caves for six months had, in their ignorance and boredom, scratched their names on the walls and built fires in the caves, to Warner's horror. 'It was with shock that I traced, on the oval faces and calm mouths, the foul scratches of Slavic obscenity and the regimental numbers which Ivan and his folk had left there. Two years before, a little group of four hundred Russian soldiers, harried from pillar to post, beaten and pursued by the

Red Armies, had fled through Turkestan. The Chinese Governor, more fearful of the Bolsheviks than of the thinning ranks of the old regime, had stripped them of their arms and horses and interned them at the Chapels of the Thousand Buddhas, while their general was clapped into the Chinese prison at Urumqi, mercifully supplied with enough opium to forget the filth and hideous fare and to achieve a reasonably swift death.'[16]

Warner's conclusion was that, 'Obviously, some specimens of these paintings must be secured for study at home, and, more important still, for safe-keeping against further vandalism.'[17] Though the second objective was a worthy one and, as he tells it, arose from the sight of the vandalised paintings, Warner had come to Dunhuang fully pre- pared to remove wall-paintings. 'Before leaving Peking I had provided myself with a quantity of the fixative recommended by the chemists to tie together the ancient pigment, now as delicate and easily dislodged as chalk dust on a blackboard. Also I had with me the ingredients for the soluble bed which must be applied to the painting after the colour was judged secure.'

A further sight of local worshippers was sufficient to strengthen his purpose. Three bow-legged Mongols 'slouched in to gaze and worship. They prayed respectfully enough to a hideous modern clay figure with magenta cheeks and bright blue hair but, when they rose and began talking together in a group, one placed his greasy open palm on a ninth-century wall-painting and leaned his whole weight there as he chatted. Another strolled to the pictured wall and, in idle curiosity, picked at the scaling paint with his finger-nails. As they crowded out through the narrow entrance their vile sheepskins scrubbed a row of saintly figures by the doorway, figures which, alas! no longer had middles, so many hundreds of sheep-skinned shoulders and elbows had rubbed there in the past. This was enough . . .'

Langdon Warner began work. 'I grimly set about first to apply the colourless liquid which a Peking chemist had given me to fix the crum- bling pigments, and later applied the hot glue-like bed to the paint itself. Here, however, were unexpected difficulties. The temperature in the caves was below zero, and I was far from sure that my chemical had penetrated the plaster wall before it froze, and later the boiling jelly was almost impossible to lay on that vertical surface before it stiffened . . . I chose some Tang figures which were left in fair condi- tion from partly-destroyed groups. Though far from being the most important in the place, these would prove treasures the like of which we had never seen in America, and which even Berlin, with its wealth of frescoes sawn in squares from the stucco walls of Turkestan, might envy.'

But he suffered: 'Five days of labour from morning till dark and five

nights of remorse for what I had done and of black despair, conquered with difficulty each morning, saw the fragments of paintings securely packed in felts and lashed tightly between flat boards, ready for the eighteen-weeks' trip by springless jolting cart, railroad, and ship to the Fogg Museum at Harvard.'[18]

Despite his 'black despair', Warner had not finished. This time, his reason for rescuing an artefact was not White Russian vandalism but 'the local image-maker' with his mud-trowel and paintbox, who 'was to appear in a few weeks . . . for his annual orgy of vandalism'. Stein had earlier encouraged the local image-maker by giving money to Wang Yuanlu, who was trying to restore the decaying site to some of its former glory, for the restoration of some sculptures. As Warner wrote, 'It seemed that these statues were his pride. He had spent months in begging from oasis to oasis for money to have them made, and now came a mad foreigner who, though he had given a handsome present, expected to carry one away. He suggested that one could save trouble and carriage by stopping at the market town and ordering a statue made by the very sculptor whom he employed. One might even wait till Peking was reached to have one constructed by the metropolitan artists. Reasonable as this suggestion was, I insisted that I valued more an image hallowed by his chapels.'19*

Wang Yuanlu, with his pious desire to restore, was effectively cornered by Warner's proposal 'to take only an old and tarnished example instead of one of his recently constructed and paid-for works of art. Thus it was that I was enabled to set about a labour of love and reverently pry from its pedestal a figure halting upon one knee, and with sensitive hands clasped in adoration before its bosom . . . Dusty though the colours were on the prim folds of the garment, a gentle breath and the flick of a silken scarf cleared them to fresh blue and crimson and gold. The yellow ivory of the cheeks shone out anew and the necklace glowed.'

In order to transport his treasure he wrapped it in 'my blankets, my sheepskin breeches turned Brian O'Lynn fashion, the incomparable underthings constructed by the woolly Dr Jaeger, and the very BVD's to be seen in shameless display in our American magazine'.20

On his return journey, in Lanzhou, Warner met Dr Andersson, the Swedish head of the Chinese Geological Survey who had made many excavations of the neolithic sites in the area, unearthing wonderful red clay funerary pots decorated with whorls and swirls in black. They drank schnapps and looked over Andersson's latest finds. Such meetings constantly occur in the accounts of travellers in Central Asia, like Stein bumping into Sir Cecil Clementi near Hami. One day they are alone, trekking across the desert, the next they encounter another of their tribe. Accounts of arrivals in Kashgar, for example, create a picture of busy traffic, with explorers from Russia, Britain, Sweden and Germany practically falling over one another.

Warner returned to China the following year on a second Fogg expedition. This was doomed almost before it had begun, for when a

---

* The matter is a delicate one. Should temples or churches remain frozen in some idealised time or should they change as fashions for religious decoration change? I remember going to the Yungang caves in January 1976 with their massive, majestic yellow-grey central Buddha figure and the rows of little caves carved out of the yellow earth. The long dry yellow cliff stood beside a dry yellow river-bed under the blue winter sky: it was an ancient and peaceful site. The bus driver, however, told me as he dropped us beside the main temple in the centre of town, 'You'll like this one, it's much better than those old caves.' The temple frescoes had been repainted in the late nineteenth century; they were bright and busy, full of caricatures of lohan (Buddhist 'saints') with infinitely long arms (all the better to point the way) or crazy overgrown eyebrows. This was popular religion, more to the taste of even Communist bus-drivers; of course the foreigners, with their taste formed by Gothic cathedrals and carefully preserved sites, all preferred the dusty old caves.

British policeman ordered his men to fire on a crowd of demonstrating students in Shanghai and killed eleven of them, feelings against foreigners in China reached a dangerous point. As missionaries were recalled from the interior to the relative safety of the coastal treaty ports, Langdon Warner's party reached Dunhuang. This time he had brought with him, not just fixatives and glues from a Peking chemist, but a young American fresco specialist. But at the caves they were faced by an angry mob of farmers and, when they tried to set up camp at a lesser group of caves not far away, the same thing happened. China had finally begun to close its doors to Western treasure-seekers and the second Fogg expedition had to be abandoned. Warner returned to teaching in America and to visiting Japan instead.

The contents of Cave 17 at Dunhuang are now dispersed between Peking, St Petersburg, Paris and London, with other smaller collections scattered around the world. One of the most extraordinary dispersals of Dunhuang manuscripts and other Silk Road finds was that of the collection amassed on behalf of Baron Kozui Otani, leader of the *Jodo Shinzu* (Pure Land Sect) by various Buddhist missions between 1902 and 1908, when they came to the attention of Captain A. R. B. Shuttleworth, standing in as consul at Kashgar whilst George Macartney was on leave. The Otani manuscripts appear to have been sold when the baron had to sell his mansion (where they were kept) owing to a sudden cash-flow crisis. The new owner, a former Finance Minister, seems to have given about a third of the collection to the Japanese governor-general of occupied Korea in return for mining rights and this portion is rumoured to be in the National Museum in Seoul. Otani himself is thought to have given another third to the Japanese governor-general of Lushun in Manchuria, and the remainder stayed in Japan, ending up in the Tokyo National Museum. The German collections reflect the oases where they worked, around Turfan, Kucha and Kumtura, and those in St Petersburg contain many Dunhuang fragments (Kozlov was a late visitor to the Caves of the Thousand Buddhas) and the best collection of Kharakhoto finds.

- 15 -

The Baby General:
travel on the Silk Road in the 1930s

JUST AS THE Chinese government, pushed by Chinese scholars,[1] was beginning to try to stop the ingress of foreign collectors on the Silk Roads and the consequent exit of treasures, Russo-British rivalry in Central Asia was officially ended in 1907 with the signing of the Anglo-Russian Convention in St Petersburg. Both sides agreed not to interfere in Tibet, not to seek concessions for railways, mines, roads or telegraphs and, acknowledging China's traditional suzerainty, to deal with Tibet only through the Chinese. Russia acknowledged that Afghanistan lay within 'Britain's sphere of influence'.[2]

The Convention did not, of course, put an end to espionage and intelligence-gathering in the area, and the rise of Soviet Russia after 1917, taking in many of the cities of the western end of the Silk Roads such as Samarkand and Bokhara, did nothing to allay British suspicions of Russian interests in Central Asia. Many White Russian soldiers fled into Central Asia, including the band of soldiers whose defacement of the wall-paintings at the Caves of the Thousand Buddhas gave Langdon Warner an excuse to remove artefacts in order to preserve them. In Mongolia, an extraordinary White Russian General from Riga, Baron Roman Nicolaus Fyodorovich von Ungern-Sternberg (1887–1921), a Buddhist convert who saw himself as the heir to Genghis Khan, led an army to attack Urga (now Ulaanbaatar), the Mongolian capital, in 1921. Despite his Buddhist beliefs, once the city was taken he presided over a four-day bloodbath of burning, raping and looting. Drunken soldiers were quite out of control: 'one Cossack began killing his own comrades, until he himself was shot dead. One particularly sadistic Russian . . . liked strangling old women "because he enjoyed seeing them quiver under the grip of his fingers as he broke their necks" . . . A baker's boy suspected of Bolshevik sympathies was baked alive in his own oven. Young women were raped to death by whole squadrons of Mongol cavalry.'[3] Flushed with his success, Ungern-Sternberg announced that he would plant 'an avenue of gallows' from Mongolia to Moscow, and on 27 May 1921 proclaimed himself Emperor of all Russia.[4] His foray into Russia was met by determined resistance and he fled back to Chinese Turkestan where his own men tried to kill him. He was as difficult to murder as Rasputin, surviving a machine-gun attack, rising covered in blood to mount his horse and gallop away, but was eventually captured by a Red Army unit and executed.

Further south, since 1911, Xinjiang had been ruled by a Chinese general, Yang Zengxin. 'Nominally the representative of China's central government, he was in fact the Xinjiang's absolute master, merely advising Peking of his decisions. He kept the key of the radio station attached to his own belt... he read every message himself and destroyed any of which he did not approve.'⁵

Yang's deputy, Fan Yaonan, aspired to higher things and, on 7 July 1928, at a banquet in Urumqi which was attended by many high-ranking Chinese officials as well as the Soviet consul-general and his wife, shot Yang dead. The consul-general and his wife fled to the safety of the lavatory. Fan was beheaded on the order of Jin Shuren, another of Yang's ministers, and Jin Shuren took over.

In 1930 one of the last of the Moslem Khans, the ruler of the oasis of Hami, died, and the Chinese government determined to bring Hami under Chinese control. A rebellion ensued and a young Chinese Moslem soldier based in Dunhuang, Ma Zhongyin (trained in the military academy in Nanjing), took over the Moslem rebel band. For the next four years Xinjiang was in turmoil: Ma Zhongyin tried to take Hami but was driven back towards Kashgar where, in 1934, he set up a Dongan (Chinese Moslem) government. Ma was referred to as 'the Baby General', described by the British missionary, Mildred Cable, as 'handsome, elegant, wilful', and by a 'wise old Chinese diplomat', whom she quotes, as 'vain ... profoundly ignorant'.⁶

Throughout the oasis towns, Dongans and other disaffected groups rebelled. Travellers were caught up in the unrest. In Cherchen in 1933, one of Sven Hedin's Sino-Swedish expedition scientists, Dr Nils Ambolt, who was in the area taking astronomic readings, was trapped by a mob. He reported, 'This was the first time I had ever seen a revolutionary mob, wild with lust, without a trace of responsibility, fanatical, excited and terrifying, and it was not a pretty sight.'⁷ Georg Vasel, a German engineer building landing strips for the Chinese government, was travelling between Hami and Urumqi when he passed an area that had been attacked and burnt. His lorry drove over piles of corpses, their bones crunching beneath the wheels. Outside the town were piled the bodies of Chinese soldiers killed by Ma Zhongyin's troops. Von Hannekan, a German whose name was 'well and honourably known in Tientsin and the North China Treaty ports' had 'set out from Hami during the rebellion to travel to Urumqi and was never seen again. The Silk Road Chinese say he was killed by Kazakh robbers in the neighbouring ranges of the Tianshan.'⁸

Where oases were not destroyed by warfare, sickness struck. In Dunhuang, Mildred Cable, who had been forced by Ma Zhongyin to

224

treat the bullet wounds to his legs, saw the effects of a typhus epidemic. At the Caves of the Thousand Buddhas, 'the temple entrances were full of men and women muttering in delirium and calling on passers-by for a drink of water to slake their intolerable thirst. Dogs and wolves had a good time outside the north gate, for by ancient custom the bodies of all who died in the roadways were wrapped in matting and buried there in shallow graves.'9

Ma Zhongying, who had driven the local Turkic ruler from Kashgar, was himself driven out in 1934 by a combined force of Manchurian and Turkic troops under General Sheng Shizai. Ma's Dongan troops withdrew to Khotan and Yarkand whilst he 'caused general surprise by fleeing across the border into Russian Central Asia'.10 It is thought he may have been killed on Stalin's orders as he was of no particular use.11

With bandits, frightening local unrest and failing control from the Chinese government as Japan invaded, the Silk Roads became increasingly dangerous. As the British diplomat Sir Eric Teichman (who crossed the Gobi by car in 1935) concluded, 'Chinese Turkistan was formerly the happy hunting ground of big-game hunter, explorer and archaeologist. But, with the arrival of inevitable change, it is no longer so. Gone is the old orderly Xinjiang, with its venerable Chinese Ambans [magistrates], peaceful, submissive Turki peasants, and ragged, opium-soaked Chinese soldiery; a quiet and attractive backwater in the stream of human life. And, with the disappearance of the old Xinjiang, gone are the days of pleasant, easy wanderings in Chinese Turkistan.'12

The dangers did not deter a considerable number of travellers and explorers. Mildred Cable and Francesca French spent many years travelling on the Silk Roads (after twenty years' mission work in North China), meeting the Baby General Ma in Dunhuang in about 1931. Sir Eric Teichman himself, travelling in 1937, arrived in Kashgar only a year or so after Peter Fleming and the Swiss ski champion Ella Maillart, who had travelled the southern Silk Road together. Preceding them were Owen Lattimore and his wife Eleanor who, after Owen made a solo camel trek across Mongolia, decided to join forces and spend their honeymoon exploring both the northern and southern Silk Roads in 1927 with their servant Moses.

Owen Lattimore (1900–89) had been born and grew up in China. His family could not afford to send him to university (after he failed a scholarship exam to Oxford) so he joined a British import–export firm based in Tianjin, Arnhold and Co., and got the chance to travel widely in China. His first experience of Central Asia came in 1925 when he was sent to Inner Mongolia to negotiate the release of a 'trainload of wool that had been held up by a feud between two warlords'.13 Despite his lack of formal higher education, later Lattimore

Crossing the Astore river near its confluence with the Indus, photographed by Skrine

was to become a lecturer at Johns Hopkins University and a specialist on Mongolia. In the late 1940s he became a prime target for the anti-Communist movement in America that was to culminate in Senator McCarthy's witch-hunts. Though he was never convicted of whatever it was McCarthy wanted to convict him of, his academic career in America was brought to a premature end and he moved to the University of Leeds, where he built up a new department of Chinese and Mongolian studies over which he presided until his retirement.

Eleanor travelled by train across Siberia, whilst Owen traversed Inner Mongolia on horseback. He crossed into Russian Turkestan to meet her at Chuguchak: 'She stood, almost unrecognisable to me in her furs, beside a small heaped sledge in the middle of the street. She had brought off the incredible, and we were together, and in Central Asia.'[14] After 'becoming an expedition' they made their way to Urumqi, the provincial capital of Xinjiang. 'On the edge of Urumqi town, the spring thaw was over and done with and a tinge of green refreshed the land. In the town itself, all was not yet well. We had to dismount at the outermost suburb and walk to our lodging. Through-

226

out the winter the snow is trodden deep and hard in the streets. As it melts, the streets become channels filled with black liquid mire of an amazing viscosity; it may be two feet or a yard deep. For more than a month this must be laboriously scooped, swept, pushed, and carted out of the way, leaving sunken passages that show the foundations of houses and walls. During this period one must go abroad either in a small city cart, or capering with the best agility one can summon along little raised footways at the side, where the drier mud has been heaped. In the summer, the streets become carpeted with soft dust, several inches thick, a chief ingredient of next year's mire.'[15]

In Urumqi they stayed with a friend of Owen's, Pan, son of the late governor of Khotan, and Aksu who 'had done a great deal to further the explorations of Sir Aurel Stein', and enjoyed picnics with 'McLorn, the Irishman, and his wife; a Russian friend of ours, formerly in charge of the Russo-Asiatic Bank, until its collapse which left him stranded in Central Asia; Mr A Hsing-a (the Chinese form of his name) a Sibo from the Ili Valley who was in the postal service and spoke Chinese and Russian perfectly . . . The presence of my wife and Mrs McLorn allowed the wives of some of the Chinese to accompany them – mixed company still being a stiff hedge for the Chinese to jump except when following a foreign lead. Mrs McLorn spoke no Chinese but perfect Russian, having been born in Petrograd, whither her parents had gone from England. Thus with Russian, English and Chinese no-one was baulked of conversation.'

They soon set out for Turfan, 'travelling in a new style. My wife and I had saddle ponies, while Moses travelled more slowly in a two-wheeled Turki cart, with our kitchen battery and a few effects. My wife rode a splendid black which we had just purchased in Urumqi, while I rode a raking bay lent to me by Mr Pan.' Eleanor described how 'At sunrise we rode past domed clay tombs and an encamped caravan and irrigated fields into the picture-book streets of the Turki city of Turfan. It is a blissful wandering life and full of beauty and elemental joys and we are greedily wishing it could go on forever. It is already stifling hot here. We have come down suddenly from Urumqi on a high plateau to a depression below the level of the sea. Even now the streets are roofed with matting, and the vines and trees are trained to grow over them for shade. They are clean, too, and sprinkled wet for coolness, so there is a surprising difference between the temperature of the shady streets and the desert just outside the city walls . . . [The streets] are lined with colour and riding into them yesterday I was ecstatic. They are lined with shops hung with gay wares, brightly woven rugs and saddle bags and long festoons of yellow and red cotton cloth and counters of dried apricots and raisins and nuts and red pepper all laid out in neat lines.'[16]

The city was 'completely Turki' unlike Urumqi, and the 'women and girls wear blatantly gorgeous clothes, a sort of Mother Hubbard gown of bright figured cotton or silk, black braided jackets, and kerchiefs or caps on their heads. The little girls are most picturesque of all in the bright quaint long skirts just like their mothers and little embroidered caps. They wear their hair in two long braids over their shoulders and often paint their cheeks and eyebrows, both they and the women frequently connecting their eyebrows by a streak of black paint which has a rather striking effect. The men are impressive in long striped coats and white turbans or little embroidered skull caps.'[17]

As they moved on along the northern Silk Road, they reached Kulja, where they stayed with the Russian manager of the local branch of the Russo-Asiatic Bank. Madame Dubina was a Russian matron who took great pride in her housekeeping. 'Her servants are Russians, a cook who lives with his family in the huge kitchen, a laundress who according to Russian custom takes all the clothes to the baths to wash and brings them home to dry and iron, and a coachman who lives with his family in a little house by the stables. They have their own vegetables, milk and butter and the food was delicious. We especially loved their beautiful garden full of roses and peonies and rows of poplar trees which seemed heavenly after our hot dusty days on the road.'[18]

They rode through Aksu and on to Kashgar. 'The heat was so unbearable that we travelled entirely at night, in the most sweet and delightful cart you can imagine. It was a "house-cart", a sort of Wendy house on wheels, and it had been built for postmaster Wang in which to bring his pretty wife from Urumqi to Aksu . . . we covered the bottom of the cart with our boxes and bags, then spread on them everything soft we had, tent, furs, felts and sleeping bags . . . Wang T'ai-t'ai had washed the blue curtains for us and the blue canopy at the front that serves as the awning.'

Like Stein before her, Eleanor Lattimore waxed lyrical about the comforts of the British consulate in Kashgar: 'After fifteen breathless sticky vagabond days of desert we have reached an oasis of civilisation, of all Central Asia the most civilised, British India transplanted to Turkestan, the British Consulate-General at Kashgar . . . We are loving the contrast of its comfort with our recent vagabondage – hot baths, clean sheets, dainty food, nice dishes, white-robed servants, a library of books, shady terraces and an enchanting garden riotous with fruit and flowers.'[19]

The same oasis of British comforts awaited Ella Maillart and Peter Fleming after their crossing of the southern Silk Road ten years later. Ella Maillart described how she had looked longingly towards the Tian Shan from Russian Turkestan in 1932 but that it took her three years, 'owing to political troubles' in the area (with the Japanese

occupation of Manchuria), to reach Peking and begin trying to get to Chinese Turkestan. 'At the Geological Institute of China, Père Teilhard de Chardin, who, in 1931, had crossed Asia with the Citroën Expedition, could only confirm me in my fears.'[20] A Swedish geologist with whom she discussed the possibilities mentioned the chance of travelling with a Russian couple, the Smigunovs, who 'would serve me as guides and as interpreters in Chinese, Mongolian, Tibetan and Turki . . . He would write to them at once and ask them to get in touch with me.' Another Swede she met in the bar of the Hôtel du Nord, Peking, was going by lorry into the desert. ' "It's a pity I never take women," he said as he left; "but you'll find other lorries that will carry you as far as Lanzhou." ' And then she bumped into Peter Fleming of *The Times*. 'Hearing me speak of the Tsaidam and the Smigunovs, he had said coldly: "As a matter of fact, I'm going back to Europe by that route. You can come with me if you like . . ." "I beg your pardon," I had answered, "It's my route and it's I who'll take you, if I can think of some way in which you might be useful to me." '[21]

Without relaying any such conversation, Peter Fleming described how, faced with dangers and official impediments, 'gradually the plan

229

and the party took shape. I was only intermittently in Peking between trips to Shanghai, Tokyo and Mongolia; and Kini [Ella Maillart], who had been the first to hear of the Smigunovs, had first claim on their services. We still felt a perhaps unreasoned aversion from the idea of travelling together; but that sentiment was as nothing to our not less unreasoned desire to do the journey somehow. And at last – reluctantly, rather suspiciously – we found ourselves joining forces.

'It was against our principles. Kini's last book had been called *Turkistan Solo*; my last book had been called *One's Company*. If we felt foolish starting together, what would we be made to feel when we came back?'[22] It was more awkward for him, for he had a wife at home who might not have enjoyed the idea of his travelling across Central Asia with an attractive, unattached Swiss girl.

Fleming described their preparations: 'Both Kini and I preferred, on principle and from previous experience, to travel light. Moreover, in view of the very limited scope of our ostensible itinerary, large quantities of baggage, stores and tents would have stimulated the curiosity of officials to a dangerous degree (to say nothing of their cupidity); and as it turned out we should often have found it impossible to get animals to carry the stuff. Our staple foodstuffs we knew that we could buy as we went along, and tents and sleeping bags could be made for us in Xining, on the edge of the Tibetan plateau. So apart from old clothes, a few books, two compasses and two portable typewriters, we took with us from Peking only the following supplies: 2 lb of marmalade, 4 tins of cocoa, 6 bottles of brandy, 1 bottle of Worcester sauce, 1 lb of coffee, 3 small packets of chocolate, some soap and a good deal of tobacco, besides a small store of knives, beads, toys etc. by way of presents, and a rather scratch assortment of medicines . . .

'Our clothes were a random collection and call for little comment.'[23] This is possibly disingenuous: on a subsequent trip to China to visit the war front, Christopher Isherwood (whose 'trousers were still soaked, my shirt had a large burn on the front – it had lain too near the coals – my shoes were shrunken and stiff with mud') described Peter Fleming thus: 'In his khaki shirt and shorts, complete with golf stockings, strong suede shoes, waterproof wristwatch and Leica camera, he might have stepped straight from a London tailor's window, advertising Gents' Tropical Exploration Kit.'[24]

At Lanzhou they were forced to leave the Smigunovs behind because the Chinese authorities would not allow them to proceed, and they set off with only Wang the muleteer. Unlike the honeymooner Eleanor Lattimore, Ella Maillart described the places they passed as depressing: 'Life in Gansu is really wretched.'[25] They made a loop south of the southern Silk Road, to Xining and the Kumbum lamasery, and proceeded through Qinghai until they reached Cherchen on the

Silk Road. Their camels suffered from stinking, suppurating sores and Ella Maillart's little horse, Slalom, collapsed and was left to die on the edge of the Tsaidam, at which Peter Fleming cried, as he had not done for years.

As they rode into the Cherchen oasis on the southern Silk Road, 'the countrywomen fled, hiding their faces with a fold of their white veils . . . The men rose and, joining their hands on their breasts, salaamed to us. Those who were on horseback hastened to dismount as a gesture of respect. There were ripe apricots on the branches above our heads and I had my first taste of fruit that year.'

Trekking along the southern edge of the Taklamakan, Maillart found that 'Mosquitoes were welcome messengers, forerunners of humidity. The wind brought me – I say "me", for Peter admittedly had no sense of smell – a scent of pinks that came, in fact, from clusters of pink flowers like little bells. Then the reeds in the sand would become more dense. And suddenly, in the shadow of ground that was itself whitened by salt, there would be the dark water-hole. We would get down on our knees and fill our bowls with cool, sometimes magnesian, water. Afterwards it would be the animals' turn.'[26]

They got along by dividing tasks according to temperament. Fleming, who invariably characterised himself as the hopeless amateur and Ella Maillart as the professional, said:

> I did: all the shooting
> most of the heavy manual labour
> all the negotiating
> all the unnecessary acceleration of progress
> all the talking in Chinese and (later) Turki
> Kini did: all the cooking
> all the laundering
> all the medical and veterinary work
> most of the fraternizing
> most of the talking in Russian.[27]

Beyond Cherchen, the camels were in a bad way. Pearl had 'a cavity as big as a man's fist just below the spine and this cavity was crawling with maggots massed so closely as to constitute a kind of whitish stuffing – like the core of an artichoke'. The camel kept driving his nose-peg into the wound, but Ella Maillart treated it with concentrated permanganate and 'threw xeroform into the open mouths of the uneasy worms' so that they turned black and fell out. 'Number Two, Tuzun, had been pulling so hard on his nose that it bled, and the flies had quickly gathered for the feast provided . . . At the first village we got to, I went to an old camel-driver for advice. He

Shopping in Kumbum, photographed by Peter Fleming, 1935

made me buy some black pepper and pound it up. With this he filled up the wound, and in three days it had healed.' At Keriya, they sold their camels and bought horses for the shorter distances between the remaining oases. 'But Peter's rejoicings at having an animal suited to his height were of short duration. He had to finish the stage on foot. The authorities had hired us thin animals that they had no use for themselves. Next day, my companion left Domoko mounted on a donkey once more. Peter made no complaint but he had to admit that donkey-riding as a method of locomotion kept one's mind at a very prosaic level.'[28]

At Khotan, 'while the animals ate, we fought off the flies in a poor inn'.[29] Ella Maillart, who had expected it to be 'of obvious archaeological interest like Samarkand', was disappointed. 'Stagnant water stank in muddy alleys, the booths were black with flies and I noticed that most of the inhabitants, even the young girls, were afflicted with enormous goitres.'[30] They encountered their first 'British officials'; though the local representative was away, his assistant, 'a young Afghan with a terrifying squint', entertained them with a long story: 'It was, to say the least of it, a sensational story, but at first we found it difficult to fit into the political and geographical conditions obtain-

232

ing in these parts. Comprehension dawned slowly: it was a synopsis of M. Jules Verne's *Twenty Thousand Leagues Under the Sea*, which had been translated into Afghan in Kabul.'

Later when they 'were eating breakfast in a dense cloud of flies . . . there ambled up the steps into the garden a small donkey, flying the Union Jack. The bearded, weatherbeaten Turki in charge of him bore on his chest the legend BRITISH INDIAN POSTMAN. The mail had come in.' They devoured the three-month-old copies of *The Times* destined for Mr Moldovack, 'who turned out to be an Armenian by birth'. He was a carpet-trader, now eighty-five and 'crippled by elephantiasis', who had lost all his money and his carpets as a result of the Russian Revolution and had been living in exile in Khotan for fifteen years.[31]

Between Yarkand and Kashgar a donkey nearly drowned in a ditch, ruining Peter Fleming's plans for appearing refreshed and respectable when they arrived at the British consulate in Kashgar. His razor was rusted and as he picked through his damp luggage, 'The suit, the precious suit, came out last of all. Wet it was bound to be, and soiled with mud; what I had not bargained for was that it should turn out to be bright green in colour. The dye from a sash bought in Khotan had run . . . I had now to decide whether to enter Kashgar disguised as a lettuce, or looking like something that had escaped from Devil's Island. It seemed to me that, if there is one thing worse than wearing bright green clothes, it is wearing bright green clothes that are also soaking wet; I therefore sadly resumed the shirt and shorts of every day and prepared to let down the British Raj.'[32]

They saw the New Town of Kashgar but soon discovered that the consulate and the old town were a two-mile ride further on. 'Somebody was riding out to meet us: a tall, immaculate young man (with a topee) on a grey polo pony . . . "I'm Barlow," said the tall young man. "The Consul-General's away in the hills on holiday. I'm glad you got here all right. Let's go on up to the house" . . . "I don't know whether you drink beer . . ." Barlow was saying. He very soon did.'[33]

Ella Maillart described their destination: 'The garden was a riot of flowers. Young ducks waddled about on the English lawn. And then, the house! It was a long house with a verandah, a cool hall, and well-polished furniture; armchairs covered with chintz, books and newspapers everywhere . . . There was a youngish man, the English doctor at the Consulate, and a slight old lady who seemed to emerge out of a lace collar, "May I introduce . . . Miss Engwall of the Swedish Mission." And last of all, there was a table piled high with sandwiches and hot scones swimming in melting butter . . .

'Behold me, obliged to try and keep my cup of tea straight on a slippery saucer, and saying with my very best "fashionable society" smile:

"Two lumps, please . . . Yes, thanks, we had an excellent journey." '34

She enjoyed sleep without 'having to fight off fleas', vegetables, salad, black coffee, bread and honey for breakfast. Peter Fleming, who entitled his chapter 'Kashgar-les-Bains', revelled in the contrast: 'One night we slept on the floor, drank tea in mugs, ate doughy bread, argued with officials, were stared at, dreaded the day's heat; twenty-four hours later we were sitting in comfortable armchairs with long drinks and illustrated papers and a gramophone playing . . . We stayed a fortnight in Kashgar, leading a country-house life against an exotic background coloured, in the early John Buchan manner, with international melodrama . . . We idled shamelessly in Kashgar, eating and sleeping and asking interminable questions of our long-suffering hosts. The city is, not without reason, very prone to spy-fever, and the night we arrived the bazaar rumour ran that a British agent had ridden in from Khotan, accompanied by a White Russian agent disguised as a woman. This was hard on Kini; but the next evening we both played Association Football with the Consulate guard of Hunzas, so that rumour had a longer life than most.'35

The comforts of the British consulate in Kashgar close most accounts of Silk Road travel in the 1930s, with the exception of that of the missionaries of the China Inland Mission. Mildred Cable, Francesca French and Evangeline French spent most of the period between 1928 and 1932 travelling and preaching on both the northern and southern Silk Roads. They wrote several books about their experiences. *A Desert Journal: letters from Central Asia* by all three, published in 1934, stressed the religious aspect of their travels, describing happy Christian communities in far-flung oases, but a volume entitled *The Gobi Desert*, by Mildred Cable and Francesca French, is a detailed account of the contemporary situation of the oasis towns of the Gobi and Lop deserts, along the old northern Silk Road.

Jiayuguan, the ancient fort which marked the westernmost end of the Great Wall, was still, in the early 1930s, a busy stop on the old trade route. There were shops where travellers could buy 'tobacco, cigarettes, matches and rough paper made from the pulped leaf of the dwarf iris, small screws of red pepper mixed with coarse salt as condiment to the tasteless inn food, strong hand-woven braid for tying a man's trousers round his waist and ankles, and leather thongs for mending harness . . . The blacksmith's shop was always lively. In front of it a strong construction of wooden posts, ropes and pulleys looked like a medieval instrument of torture, but it was only a contrivance used for slinging difficult beasts who would not be quiet during the process of shoeing. With some mules it was sufficient to tie the hair of the tail to the tongue in order to quell the rebellious spirit, but others

had to be lifted from the ground and thoroughly incapacitated before they would stop kicking.

'The blacksmith was, incidentally, the veterinary surgeon of the place, and there was constant entertainment for carters in watching the dosing of desert-tried beasts, the ramming of needles into the tongue of a sick mule, and the more delicate operation of cutting the cartilage of the nostrils to cure spasms.'

The Jiayuguan inn was constantly busy with 'the travellers who came, lodged for a night or two . . . and forthwith went their way. Every sunset and every sunrise they arrived, some taking night stages and some travelling by day, but all were travel-worn and weary. They hailed from every part of China's dominion and were bound for her remotest frontiers . . . These formed the stream of living men and women who moved up and down the great road, acquainted with life and full of knowledge about distant places.'[36]

They visited Dunhuang (once tending Ma Zhongyin's bullet wounds there) and were properly sensitive to the sanctity of the place and the beauty of the painted caves. The fertility of the Dunhuang oasis itself, not far from the sand-filled Caves of the Thousand Buddhas, was described in evocative detail: 'During the spring the fruit orchards show masses of pear, peach and nectarine blossom; all the fields are green with sprouting corn and every bank is covered with

Mildred Cable in a courtyard, on her China expedition

A desert oasis: the Cres-cent lake, Dunhuang

blue desert iris. A little later, when the fruit blossom has disappeared, the opium poppy bursts into flower, covering a wide acreage as with a veil of gossamer, sometimes shaded with the faintest touch of pink to deep rose, and at other times scarlet streaked with silver-grey. All through the summer the land yields a succession of crops which include wheat, Indian corn, millet, sorghum, hemp and field peas, with a profusion of vegetables such as aubergines, scarlet capsicum, potatoes, many kinds of beans, carrots, celery, onions, leeks, golden pumpkins and green cucumbers. At different seasons, fields are gay with patches of blue flax, pink buckwheat and yellow colza.

'Fruit harvest in Dunhuang is a thing to be remembered, for it is scarcely ever known to fail. In each farmyard there are piles of apricots and plums, then peaches and nectarines, followed by the early "long-stemmed" pear, grapes and finally the large late pear which is carefully kept and stored to be eaten at mid-winter. The market stalls show piles of juicy melons, and late peaches of the kind that has been grafted on to the willow tree and which bears large, green, juicy fruit, handsome but flavourless. The rich brown jujubes and freshly gathered walnuts are so abundant that one may help oneself freely to them. The sight of such plenty is refreshing to the hungry and desert-weary traveller. Even in

236

early spring, when the other oases have no green vegetables to offer, the stalls at Dunhuang are covered with little bunches of the first shoots of lucerne [alfalfa, used to feed 'heavenly horses' since the Han dynasty], and this *primeur* is followed by branches of flowering elm, the blossom of which, rolled in flour and cooked in a special earthenware steamer, is served as a spring delicacy.'37

Despite their occasional meetings with General Ma and typhus epidemics, the missionaries' descriptions of the desert fringes are remarkably serene. Pottering from oasis to oasis (not for them the dry, uninhabited central desert), they note that 'bird life is scarce, but everywhere the approach to water is heralded by the water-wagtail, and there is a sand-coloured bird which is found at every oasis.' They were struck, like so many others, by the people of the oases and trade routes. 'No one can travel on these trade routes without receiving a vivid impression of the varied races, nations and tribes which make use of them . . . Chinese competency in the banking business . . . is universally recognised, while the native of Turkestan is relied on for the quickest transport . . . Mongolian and Tibetan hunters supply furs . . . By means of the hardy traffickers of the Himalayan passes, Indian produce such as precious stones, silk scarves, muslins and laces for women's veils are exchanged for Kashgarian carpets and rugs, and the artist craftsmen from Peking, seeking jade, depend on the rough Khotan "jade-fisher" to fetch it from the bed of the river.'

The languages of the Silk Road still presented a problem. 'The two prevailing languages are Chinese and Turki, but each is spoken in a wide range of varied dialects. For official business Chinese is the language most generally used, and from Peking to the border of Siberia, Mandarin Chinese serves the traveller for all necessary purposes, though over a very wide area north and south of Lop, Turki is commonly spoken, and Arabic, being the language of the mosque, can be used right across Central Asia.'38

In the bazaars, Kazakh women always formed a conspicuous group: 'Their intelligent, strong faces are framed with white wimples, and they are alert and interested in all that is happening . . . Another frequent sight in the bazaar is the Kirghiz, wearing a pointed cap of bright chintz bordered with lambskin, and a heavy fur coat even though the day is hot. His boots have high heels and he rides a bullock right up to the shop door . . . He sometimes carries a hooded falcon chained to his wrist . . . The Mongol was never in his element in the bazaar crowd, and only necessary business took him there. He generally pulled a camel bulkily laden with skins . . . One strange group of people sometimes appeared in the bazaar. A man, leading his donkey, would push his way through the jostling crowd. He wore a small cap embroidered with silver thread, and a long coat, unbuttoned and

hanging loosely round him. A few paces behind there walked a pathetic figure whose face and form were completely covered with a thick black veil woven from horsehair. Over the head was thrown a long black coat with its empty sleeves hanging at the sides. Something moved vaguely where the arms should be, which revealed this shapeless mass to be a woman with her baby in her arms. It was an Uzbek family party, and illustrated the humiliation of woman and the degradation imposed on her in that Moslem state.'39

Cable and French observed the transport of the Silk Roads. The most common form of inter-oasis transport was 'the Turki with his drove of little donkeys' laden with 'melons, early vegetables and fruit – apricots, peaches, grapes and pears according to season'. He made up the load with 'rolls of loosely woven, undyed cotton'. The Chinese preferred carts, pulled by large, sleek mules which were sold to rich Dongans at Suzhou at a tremendous profit, whereupon the carter acquired 'rough but desert-hardened beasts' for his return trip and invested his profit in 'good Turkestan horses, which are very cheap in Dzungaria but fetch a big price in Central China'.40

For longer distances, the camel was pre-eminent. 'The Central Asian camel is a very different creature from the fleet dromedary of the Arabian desert. This is the bulky Bactrian species, with two humps forming a natural saddle for riders, and whose caravan training has made its pace slow and steady. From calfhood it walks with the caravan, and the even progress of the long train has become part of its nature. It is born by the wayside, and for the first few days of its life is carried by its mother in a wooden cradle on her back, but before it is a week old the little angular creature, which seems to be all legs and hump, runs fitfully by her side, always pushing its nose toward her udder. The cradle still serves for an occasional rest and doze, but the young camel develops very quickly, and soon it is learning to follow the trail. Its burden is very carefully regulated to its strength and it is about four years before it carries a full load, but besides its merchandise, the caravan always has a miscellaneous lot of goods to transport, and there is bedding, spare clothes, tent-poles, big iron pots for cooking, trivets and smaller cooking utensils, besides sacks of flour and of *zamba* [roasted barley]. Such odds-and-ends are bulky but not heavy, and half-grown beasts can help by carrying some of these lighter things.

'The strength of the camel varies according to size and age, but the driver has an unfailing test by which he knows if each beast's burden is suitable to its capacity. When it kneels to be laden it always grumbles, growls and shows resentment, but of this the driver takes no notice. He goes on loading up until the moment when the camel becomes silent; then he knows that the burden is heavy enough, and nothing more is added. By the time it is four years old the young camel

239

has a wooden pin through its nostril, to which a rope is fastened and by means of which it is controlled and taught to kneel and to rise at a given signal. This pin is a thin peg of wood, sharpened at one end and thrust through the nostril. It is fitted with a wooden or leather washer to avoid chafing the delicate cartilage, and the exact spot for piercing the camel is very carefully chosen . . . The camel is proverbially surly and resentful, and its only response to friendly advances is a shower of loathsome cud which the creature has regurgitated in its annoyance and sprays over the troublesome human.'[41]

The postmen of the Gobi desert, inheritors of a system that dated back to the Han dynasty, used little donkeys to deliver mail. Mildred Cable described the arrival of the postman at an inn: 'I sat on the edge of the *kang* [brick platform bed] lazily watching the carter as he settled the harness, sprinkled water on the wheels, and fed the mules, when . . . I saw a daintily dressed Chinese appear at the main entrance, looking from one side to the other and evidently trying to find someone who could direct him. I felt sure that this was our first caller, and a moment later the servant came in, holding a large scarlet visiting-card in his hand, which informed me that Postmaster Hu, Stamper of the Skies, was asking permission to present his respects. Encased in grime as I was, sitting on the earth and surrounded by earth, I felt quite inadequate to the task of receiving such a dainty visitor as the one I had just sighted, but by the time he reached the doorway I was standing there to greet him . . . The Stamper of the Skies was small and daintily built. He would take no larger size than fours in shoes and sixes in gloves. He wore a dove-coloured silk gown which reached his ankles, and on his head a round satin cap. On his feet were black satin shoes, and he had picked his way so carefully through the courtyard litter that they showed no trace of mud . . .

'This frail being was just back from a six months' journey taken in order to convey the body of his father from its temporary resting-place in the Gobi Desert to the family vault in Hunan. The coffin had lain in a temple courtyard outside the city, and the son was free of the three years' mourning before he was able to perform this last filial duty which required him to carry the body, by litter, to the home of its forefathers.'

He announced that he had sackloads of letters for the ladies: ' "There are letters from England, America, Norway, and there is a small parcel from Denmark which looks as if it might contain something to eat. Among the mail-matter there are many Chinese magazines, and as books are scarce here, I opened and read them with the greatest interest. I have passed some to a friend, but now that you have come, I will get them back for you at once . . . There was also a parcel addressed to you from Hankow and in it was one single shoe. I was sure that the other shoe must have been stolen in the post, so I sent a tracer to every office

A river crossing, of sorts, at Tsang-po near Pun-Tso-Ling, Tibet, photographed by Hedin in 1894

on the way, and there will be a thorough investigation." This had, in fact, been a dodge of my own to get a pair of sand-shoes safely through the hands of many covetous clerks by having them posted one at a time, but, thanks to the energy of the Stamper of the Skies, it only resulted in an immense amount of work for a number of offices, and a personal triumph for Mr Hu when the second shoe arrived.'[42]

Mr Hu was the last of his line, in his silk gown, travelling upon a small donkey. Motor traffic was beginning to rumble along the Silk Roads. Some ten years before, Owen Lattimore (who travelled on horseback or in a cart), witnessed the arrival of the Russian consul-general in a tiny hamlet, six days by horse out of Urumqi. ' "The gas-cart! The gas-cart!" . . . the whole population rushed to doors and windows, or clambered to the flat mud roofs. The car went by, roaring and stinking.'

A worldly-wise boy, with unconscious reference to *The Wind in the Willows*, said: ' "Nothing but a frog-cart after all" . . . using the Tientsin slang, which refers to the raucous motor horn. But the people of that mud village, roused from the apathy of their dusty hole in the desert, chattered in subdued amazement. "How does a thing like that cross the Manass river?" asked a moon-faced man.'[43]

The question of how things like that crossed rivers preoccupied Sir

241

Eric Teichman, who travelled from Peking to Kashgar in 1935 in two Ford V8 trucks, one new, one inherited from one of Sven Hedin's Sino-Swedish expeditions. Not only did he use one of Hedin's secondhand trucks, he also took one of Hedin's drivers, 'Serat, a Chahar Mongol'. With Hedin's reputation for losing men on his trips, it was hardly surprising that, when first approached 'on the subject of another journey to Xinjiang, Serat looked very glum and intimated that nothing would induce him, after his experience with Sven Hedin on the latter's last to Chinese Turkestan, to venture there again.'[44]

The trucks had to be ferried across rivers and even the desert could prove difficult. After rain, 'it was a case of dig and dig again, with frequent recourse to the rope mats; and a desperately disheartening job at that',[45] and Teichman feared that his expedition was particularly vulnerable to bandit attack when bogged down. Postmaster Hu, on the other hand, bravely announced that he would embrace the motor-lorry, but he was nearly killed when his lorry almost overturned while crossing an irrigation canal, and he died of shock three days later.

Today in Kashgar the British consulate still stands, in part, dwarfed by the taller hotel buildings that surround it. The site of the old Russian embassy, where British interests were watched carefully from the late nineteenth century through to the end of British rule in India, has also had a hotel built on it, but it is safe to say that the facilities offered in both do not match the country-house hospitality once offered to dusty Silk Road travellers by the British consulate-general.

Epilogue

The Silk Road today

MILDRED CABLE and Francesca French left the Silk Roads as the Chinese Communist Party began its resistance against the Japanese invasion in the nearby province of Shanxi. The situation was complicated, for the munition lorries they saw in increasing numbers were sent from the Soviet Union, not to supply their Chinese Communist comrades, but Chiang Kai-shek. Stalin refused to accept the validity of the Chinese Communist Party, insisting that it should ally itself with Chiang Kai-shek and pass through various revolutionary hoops like mobilising the proletariat before it could be considered truly Communist. As China was a predominantly agrarian state, and the small urban proletariat firmly in the control of Chiang Kai-shek, Mao Zedong decided to abandon urban struggle and mobilise the peasants. Slightly confusing the issue, Cable and French left as 'Japan invaded China, armies began to march . . . heavily laden lorries thundered down from the Siberian railhead, for munitions were needed in China and the old desert trade route was the direct road by which to convey them. The trucks carried war material, some of which had come by way of the Old Silk Road, along the banks of the Oxus, and southward over those Gobi trade routes which my companions and I had covered so often on our missionary journeys. New conditions required a new name, and the main artery through Turkestan was soon spoken of as The Red Highway . . .'[1]

The governor of Xinjiang, Sheng Shizai, who had taken control in 1933, showed the confusion of the times in his shifts of allegiance. He had requested military assistance from Stalin to crush Ma Zhongyin in 1934, but in 1942 claimed that he had discovered a Soviet plot to take over Xinjiang. Soviet advisers withdrew and Sheng launched a merciless suppression of local Communists, killing Mao Zedong's own brother amongst many others. He then pledged allegiance to Chiang Kai-shek but, as it became apparent that Chiang's Nationalists were losing out to the Communists, announced the discovery of a plot by Chiang Kai-shek to overthrow him. In 1944 he fled to Taiwan with a considerable fortune acquired by dubious means, but he soon died.

In 1949 the Chinese Communist Party took control, and by the early 1950s Xinjiang had been brought back under Chinese control, not without a terrible fight. Military 'farms' were established throughout the region and Chinese settlers despatched to dilute the Uighur population. For many of the people of the Silk Road, boundaries such as that between the Soviet Union and China were meaningless. There were Kirghiz on both sides of the border, there were Kazakhs on both sides of the border, and mass defections from China to Soviet areas took place in the late 1950s.

For the Uighurs, the cruel but restricted regime of the Chinese Nationalists may not have brought stability or prosperity to Xinjiang but it left most of them to continue to pursue their livelihood and practise their religion. The Communist regime was more invasive. Top political, administrative and academic jobs were occupied by Chinese who, though they had come to settle, rarely made any effort to learn Uighur, proscribed the teaching of Arabic and the use of the Arabic script and restricted religious practice. Aware of the vast mineral resources of the Central Asian deserts, the Chinese began oil exploration and mining. The carefully guarded gold mines, whose produce was all destined for China, were a particular source of irritation to the local people (and the same methods, with the same consequences, were used in Tibet).

With the break-up of the Soviet Union, some of the peoples of the Silk Roads achieved independence from Moscow, setting up their own republics of Kazakhstan, Kirghistan and Uzbekhistan, and were able to exploit some of the wealth of the area themselves, although corruption became widespread and resulted in persistent poverty for the majority of the inhabitants. But as technology improves and mineral resources elsewhere become exhausted, the potential of the gas and oil fields becomes easier to exploit.

The Silk Roads, as trade routes, have largely returned to their earlier form, with traders travelling shorter distances, from oasis to oasis, and most goods moving shorter distances rather than being carried by land to Rome or Iran. One exception is the Chinese supply route to Tibet which still, until the proposed railway is constructed, runs past Dunhuang. Long 'caravans' of petrol-tankers rumble past Jiayuguan and Dunhuang on a regular basis.

Many of the Silk Road travellers today, however, are tourists. Under the Soviet Union tourism was encouraged, with organised tours of Samarkand and Bokhara, and, under the Chinese, Silk Road tourism expanded greatly in the late 1980s and continues to flourish. Old sites were restored: the blue and turquoise domes of Samarkand gleam brighter than ever in the sun and the great open square of the Registan still impresses. In China, the old Great Wall fort at Jiayuguan was rebuilt, and the temples surrounding the Crescent lake, in the dunes behind the Caves of the Thousand Buddhas, were reconstructed.*

* Sir Fitzroy Maclean remarked in the late 1980s that 'new' ancient monuments were springing up all over Central Asia, evidence more of enthusiasm than of strict historical accuracy.

Yet, whilst China and the ex-Soviet Central Asian states prepared to make money out of tourism – restoring ancient buildings, linking Kashgar to the Chinese rail network and supplying camels for desert trips – on the far side of the Pamirs, Afghanistan remained locked in tribal feuds and a prey to the superpowers, as if the Great Game had never ended. The sudden eruption of the Taliban, a fanatically militant Islamic group, precipitated the uncompromising destruction of cultural monuments that had stood for hundreds of years. The great Buddhas of Bamiyan, which had withstood earlier iconoclastic depredations, were completely erased by modern bombs. The contents of the museums of Kabul and Kapisa were scattered and may never reappear. Silk Road treasures, evidence of the movement of cultural influence from west to east and back again, have disappeared. For those with a love of history, for whom such treasures are the legacy of a two-thousand-year odyssey, embracing the caravanserai of nations and a stream of missionaries, explorers and adventurers, this kind of cultural annihilation takes the breath away. It is too potent a reminder of the caprice that governs (and has always governed) our knowledge of the past. Yet the history of the Silk Road continues to exert its powerful fascination – a fascination which, as James Elroy Flecker's merchants recognised, was as much a matter of imagination as of trade, and perhaps more:

> We travel not for trafficking alone
> > By hotter winds our fiery hearts are fanned,
> For lust of knowing what should not be known
> > We make the Golden Journey to Samarkand. [2]

References

CHAPTER 1

'A ceaselessly flowing stream of life'

1 James Elroy Flecker, *The Golden Journey to Samarkand*, London, Max Goschen, 1913, p. 4.
2 A. F. P. Hulsewe, *China in Central Asia: the early stage, 125 BC–AD 23*, Leiden, Brill, 1979, pp. 72–3.
3 Mildred Cable with Francesca French, *The Gobi Desert*, London, Hodder and Stoughton, 1942, p. 13.
4 Colonel Sir Henry Yule, *Cathay and the Way Thither, being a collection of medieval notices on China*, London, Hakluyt Society, 1866, vol. 1, pp. cxxxv–cxxxvi.
5 See John Gittings, *A Chinese View of China*, London, BBC, 1973, pp. 41–50.
6 George Babcock Cressey, *China's Geographic Foundations: a survey of the land and its people*, New York and London, McGraw-Hill, 1933, p. 264.
7 Cressey, p. 252.
8 Cable with French, pp. 184–5.
9 Christopher Dawson, *Mission to Asia*, Toronto, University of Toronto Press, 1980, p. 152.
10 C. Skrine, *Chinese Central Asia*, London, Methuen, 1926, p. 120.
11 Ronald Latham, *Marco Polo: the travels*, Harmondsworth, Penguin, 1958, p. 80.
12 Latham, p. 83.
13 Dawson, p. 113.
14 Latham, p. 82.
15 Latham, p. 84.
16 Owen Lattimore, 'The Caravan Routes of Inner Asia' in *The Geographical Journal*, vol. LXXII, no. 6, London, 1928, pp. 500–2.
17 Latham, pp. 84–5.
18 E. Delmar Morgan and C. H. Coote (eds), *Early Voyages and Travels to Russia and Persia by Anthony Jenkinson and other Englishmen* London, Hakluyt Society, 1886, vol. 1, pp. 78–80.
19 Cable with French, pp. 95–6.
20 John Hare, *The Lost Camels of Tartary: a quest into forbidden China*, London, Abacus, 1999, pp. 127–8.
21 Ella Christie, *The Golden Road to Samarkand*, London, Seeley, Service and Co., 1925, p. 149.
22 Christie, p. 26.
23 Skrine, pp. 106–8.

CHAPTER 2

Coiled dragons and filmy fleeces: jade and silk

1 Jessica Rawson (ed.), *Chinese Jade from the Neolithic to the Qing*, London, British Museum, 1995, p. 28.
2 Rawson, pp. 111–18.
3 James Legge, *The Chinese Classics*, Oxford, 1893, quoted in Rawson, p. 13.
4 Michael Dillon (ed.), *China: a cultural and historical dictionary*, London, Curzon, 1998, p. 286.
5 Michèle Pirazzoli-t'Serstevens, *The Han Dynasty*, translated by Janet Seligman, New York, Rizzoli, 1982, pp. 52–4.
6 *The Oxford Classical Dictionary*, edited by Simon Hornblower and Anthony Spawforth, Oxford University Press, 1999, pp. 1141–2.
7 *The Geography of Strabo*, translated by Horace Leonard Jones, London, Heinemann, 1917–32, vol. 3, p. 33.
8 Georgic 11, *The Georgics of Virgil in English verse*, translated by Arthur S. Way, London, Macmillan, 1912, p. 37.
9 *The Geography of Strabo*, vol. 8, p. 33.
10 *The Elder Seneca: Declamations*, vol. 1, *Controversiae*, translated by M. Winterbottom, London, Heinemann, 1974, p. 375.
11 ibid., p. 367.
12 *Oxford Classical Dictionary*, p. 471.
13 *The Silk Book*, London, The Silk and Rayon Users' Association, 1951.
14 J. Dyer Ball, *Things Chinese*, London, Samson Low; Hong Kong, Shanghai, Yokohama and Singapore, Kelly and Walsh, 1892, pp. 331–8.
15 Chiang Yee, *A Chinese Childhood*, London, Methuen, 1940, pp. 217–21.

CHAPTER 3

From Greece and Rome to China – and back again

1 Frank L. Holt, *Alexander the Great and Bactria: the formation of a Central Asian Empire*,

Leiden, Brill, 1988, Mnemosyne: Bibliotheca Classica Batava, Suppl. 104, p. 13.

2 Holt, p. 67.

3 A. B. Bosworth, *Alexander and the East: the tragedy of triumph*, Oxford, Clarendon Press, 1996, pp. 18, 8.

4 Bosworth, pp. 70–1.

5 Bosworth, pp. 82–4.

6 Wladimir Zwalf, *The Shrines of Gandhara*, British Museum, 1979, pp. 27–9.

7 Buddha Rashmi Mani, *The Kushan Civilisation*, Delhi, B. R. Publishing Corporation, 1987, p. 1.

8 Francis Watson, *India: a concise history*, London, Thames and Hudson, 1999, pp. 65–7.

9 Watson, p. 56.

10 *Pliny: the natural history*, translated by H. Rackham, London, Heinemann, 1942, vol. II, pp. 377–9.

11 Yu Ying-shih, *Trade and Expansion in Han China: a study in the structure of Sino-Barbarian economic relations*, Berkeley, University of California Press, 1967, p. 218.

12 *Oxford Classical Dictionary*, p. 1447.

13 *Oxford Classical Dictionary*, p. 1392.

14 D. D. Leslie and K. J. H. Gardiner, *The Roman Empire in Chinese Sources*, Rome, Bardi, 1996 (Università di Roma 'La Sapienza', Studii Orientali XV), pp. xvii–xix.

15 John Goodall, *Heaven and Earth: 120 album leaves from a Ming encyclopaedia, San-ts'ai t'u-hui 1610*, London, Lund Humphries, 1979, pp. 65–83.

16 Leslie and Gardiner, p. 43.

17 Leslie and Gardiner, pp. 47–50.

18 Leslie and Gardiner, p. 245.

CHAPTER 4

A people abandoned by Heaven: the Xiongnu and trade during the Han dynasty

1 Pirazzoli-t'Serstevens, p. 13.

2 Pirazzoli-t'Serstevens, p. 40.

3 Denis Sinor, *The Cambridge History of Early Inner Asia*, Cambridge University Press, 1989, pp. 177–8.

4 Luc Kwanten, *Imperial Nomads: a history of Central Asia 500–1500*, Leicester University Press, 1979, p. 12.

5 Yu, pp. 40–1.

6 See James Hevia, *Cherishing Men from Afar:*

Qing guest ritual and the Macartney Embassy of 1793, Durham, NC, Duke University, 1995.

7 Patricia Buckley Ebrey, *The Cambridge Illustrated History of China*, Cambridge University Press, 1996, p. 70.

8 Pirazzoli-t'Serstevens, pp. 38–40.

9 Yu, p. 40.

10 A. F. P. Hulsewe, *China in Central Asia: the early stage, 125 BC–AD 23*, Leiden, Brill, 1979, pp. 40–1.

11 Hulsewe, p. 207.

12 Hulsewe, p. 210.

13 Hulsewe, pp. 80–1.

14 Hulsewe, p. 88.

15 Yu, p. 197.

16 Hulsewe, pp. 133–5.

17 Austin Coates, *China Races*, Hong Kong, Oxford University Press, 1994, pp. 3 and 23.

18 Colin Ronan and Joseph Needham, *The Shorter Science and Civilisation in China*, Cambridge University Press, 1994, vol. 4, pp. 43–51, 157 *et seq.*

19 Pirazzoli-t'Serstevens, p. 28.

20 Arthur Waley, 'The Heavenly Horses of Ferghana: a new view' in *History Today*, February 1955, pp. 96–7.

21 See, for example, John Goodall, pp. 62–3.

22 Waley, p. 99.

23 Hulsewe, pp. 148–9.

24 Hulsewe, pp. 199–200.

25 K. C. Chang (ed.), *Food in Chinese Culture: anthropological and historical perspectives*, Yale University Press, 1977, p. 80.

26 Edward H. Schafer, *The Golden Peaches of Samarkand: a study of T'ang exotics*, Berkeley, University of California Press, 1963, p. 142.

27 Yu, p. 128.

28 Yu, pp. 153, 157, 199.

29 Yu, pp. 153, 157, 199.

CHAPTER 5

The spread of trade and religions: Tocharians and Sogdians

1 Stein quoted in Elizabeth Wayland Barber, *The Mummies of Urumqi*, New York, Norton, 1999, pp. 93–4.

2 Illustrated in the plates in Wayland Barber.

3 E. O. Reischauer and J. K. Fairbank, *East Asia: the great tradition*, Boston, Houghton Mifflin, 1960, p. 18.

4 Pirazzoli-t'Serstevens, pp. 109–10.

5 Quoted in John Hare, *The Lost Camels of Tar-*

tary: a quest into forbidden China, London, Abacus, 1999, p. 155.

6 Hare, p. 137.

7 *Oxford Classical Dictionary*, p. 58.

8 Nicholas Sims-Williams, 'The Sogdian Merchants in China and India' in *Cina e Iran: da Alessandro Magno alla dinastia Tang*, Florence, Olschki, 1996 (*Orientalia Veneziana*, V), p. 46.

9 Tsien Tsuen-hsuin, 'Paper and Printing' in Joseph Needham, *Science and Civilisation in China*, vol. 5: *Chemistry and Chemical Technology*, part 1, p. 297.

10 Sims-Williams, pp. 46–62.

11 Kathleen Hopkirk, *A Traveller's Companion to Central Asia*, London, John Murray, 1993, p. 9.

12 *Along the Ancient Silk Routes: Central Asian art from the West Berlin State Museums*, New York, Metropolitan Museum of Art, 1982, pp. 176–9.

13 Susan Whitfield, *Life along the Silk Road*, London, John Murray, 1999, p. 29.

14 Quoted in Whitfield, p. 27.

15 Victor Mair, 'Old Sinitic *Myag, Old Persian Magus and English Magician' in *Early China*, 15, 1990, pp. 44–7.

16 Richard C. Foltz, *Religions of the Silk Road*, London, Macmillan, 1999, p. 31.

17 Foltz, pp. 28–9.

18 Steven Runciman, *The Medieval Manichee: a study of the Christian dualist heresy*, Cambridge University Press [1947], 1991.

19 Foltz, pp. 74–5.

20 *Along the Ancient Silk Routes*, New York, Metropolitan Museum of Art, 1982, pp. 176–7.

21 S. N. C. Lieu, *Manichaeism in Central Asia and China*, Leiden, Brill, 1998, p. 138.

22 *Along the Ancient Silk Routes*, pp. 175 et seq.

23 Peter Bryder, 'Where the Faint Traces of Manichaeism Disappear . . .' in *Altorientalische Forschungen*, 15/1, 1988, pp. 201–8, and Bryder, 'Caoan Revisited' in *Research into China Overseas Communication History*, 16/2, 1989, pp. 32–45.

CHAPTER 6

The fashion for all things Central Asian

1 Schafer, p. 8.

2 Schafer, p. 14, quoting the *Bei shi/History of the Northern Dynasties*, comp. AD 630–50.

3 Ann Bridge, quoted in A. C. Grayling and Susan Whitfield, *A Literary Companion to China*, London, John Murray, 1994, p. 80.

4 Schafer, p. 70.

5 Schafer, p. 71.

6 Schafer, p. 74.

7 Schafer, p. 77.

8 Arthur F. Wright and Denis Twitchett, *Perspectives on the T'ang*, New Haven and London, Yale University Press, 1973, p. 7.

9 Wright and Twitchett, pp. 387–91.

10 See Arthur Waley, *The Life and Times of Po Chu-I, 722–846 AD*, London, George Allen and Unwin, 1949, p. 44.

11 Schafer, pp. 66–9.

12 Schafer, pp. 94–5.

13 Schafer, p. 102.

14 Schafer, pp. 125–6.

15 Schafer, p. 147.

16 Schafer, pp. 191–2.

17 Schafer, p. 212 and Wright and Twitchett, p. 400.

18 Schafer, pp. 218–20.

19 Schafer, p. 200.

20 Schafer, pp. 197–202.

21 Schafer, pp. 236–7.

22 C. P. Fitzgerald, *Barbarian Beds: the origin of the chair in China*, London, Cresset Press, 1965, p. 4.

23 Reischauer and Fairbank, pp. 473–502.

24 Fitzgerald, p. 28.

25 Fitzgerald, pp. 5–6.

26 Fitzgerald, pls. xiii, xv.

27 See Frances Wood, 'Closely Observed China: from William Alexander's sketches to his published work' in *British Library Journal*, vol. 24, no. 1, Spring 1998, p. 105.

CHAPTER 7

The Caves of the Thousand Buddhas: Buddhism on the Silk Road

1 Arthur W. Hummel, *Eminent Chinese of the Ch'ing Period (1644–1912)* [Washington, 1943–4], Taipei, Literature House, 1964, p. 761.

2 Wladimir Zwalf (ed.), *Buddhism: art and faith*, London, British Museum, 1985, pp. 9, 11.

3 Zwalf, p. 12.

4 Erik Zürcher, *The Buddhist Conquest of China: the spread and adaptation of Buddhism in early medieval China*, Leiden, Brill, 1958, p. 2.

5 Zürcher, p. 40.

6 Zürcher, pp. 23–4.

7 Zürcher, p. 2.

8 Zürcher, pp. 65–6.

9 Zürcher, pp. 66–9.

10 René Grousset, *The Empire of the Steppes: a history of Central Asia*, translated by Naomi Walford, New Brunswick, Rutgers University Press, 1970, pp. 49–50.

11 Zürcher, pp. 140–1.

12 H. A. Giles, *The Travels of Fa-hsien (399–414 AD) or Record of the Buddhistic Kingdoms*, Cambridge University Press, 1923, p. 12.

13 Giles, pp. 8–9.

14 Robert Byron, *The Road to Oxiana* [1937], London, The Folio Society, 2000, pp. 303–4.

15 *The Encyclopaedia of Islam*, Leiden, Brill, 1986, vol. VI, p. 65.

16 'The Taliban Order All Statues Destroyed', *Guardian*, 27 February 2001, p. 17.

17 Jeannette Mirsky, *The Great Chinese Travellers*, London, Unwin, 1965, p. 29.

18 *The Life of Hiuen-tsiang by the Shaman Hwui Li*, translated by Samuel Beal, London, Kegan Paul, 1911, p. 2.

19 Beal, pp. 3, 10.

20 Beal, pp. 15–16.

21 Beal, p. 17.

22 Beal, pp. 21–3.

23 Tsien, p. 40.

24 Michael Loewe, *Records of the Han Administration*, vol. 2, Documents, Cambridge University Press, 1967, pp. 122–3, 125.

25 For an overview of about half the collection from Dunhuang in the British Library see Lionel Giles, *Descriptive Catalogue of the Chinese Manuscripts from Tunhuang in the British Museum*, London, 1957. There is a series of catalogues of the Pelliot collection in Paris at the Bibliothèque nationale and a fine exhibition catalogue with many of the holdings from the BN and the Musée Guimet: Jacques Gies and Monique Cohen, *Sérinde, Terre de Bouddha*, Paris, Réunion des Musées Nationaux, 1996. See also Anne Farrer and Roderick Whitfield, *Caves of the Thousand Buddhas: Chinese art from the Silk Route*, London, British Museum, 1990.

CHAPTER 8

Tanguts, Mongols, Nestorians and Marco Polo

1 David Morgan, *The Mongols*, Oxford, Blackwell, 1986, p. 74.

2 Herbert Franke, 'Sino-Western Contacts under the Mongol Empire' [1965] in Herbert Franke, *China under Mongol Rule*, Basingstoke, Variorum, 1994, vii, p. 50.

3 Morgan, p. 145.

4 For John of Plano Carpine's account of his trip see C. R. Beazley, *The Text and Versions of John de Plano Carpine and William de Rubruquis*, London, Hakluyt Society, 1903, and for a simple overview (with bibliography) see Frances Wood, *Did Marco Polo Go to China?* Boulder, Westview Press, 1996, pp. 16–28.

5 Foltz, p. 85.

6 J. Dyer Ball, *Things Chinese*, 1892, p. 384.

7 See Peter Jackson, *The Mission of William of Rubruck*, London, Hakluyt Society, 1990, and the wonderful little book by Leonardo Olschki, *Guillaume Boucher, a French artist at the court of the Khans*, Baltimore, Johns Hopkins Press, 1946.

8 Colonel Sir Henry Yule, *Cathay and the Way Thither*; second edition revised by Henri Cordier, London, Hakluyt Society, 1915, vol. 1, pp. 169–72; and Jack Dabbs, *History of the Discovery and Exploration of Chinese Turkestan*, The Hague, Mouton, 1963, p. 19.

9 William Dalrymple, *In Xanadu: a quest*, London, Fontana, 1990.

10 Italo Calvino, *Invisible Cities*, London, Secker and Warburg, 1974, p. 5.

11 Colonel Sir Henry Yule and Henri Cordier, *The Travels of Marco Polo: the complete Yule–Cordier edition* [1920], New York, Dover, 1993, vol. 2, pp. 160–1.

12 Yule and Cordier, vol. 2, p. 167.

13 Yule and Cordier, vol. 2, pp. 117, 130.

14 Paul Pelliot, *Notes on Marco Polo*, Paris, Imprimerie nationale, 1959–1963.

15 F. Rouleau, 'The Yangchow Latin Tombstone as a Landmark of Medieval Christianity in China' in *Harvard Journal of Asiatic Studies*, 17, 1954, p. 363.

16 A. C. Moule and Paul Pelliot, *Marco Polo*, London, Routledge, 1938, vol. 1, p. 49.

17 Morris Rossabi, *Voyager from Xanadu: Rabban Sauma and the first journey from China to the West*, Tokyo, Kodansha, 1992, p. 52.

18 Rossabi, p. 117.

19 Rossabi, p. 154.

CHAPTER 9

A parterre of roses: travellers to Ming China and Samarkand

1 L. C. Carrington Goodrich and Chaoying Fang (eds), *Dictionary of Ming Biography*, Columbia University Press, 1976, pp. 194–200.
2 K. M. Maitra (transl.), *A Persian Embassy to China*, Lahore, Hindi Press, 1934, p. 12.
3 Maitra, pp. 16–17.
4 Maitra, pp. 20–5.
5 Maitra, pp. 111–15.
6 Goodrich and Fang, p. 362.
7 Goodrich and Fang, pp. 472–3, and the entry for Matteo Ricci, pp. 1137–44; see also Yule, *Cathay and the Way Thither*, vol. IV, p. 169.
8 E. Delmar Morgan and C. H. Coote (eds), *Early Voyages and Travels in Russia and Persia by Anthony Jenkinson and other Englishmen*, London, Hakluyt Society, 1886, vol. 1, pp. 87–9.
9 Goodrich and Fang, p. 6.
10 Morgan and Coote, vol. 1, p. 83.
11 Christie, p. 128.
12 Sinor, p. 187.
13 Quoted in Hilda Hookham, *Tamburlaine the Conqueror*, London, Hodder and Stoughton, 1962, p. 1.
14 MS Bodley 264.
15 Sinor, p. 191.
16 Sinor, pp. 189–90.
17 *Clavijo: Embassy to Tamerlane 1403–1406*, translated by Guy Le Strange, London, Routledge, 1928, p. 280.
18 *Clavijo*, pp. 218–19.
19 *Clavijo*, pp. 263–4.
20 *Clavijo*, pp. 222–3.
21 *Clavijo*, pp. 227–8.
22 *Clavijo*, p. 228.
23 *Clavijo*, pp. 224–5, 267.
24 F. W. Barthold, *Turkestan Down to the Mongol Invasion*, London, Luzac, 1968, pp. 235–6.
25 Byron, p. 109.
26 Christie, pp. 146–7.
27 Christie, pp. 150–1.
28 Wilfred Blunt, *The Golden Road to Samarkand*, London, Hamish Hamilton, 1973, p. 11.
29 *The Poems of Matthew Arnold*, edited by Kenneth Allott; second edition edited by Miriam Allott, London, Longman, 1979, pp. 86–7.
30 *Poems of Matthew Arnold*, p. 323.
31 *Poems of Matthew Arnold*, pp. 326–7.
32 *Fitzgerald: Selected works*, edited by Joanna Richardson, London, Rupert Hart-Davis, 1962, pp. 243–5.
33 Oscar Wilde, *The Complete Works*, vol. 1, Oxford University Press, 2000, pp. 136–7.
34 *The New Oxford Book of English Verse*, edited by Helen Gardner, London, Oxford University Press, 1972, p.852.
35 See Edward Said, *Orientalism*, New York, Random House, 1978.

CHAPTER 10

The Great Game and the Silk Road

1 Hummel, p. 265.
2 Isenbike Togan, 'Inner Asian Moslem Merchants at the Closure of the Silk Routes' in Vadime Elisseeff (ed.), *The Silk Roads: highways of culture and commerce*, New York and Oxford, Berghahn Books/Unesco, 2000, p. 253.
3 Hummel, p. 265.
4 Hummel, pp. 371–2.
5 Jonathan Spence, *The Search for Modern China*, New York, Norton, 1990, pp. 97–100.
6 Togan in Elisseeff, pp. 255–6.
7 Jack Dabbs, *A History of the Discovery and Exploitation of Chinese Turkestan*, The Hague, 1963, Central Asiatic Studies VIII, p. 87.
8 Peter Hopkirk, *The Great Game: on secret service in High Asia*, Oxford University Press, 1991, p. 3.
9 Hopkirk, *Great Game*, p. 5.
10 Peter Hopkirk, *Foreign Devils on the Silk Road*, London, John Murray, 1980, p. 35.
11 Karl E. Meyer and Shareen Blair Brysac, *Tournament of Shadows: the Great Game and the race for empire in Asia*, London, Little, Brown, 2001, p. 211.
12 Sir Aurel Stein, *Ruins of Desert Cathay: personal narrative of explorations in Central Asia and westernmost China* [1912], New York, Dover Publications, 1987, vol. 1, pp. 130–4.
13 Captain Frank E. Younghusband, *The Heart of a Continent: a narrative of travels in Manchuria, across the Gobi Desert, through the Himalayas, the Pamirs and Chitral, 1884–1894*, London, John Murray, 1896, p. 177.
14 Hopkirk, *Foreign Devils*, pp. 38–9.
15 Yule and Cordier, vol. 1, p. 188.
16 Stein, *On Ancient Central Asian Tracks,*

pp. 135, 171.

17 Yule and Cordier, vol. 1, pp. 180–2.

18 Hummel, p. 74.

19 Quoted in Meyer and Brysac, p. 231.

20 Meyer and Brysac, pp. 230–3.

21 Gerald Morgan, *Ney Elias: explorer and envoy extraordinary in High Asia*, London, Allen and Unwin, 1971, p. 135.

22 Lady Macartney, *An English Lady in Chinese Turkestan* [1931], Hong Kong, Oxford University Press, 1985, pp. 119–20.

23 Younghusband, p. 316. For 'defrocked' see, for example, Patrick French, *Younghusband: the last great imperial adventurer*, London, Flamingo, 1995, p. 86.

24 Younghusband, pp. 311–13.

25 Younghusband, pp. 320–1.

26 Patrick French, p. 75.

27 Patrick French, pp. 75–7.

28 Younghusband, p. 328.

29 Younghusband, pp. 326–38.

30 Burnes's *Travels into Bokhara* (1834) quoted in Kathleen Hopkirk, *A Traveller's Companion to Central Asia*, London, John Murray, 1993, p. 42.

31 Togan in Elisseeff, p. 251.

32 Meyer and Brysac, p. 122.

33 K. Hopkirk, p. 45.

34 K. Hopkirk, p. 47.

35 K. Hopkirk, p. 128.

36 Fred Burnaby, *A Ride to Khiva: travels and adventures in Central Asia*, London, Cassell, Petter and Galpin, 1876, p. 301.

37 Burnaby, pp. 179, 339.

38 Evan Charteris, *The Life and Letters of Sir Edmund Gosse*, London, William Heinemann, 1931, p. 121.

CHAPTER 11

Asia held them captive in her cold embrace: explorers on the Silk Road

1 Donald Rayfield quoted in Meyer and Brysac, p. 225.

2 Meyer and Brysac, p. 527.

3 Morgan, p. 28.

4 Meyer and Brysac, p. 229.

5 Peter Hopkirk, *Trespassers on the Roof of the World: the race for Lhasa*, London, John Murray, 1982, p. 37.

6 Meyer and Brysac, p. 236.

7 Meyer and Brysac, pp. 236–9.

8 Dabbs, pp. 91–2.

9 Sven Hedin, *My Life as an Explorer*, London, Cassell, 1926, p. 1.

10 Hedin, pp. 46–8.

11 Hedin, pp. 95–7.

12 Hedin, pp. 97–9.

13 Hedin, pp. 114–41, 211.

14 Hopkirk, *Foreign Devils*, p. 65.

15 Hopkirk, *Trespassers*, pp. 157–8.

16 Hopkirk, *Trespassers*, p. 198.

17 Peter Fleming, *Bayonets to Lhasa*, London, Rupert Hart-Davis, 1962, p. 135, and Meyer and Brysac, p. 300.

18 Fleming, p. 211.

19 Fleming, p. 252.

20 Hopkirk, *Trespassers*, p. 198.

21 Hedin, pp. 400–1 and Hopkirk, *Foreign Devils*, p. 55.

22 Sven Hedin, *Sven Hedin's German Diary, 1935–1942*, translated by Joan Bulman, Dublin, Eutherion Books, 1951, pp. 1–2, 73–5.

23 Hopkirk, *Foreign Devils*, p. 55.

CHAPTER 12

Trophies and tiger entrails: hunting and theorising on the Silk Road

1 Meyer and Brysac, pp. 237–8.

2 Meyer and Brysac, p. 230.

3 Ralph P. Cobbold, *Innermost Asia: travel and sport in the Pamirs*, London, Heinemann, 1900, p. 58.

4 Cobbold, p. 69.

5 Ellsworth Huntington, *The Pulse of Asia: a journey in Central Asia illustrating the geographic base of history*, London, 1907, pp. 252–3.

6 Huntington, p. 230.

7 Huntington, pp. 280–1.

8 Huntington, pp. 359–61.

9 Huntington, p. 363

10 Huntington, pp. 363–5.

11 Huntington, pp. 108–9.

12 Cobbold, pp. 12–13 and 34–5.

13 Dabbs, p. 92.

14 Cobbold, pp. 46–8.

15 Cobbold, p. 35.

16 Cobbold, pp. 61 and 76.

17 R. C. F. Schomberg, *Unknown Karakoram*, London, Martin Hopkinson, 1936, p. 110.

18 Schomberg, pp. 200–1.

19 Schomberg, p. 15. I'm not sure which Mason he means.

20 Schomberg, p. 97.
21 Alpo Ratia, 'Mannerheim's Central Asian Expedition of 1906–8' in *IDP News*, no. 15, Spring 2000, British Library, International Dunhuang Project, pp. 1–3.
22 Quoted in Ratia, p. 2.

CHAPTER 13

Securing specimens: Aurel Stein

1 Younghusband, quoted in Hopkirk, *Foreign Devils*, p. 43.
2 Rudolf Hoernle, 'A Collection of Antiquities from Central Asia' in *Journal of the Royal Asiatic Society of Bengal*, extra number 1, pp. li et seq., 1–110. For a brief overview of the stimulus to Stein via Hoernle and other scholars in India, see Frances Wood, 'From Central Asia to London: the Stein collection of manuscripts in the British Library' in Katsumi Tanabe, Joe Cribb and Helen Wang (eds), *Studies in Silk Road Coins and Culture: papers in honour of Professor Ikuo Hirayama on his 65th birthday*, Kamakura, Institute of Silk Road Studies, 1997.
3 Annabel Walker, *Aurel Stein: pioneer of the Silk Road*, London, John Murray, 1995, pp. 30–5.
4 From Kipling's *Kim*, quoted in Walker, p. 38.
5 Walker, p. 63.
6 Walker, pp. 68–9.
7 Walker, p. 108.
8 Hoernle in *Journal of the Asiatic Society of Bengal*, 1901.
9 Stein, *Ruins of Desert Cathay*, vol. 2, p. 168.
10 Stein, vol. 2, p. 172.
11 Stein, vol. 2, p. 305.
12 Stein, vol. 2, p. 344.
13 Stein, vol. 2, pp. 361–2.
14 Stein, vol. 2, p. 275.
15 Stein, vol. 2, p. 405.
16 Stein, vol. 2, pp. 466–7.
17 Stein, vol. 2, p. 483.
18 Stein, vol. 2. p. 490.
19 See Helen Wang, 'Stein's Recording Angel – Miss F. M. G. Lorimer' in *Journal of the Royal Asiatic Society*, London, 3rd series, vol. 8, part 2, July 1998, pp. 207–28.
20 See Frances Wood, 'Two Thousand Years at Dunhuang' in Susan Whitfield and Frances Wood (eds), *Dunhuang and Turfan: contents and conservation of ancient documents from Central Asia*, London, British Library, 1996,

pp. 3–4.
21 See British Library Oriental and India Office Collections, MS Or. 13114, 'Aurel Stein correspondence with M. Pelliot regarding Chinese documents, 1910–'.
22 Arthur Waley, *Ballads and Stories from Tunhuang*, London, 1960, introduction.
23 Lionel Giles, *Six Centuries at Tunhuang*, London, China Society, 1944.
24 Wang Jiqing, 'Photographs in the British Library of Documents and Manuscripts from Sir Aurel Stein's Fourth Expedition in China' in *British Library Journal*, vol. 24, no. 1, Spring 1998, pp. 23–74.

CHAPTER 14

An end to excavation: Pelliot, von Le Coq and Warner

1 Paul Pelliot, *Carnets de Pékin 1899–1901*, Paris, Collège de France, 1976, p. 34.
2 Hopkirk, *Foreign Devils*, p. 182.
3 Hopkirk, *Foreign Devils*, p. 184.
4 Bibliothèque nationale, *Trésors de Chine et Haute Asie: centième anniversaire de Paul Pelliot*, Paris, 1979, p. 14.
5 ibid. (author's translation).
6 *Along the Ancient Silk Routes*, pp. 26–7.
7 *Along the Ancient Silk Routes*, p. 28.
8 *Along the Ancient Silk Routes*, p. 35.
9 Langdon Warner, *The Long Old Road in China*, London, Arrowsmith, 1927, p. 31.
10 Warner, pp. 31–2, 40.
11 Warner, p. 49.
12 Warner, pp. 78–9.
13 Theodore Bowie (ed.), *Langdon Warner through his Letters*, Bloomington, Indiana University Press, 1966, p. 112.
14 Warner, pp. 160–3, 193.
15 Warner, p. 211.
16 Warner, p. 214.
17 Warner, p. 215.
18 Warner, pp. 217–19.
19 Warner, p. 220.
20 Warner, pp. 220–1.

CHAPTER 15

*The Baby General: travel on the Silk
Road in the 1930s*

1 Meyer and Brysac, pp. 387–90.
2 Hopkirk, *Great Game*, p. 520.
3 Peter Hopkirk, *Setting the East Ablaze: on
secret service in Bolshevik Asia*, Oxford University Press, 1986, pp. 133–4.
4 Hopkirk, *Setting the East Ablaze*, p. 137.
5 Hopkirk, *Setting the East Ablaze*, p. 215.
6 Cable with French, pp. 222–32.
7 Hopkirk, *Setting the East Ablaze*, p. 221.
8 Eric Teichman, *Journey to Turkistan* [1937],
Hong Kong, Oxford University Press, 1988,
p. 93.
9 Cable with French, pp. 240–1.
10 Teichman, p. 21.
11 Hopkirk, *Setting the East Ablaze*, p. 240.
12 Teichman, p. 184.
13 Owen Lattimore, *High Tartary* [1930], New
York and Tokyo, Kodansha, 1994, p. x.
14 Lattimore, *High Tartary*, p. 90.
15 Lattimore, *High Tartary*, pp. 141–2.
16 Eleanor Holgate Lattimore, *Turkestan
Reunion*, New York, John Day, 1934,
pp. 110–11.
17 Eleanor Lattimore, pp. 111–12.
18 Eleanor Lattimore, pp. 171–2.
19 Eleanor Lattimore, pp. 253–4.
20 Ella Maillart, *Forbidden Journey: from Peking
to Kashgar*, London, Heinemann, 1937, p. 3.
21 Maillart, pp. 6–8.
22 Peter Fleming, *News from Tartary* [1936] in
*Travels in Tartary: One's Company and News
from Tartary*, London, Reprint Society, 1971,
pp. 272–3.
23 Fleming, *News from Tartary*, pp. 275–6.
24 W. H. Auden and Christopher Isherwood,
Journey to a War [1939], London, Faber, 1973,
pp. 197, 296.
25 Maillart, p. 44.
26 Maillart, pp. 179, 190.
27 Fleming, *News from Tartary*, p. 398.
28 Maillart, pp. 192–3, 202.
29 Fleming, *News from Tartary*, p. 513.
30 Maillart, p. 224.
31 Fleming, *News from Tartary*, pp. 514–16.
32 Fleming, *News from Tartary*, p. 534.
33 Fleming, *News from Tartary*, p. 535.
34 Maillart, pp. 250–1.
35 Fleming, *News from Tartary*, p. 540.
36 Mildred Cable with Francesca French,
pp. 18–19.
37 Cable with French, p. 70.
38 Cable with French, pp. 154–5.
39 Cable with French, pp. 157–8.
40 Cable with French, pp. 159–61.
41 Cable with French, p. 162.
42 Cable with French, pp. 252–5.
43 Owen Lattimore, *High Tartary*, p. 184.
44 Teichman, pp. 3–5.
45 Teichman, p. 50.

EPILOGUE

The Silk Road today

1 Cable with French, p. 299.
2 *The New Oxford Book of English Verse*,
p. 852.

List of Illustrations

List of Illustrations

List of Illustrations

Acknowledgements

Every effort has been made to contact copyright holders; in the event of an inadvertent omission or error, the editorial department should be notified at The Folio Society Ltd, 44 Eagle Street, London WC1R 4FS.

The Folio Society wishes to thank the following writers, publishers and literary representatives for their permission to use copyright material:

Mildred Cable with Francesca French, *The Gobi Desert* (Hodder and Stoughton Limited, 1942), reproduced by permission of Hodder and Stoughton Limited.

Clavijo, *Embassy to Tamerlane, 1403–1406*, translated by Guy Le Strange (Routledge, 1928), reproduced by permission of Routledge.

Peter Fleming, *News from Tartary* (1936, reprinted 2001 by Birlinn Books) Copyright © the Estate of Peter Fleming.

Ellsworth Huntington, *The Pulse of Asia: A Journey in Central Asia* (Houghton Mifflin, 1907), reproduced by permission of Houghton Mifflin Company.

Owen Lattimore, 'The Caravan Routes of Inner Asia' in *The Geographical Journal*, vol. LXXII, no. 6 (1928), reproduced by permission of the Royal Geographical Society with IBG.

D. D. Leslie and K. J. H. Gardiner, *The Roman Empire in Chinese Sources* (Bardi, 1996), reproduced by permission of Bardi Editore.

Ella Maillart, *Forbidden Journey: from Peking to Kashgar* (Heinemann, 1937), reproduced by permission of David Higham Associates Limited.

Pliny, *The Natural History*, translated by H. Rackham (Heinemann, 1942), reproduced by permission of the publishers and the Trustees of the Loeb Classical Library from *Pliny: Volume II – Natural History*, Loeb Classical Library Volume L 352, translated by H. Rackham, Cambridge, Mass.: Harvard University Press, 1942. The Loeb Classical Library ® is a registered trademark of the President and Fellows of Harvard College.

Edward H. Schafer, *The Golden Peaches of Samarkand: a study of T'ang Exotics* (University of California Press, 1963), © 1963 The Regents of the University of California, reproduced by permission of the University of California Press.

The Emperor Wu, 'The Heavenly Horses of Ferghana', translated by Arthur Waley in *History Today* (February 1955), reproduced by permission of the Arthur Waley Estate.

Chiang Yee, *A Chinese Childhood* (Methuen, 1940), reproduced by permission of Chien-Fei Chiang.

Captain Frank E. Younghusband, *The Heart of a Continent: a narrative of travels in Manchuria, across the Gobi Desert, through the Himalayas, the Pamirs and Chitral, 1884–1894* (John Murray, 1896), reproduced by permission of John Murray (Publishers) Ltd.

Index

Index

Index

Index

Index

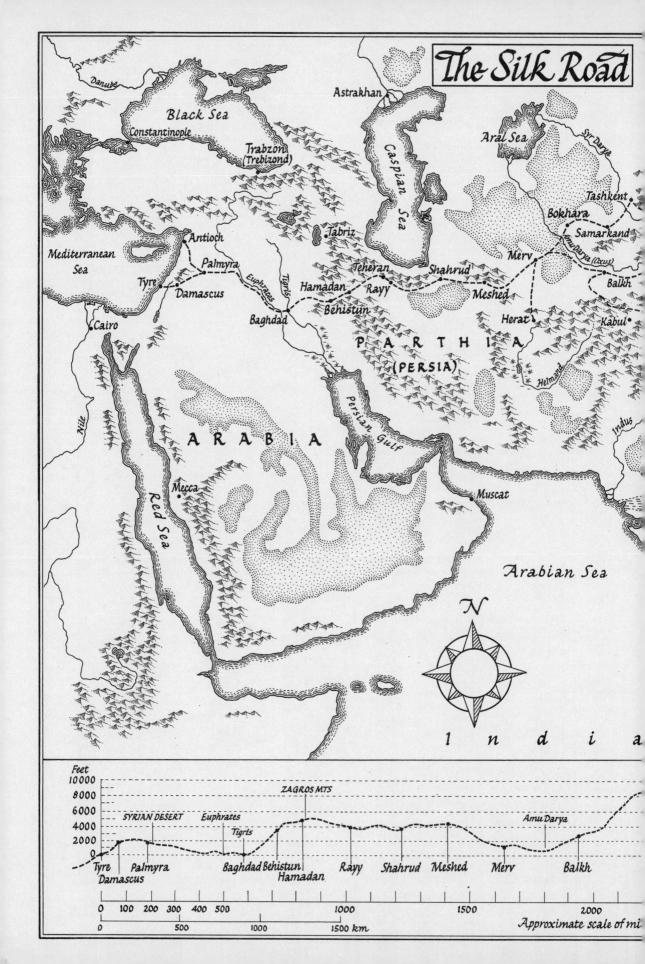

The Silk Road

Danube

Black Sea

Constantinople

Trabzon (Trebizond)

Astrakhan

Aral Sea

Syr Darya

Tashkent

Bokhara

Samarkand

Amu Darya (Oxus)

Tabriz

Caspian Sea

Mediterranean Sea

Antioch

Palmyra

Tyre

Damascus

Euphrates

Tigris

Hamadan

Teheran

Rayy

Shahrud

Meshed

Merv

Balkh

Behistun

Baghdad

Cairo

Herat

Kabul

PARTHIA (PERSIA)

Helmand

Nile

ARABIA

Persian Gulf

Red Sea

Mecca

Muscat

Arabian Sea

Indus

N

I n d i a

Feet								
10000								
8000			ZAGROS MTS					
6000								
4000	SYRIAN DESERT	Euphrates					Amu Darya	
2000		Tigris						
0								

Tyre
Damascus
Palmyra
Baghdad
Behistun
Hamadan
Rayy
Shahrud
Meshed
Merv
Balkh

0   100 200 300 400 500   1000   1500   2000

0   500   1000   1500 km

Approximate scale of mi

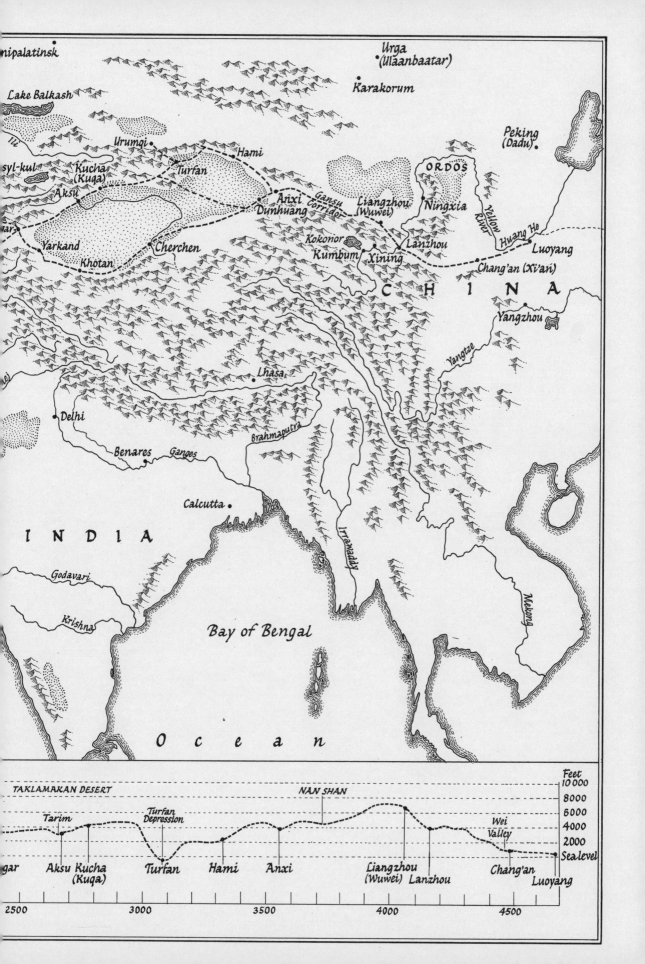

Urga
(Ulaanbaatar)

nipalatinsk

Lake Balkash

Karakorum

Peking
(Dadu)

Ili

Urumqi

Hami

ORDOS

syl-kul

Kucha
(Kuqa)

Turfan

Aksu

Anxi

Gansu Corridor

Liangzhou
(Wuwei)

Ningxia

Dunhuang

Yellow River

Hwang He

Yarkand

Cherchen

Kokonor

Lanzhou

Luoyang

Khotan

Kumbum

Xining

Chang'an (Xi'an)

C H I N A

ar

Yangzhou

Kumbum

Lhasa

Yangtze

Delhi

Benares

Ganges

Brahmaputra

Calcutta

I N D I A

Godavari

Irrawaddy

Krishna

Mekong

Bay of Bengal

O c e a n

Feet
10 000

TAKLAMAKAN DESERT

NAN SHAN

8000

Turfan
Depression

6000

Tarim

Wei
Valley

4000

2000

Sea level

gar

Aksu Kucha
(Kuqa)

Turfan

Hami

Anxi

Liangzhou
(Wuwei)

Lanzhou

Chang'an

Luoyang

2500

3000

3500

4000

4500